Interstices of the Sublime

John D. Caputo, *series editor*

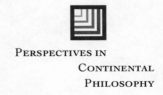

PERSPECTIVES IN
CONTINENTAL
PHILOSOPHY

CLAYTON CROCKETT

Interstices of the Sublime
Theology and Psychoanalytic Theory

FORDHAM UNIVERSITY PRESS
New York ■ 2007

Library of Congress Cataloging-in-Publication Data

    Crockett, Clayton, 1969–
    Interstices of the sublime : theology and psychoanalytic theory / Clayton Crockett.—1st ed.
       p. cm.—(Perspectives in continental philosophy)
     ISBN-13: 978-0-8232-2721-1 (cloth : alk. paper)
     ISBN-10: 0-8232-2721-9 (cloth : alk. paper)
     ISBN-13: 978-0-8232-2722-8 (pbk. : alk. paper)
     ISBN-10: 0-8232-2722-7 (pbk. : alk. paper)
     1. Psychoanalysis and religion. 2. Sublime, The. 3. Sublimation (Psychology) I. Title.
    BF175.4.R44C76 2007
    201′.6150195—dc22

                            2007016141

Printed in the United States of America
09 08 07 5 4 3 2 1
First edition

For the memory of Charlie Winquist, who taught me
what it means to think and live with a theological exigency

Contents

Acknowledgments

An earlier version of chapter 1, "On Sublimation," was published in the *Journal of the American Academy of Religion* 68, no. 4 (2000): 837–55. It is republished with the permission of Oxford University Press.

An earlier version of chapter 4, "Foreclosing God," was published in *Explorations in Contemporary Philosophy of Religion: Approaches from Continental Philosophy*, edited by Deane-Peter Baker and Patrick Maxwell (VIBS/Rodopi, Philosophy of Religion special series, Number 143, 2002), 174–88. It is republished here with the permission of Rodopi.

An earlier version of chapter 5, "Anxiety and the S(ub)lime Body of God," was published in the online *Journal for Cultural and Religious Theory* 1, no. 1 (December 1999) (http://www.jcrt.org/archives/01.1/index.html?page = crockett.html).

I gratefully acknowledge the University Research Council of the University of Central Arkansas for a Summer Stipend in 2004 that supported the writing and completion of this book. I would also like to acknowledge the continuing support for my work by the University of Central Arkansas, especially the College of Liberal Arts and my colleagues in the Department of Philosophy and Religion. In particular my chair, Charles Harvey, embodies much of what is best about being a professor, teacher, colleague, and administrator.

I want to thank Helen Tartar at Fordham University Press for her consistent dedication to and support of this project. Two readers for

Fordham University Press provided both constructive and critical comments and suggestions and helped shape the final form of the book. John D. Caputo, as series editor, expressed interest in this book for his series at an early stage, and he offered helpful advice and encouragement throughout the process. In addition, Caputo has been incredibly generous and gracious to me during some difficult times, including the sickness and death of Charlie Winquist, and for that I will always be thankful. I think it is truly fitting that Jack succeeds Winquist at Syracuse University, to continue the tradition of radical theology there.

Many people have contributed to this work and the ideas expressed therein, both directly and indirectly. Most of all I would like to thank Jeffrey Robbins, my colleague-in-arms, for his careful reading and constructive suggestions for improvement, as well as his sustaining friendship. I want to thank Creston Davis for his friendship and willingness to enter into exciting projects with me, in addition to his energy and enthusiasm for vital theological ideas. I also want to thank Oz Lorentzen for honest and searching conversations, Noëlle Vahanian for her uncompromising thinking, Martin Kavka for his penetrating questions and insights, Keith Putt and Sharon Baker for their fellowship, Heath Atchley and Andrew Saldino for their sense of humor, Chad Snyder for his hospitality and faith in my academic success, Victor Taylor and Carl Raschke for the *JCRT*, Jim DiCenso for his past and ongoing support of my work, and Jim Livingston for his continued interest in my life and career.

Students may not always realize how integral a part they play in their teachers' work. I have been inspired by and learned from my best and brightest students, including Chrystie Flournoy, Danny Finer, Dan Gill, Laurie Stahle, and Sara Harvey. Thanks to Tommy Kendrick for the glass case and for *Gaviotas*.

I want to thank my family for their love and support, including my wife, Vicki Bryan Crockett, and my children, Maria and Bryan, for making life enriching and worthwhile. I want to thank my parents, my grandmother, and particularly my brother, Clint, who knows what it means to live along the edge of the abyss, or to walk the "line of the syzygies." In many ways your experiences have forced me to think dangerous and difficult thoughts, to try to comprehend what it means to survive in a world that is often insane.

Finally, as the dedication attests, Charlie Winquist was an inspiration, mentor, teacher, and friend, and his presence is deeply missed.

Introduction

The Primal Scene of Christianity

In this book I conduct an investigation of important religious, theological, and psychoanalytic concepts, primarily through a reading of
sublimation. Sublimation is a privileged term that is closely connected with the notion of the sublime, a Kantian term that also has
psychoanalytic and theological connotations. Investigating sublimation and the sublime as important terms for theological discourse
brings together psychoanalytic theory from Freud to Lacan, Kristeva, and Žižek along with more conventional philosophical discourses, including contemporary continental philosophy. To orient
ourselves toward considering the significance of psychoanalysis for
thinking about religious and theological topics, I will begin with a
concrete example before turning to a more descriptive account of
what I am doing in the book.

For many intellectuals, watching the movie *The Passion of the Christ*
is unbearable, but not because of the violence and gore that upsets
sensitive viewers. It is unbearable partly because it dramatizes once
again the split between Christianity and Judaism that derives from
the origin of Christianity as a religion. This split can be illuminated
through psychoanalysis by considering Freud's concept of the primal
scene. Mel Gibson's film presents itself as a documentary, a true account of the last twelve hours of the life of Jesus. Many believers

came away with the mistaken impression that "that's the way it really was." Of course, biblical scholars have taught us over the last few centuries that the gospel narratives were composed decades later, near the end of the first century, and that many of these narratives of the passion were framed by the persecution of Christians by Jews, the tensions between Jewish Christians and Gentiles within the Jesus movement, and most importantly the Jewish Revolt and the destruction of the Temple in 70 CE. This event was interpreted by the Christians as God's judgment on the Jews, and the spectacular failure of the revolt (in which many Christians participated, and which mostly wiped out the Jewish Christian community in Jerusalem) taught the Christians a lesson about the futility of challenging Roman power.

This process set in motion attempts to whitewash Roman complicity in the death of Jesus, and the Jews became a convenient scapegoat. At the same time, Paul's letters and teachings, written in the 50s and 60s, became more relevant, and were seized upon to justify the spread of Christianity to the Gentiles and away from the Jews. Although Paul's desire to spread the faith to Greeks was an interim practice, and he did not desire a permanent separation between Jews and pagan Christians, this split became permanent with the destruction of the Second Temple. The cut between Jewish and non-Jewish Christians concerned the practice of circumcision and the question whether one had to be circumcised—and therefore Jewish—to become Christian. On the other hand, Paul argues in Romans 2:28–29 that circumcision binds one under the law, and literal circumcision is less important than the "true" circumcision of the heart. He believed Christ came to overcome these literal cuts or separations, to create a new humanity in which there is no Greek or Jew. Paul's rift between Jewish and Greek Christians was supposed to lead to reconciliation upon the imminent return of Christ, but with the Jewish Revolt this cut became a tear. The tearing away of Christianity from Judaism, accomplished by the failure of the Jewish Revolt, was symbolized by the tearing of the curtain in the Temple upon the death of Christ. This event, told in Luke 23:46, is magnified in *The Passion of the Christ* into an actual earthquake that rends the floor of the Temple.

This complex historical account involves the construction of what Kathleen Biddick calls the "typological imaginary," the assumption of a linear history cut into two, a "that was then," associated with Judaism, and a "this is now," identified with Christianity. In *The Typological Imaginary: Circumcision, Technology, History*, Biddick traces medieval, modern, and postmodern effects of this typological imaginary, which continues to function and is alive and well in *The Passion of the Christ*. Anti-Semitism is an effect of the typological imaginary — that is, the need to separate Christians from Jews — or the old order from the new one. The typological imaginary gives rise to graphic technologies that reinscribe it into new situations, including more recently the imagining of a strict boundary, "an impassable divide between premodernity (history with a small 'h') and modernity (history with a capital 'H')."[1] This is a fetishization of temporal periodization, modernity as the supercession of premodernity, which Biddick traces to the original periodization wrought by the distinction between Christians and Jews. Jews function within the Christian typological imaginary as an uncanny survival, a source of anxiety that compels Christians to delimit or deface Jews in contemporary history, or erase them altogether. And this strange desire is inherent in Christian identity itself from the beginning.

The beginning of Christianity, read psychoanalytically, represents a primal scene. According to Freud, the primal scene, which Lacan translates as "an-other" scene, is paradigmatically represented in his case study of the Wolf Man. In *From the History of an Infantile Neurosis*, Freud analyzes and reconstitutes a primal scene from the phobia induced by a dream of wolves in a tree, terrifying him. Freud works through various screen memories to arrive at the original scene, which is an experience of the Wolf Man at one and a half years old coming upon his parents engaging in intercourse from behind, "in the manner of animals." The dream conveys a conscious fear of castration that was sparked by this earlier experience. Freud insists upon the real historical occurrence of this primal scene, although he struggles and wrestles with the problems and difficulties concerning whether it "really" happened. Freud finally declares that he is not sure whether it really happened, but ultimately it does not matter because of its overwhelming psychic reality.

The important notion that Freud develops through this analysis is the concept of *Nachträglichkeit*, or aftereffect. The trauma is divided into two parts: the event itself, which is inaccessible in conventional symbolic and historical reality, although it is posited as real and therefore it must have happened; and the coming-to-consciousness of this event, its symptoms, and effects. Here is a different model of temporality from linear historicity because there is a timeless connection between the primal scene and its irruption into history or consciousness. The primal scene occurs at one and a half for the Wolf

Man, but it manifests itself symptomatically when he is four years old. Here is the uncanny nature of trauma, however: It cannot be traced to a simple literal origin, and it can manifest itself afresh years later.[2]

In her book, *In Search of Dreamtime*, Tomoko Masuzawa carefully works through the complicated process of Freud's analysis and his understanding of its significance, and she makes a connection between the primal scene of the Wolf Man and the murder of the father by the primal horde in *Totem and Taboo*. Masuzawa suggests that the psychic significance of Freud's thought re-founds a notion of time that is other than linear history because it is based upon the mechanism of *Nachträglichkeit*. Freud insists upon the reality of the primal patricide, even though it cannot be located anywhere in history. Instead of criticizing Freud for his mythmaking, Masuzawa suggests that Freud's thought helps to undo the distinction between modern and premodern. She suggests that the search for the origin of religion in history is impossible, not because of our ignorance and the fallibility of our historical tools, but because origins always concern dreamtime, or a trauma that occurs outside of history that distributes its effects within history, constituting history as narrative or myth. Our myths, our stories, are the dreamtime, which is "a story told on sand."[3]

We can easily make the leap from Wolf Man back to the primal horde, and then forward to *Moses and Monotheism*, which hypothesizes the murder of Moses as another primal scene, this time one that creates what becomes Judaism. Here *Nachträglichkeit* functions explicitly as the return of the repressed. Finally, the crucifixion of Jesus Christ links the other three primal scenes into a series. Freud considers the death of Jesus in relation to the hypothetical murder of Moses in *Moses and Monotheism*, and claims that in terms of its sacrifice of a strict monotheism, the primal scene of Christianity represents a regression compared to that of Judaism: "the Christian religion did not keep to the lofty heights of spirituality to which the Jewish religion had soared."[4] Despite the fact that Freud suggests that the origin of Jewish religion is Egyptian, he argues that paganism corrupts Christianity, with its polytheistic influence upon the doctrine of God that splits God into two and then three. This corruption is the cause of Christian anti-Semitism. On the one hand, Christianity is "right" in its doctrine of the killing of God, which repeats the murder of Moses and the killing of the father by the primal horde, because it acknowledges that "we" killed God. On the other hand, there is an almost schizophrenic split, because Christians divide God into Father and Son, and, in addition, blame part of their number (the Jews) for the death of God, while absolving the others. (Although Mel Gibson *says* that we are all responsible for the death of Christ, his film *shows* certain groups of people as more responsible than others.) Freud suggests that "the deeper motives of anti-Semitism have their roots in times long past; they come from the unconscious," an unconscious in which Christians are "badly christened" and remain "what their ancestors were, barbarically polytheistic."[5] At bottom, the hatred of Jews by Christians is diagnosed by Freud as a hatred for Christianity, because these Christians do not want to truly understand what Christianity is essentially about.

One of the most important notions here is the repetition of primal scenes, so that neither the primal scene of Christianity nor the primal scene of Judaism is the original primal scene. According to Freud, "it is an attractive suggestion that the guilt attached to the murder of Moses may have been the stimulus for the wish-fantasy of the Messiah."[6] The original primal scene is the killing of the father by the primal horde of *Totem and Taboo*, which founds both culture and religion. It is also the most difficult to locate in historical reality. On the other hand, the intensity of the crucifixion as the primal scene of Christianity possesses such incredible power precisely because we know that it occurred as a historical event. At the same time, we cannot precisely locate it despite the appearance of the gospel narratives as eyewitnesses and the impressive tools of biblical scholarship.

The primal scene of Christianity is presented as if everyone is there, observing the most important event in history. But the crucifixion implies that nobody was there to view it: The disciples all fled, and Jesus is alone in his agony, except for at most a couple of thieves and handful of disinterested soldiers. Its significance was delayed and deferred throughout Christian history, although these aftereffects only served to increase the explosiveness of the event itself. According to Andrew Shanks, the historical trauma inflicted upon the early Christian community was the persecution it suffered at the hands of others. The problem then came when Christianity was converted from a minority to a majority tradition.

> The trouble is that, when it eventually came to power, the machine for surviving persecution . . . so easily became a most effective machine for persecuting. The very qualities which had originally equipped the church to survive also now equipped it to persecute.[7]

The crucifixion functioned as an attractor, drawing all of these later experiences of trauma into its orbit. It is only in retrospect that the crucifixion itself took on such momentous importance, and so that importance was read back into the event, at the same time as the effects of the event tore through time and space in an enormous work of *Nachträglichkeit*, which is the return of the repressed, the killing of the Messiah that is ultimately the killing of God. The scene took decades, at least, to construct and then centuries to reconstruct, and its power and potency funded centuries of violence and anti-Semitism, although this was only one of its many effects (but not the least important by far).

Against Orthodoxy

As this discussion of the primal scene of Christianity implies, psychoanalytic insights can shed important light upon religious histories and ideas, although such insights are often controversial and unorthodox. An encounter between theology or philosophy of religion and psychoanalytic theory from Freud to Lacan and Žižek can be read as a work against orthodoxy. Its fidelity is to the intrinsic radicalism of theological thinking itself, rather than any figure, church, or school. Today, contemporary postmodern theology as represented in the works of John Milbank and Jean-Luc Marion takes up the challenges of continental philosophy to recover an orthodox theological vision. Marion and Milbank, and many of their American theological readers, take postmodern thought seriously to get beyond it. This attempt to restore orthodoxy in Christian faith and belief occurs at the same time as a cultural and political turn toward more conservative and evangelical forms of religious life, however much Milbank and Marion deplore these political and cultural forms of conservative Christianity. The postmodern theology of Milbank, Marion, and others that promotes orthodoxy betrays the radical promise and possibility of postmodern theology, at least in terms of its American origins.

Postmodern theology in the United States developed out of an engagement with the Death of God theology of Thomas J. J. Altizer, William Hamilton, Richard Rubenstein, Gabriel Vahanian, and others. By reading the German hermeneutic philosophy of Heidegger and Gadamer along with French poststructuralism and deconstruction together under the pressure of the death of God, the postmodern theology that emerged in the early 1980s with Mark C. Taylor,

Charles Winquist, Carl Raschke, and others twisted free of orthodoxy. Because Death of God theologies repudiated Barth's theology of biblical revelation, American radical theologians were able to encounter postmodern philosophy and creatively deploy it in new and important ways. As Raschke puts it in a collection of manifesto-style essays called *Deconstruction and Theology*, "deconstruction is the death of God put into writing," although in retrospect this thesis could be broadened to include postmodern theology in general.[8] Mark C. Taylor's *Erring: A Postmodern A/theology*, published in 1984, provides the *locus classicus* of postmodern theology with its four broad themes: the death of God, the disappearance of the self, the end of history, and the closure of the book.[9] In 1986, Charles Winquist published *Epiphanies of Darkness*, a densely complex epistemological work that inscribes Freudian and Lacanian themes of desire into theological thinking.[10] For Winquist, theological thinking manifests a complex desire for a "thinking that does not disappoint," but it does not thereby ignore or avoid messy and difficult questions including those posed by psychoanalytic theory.[11]

This book continues that original trajectory, despite a countermovement that has alternatively opposed and appropriated postmodern theological thinking in an attempt to restore orthodoxy. One version of postmodern theology that desires a restoration of orthodoxy is Radical Orthodoxy, which advertises itself as a post-secular philosophy. For Radical Orthodoxy, postmodern insights can be appreciated and appropriated, especially those that suggest a phenomenology of religious experience that sanctions the space for belief in a traditional or quasi-traditional manner. At the same time, the insights of psychoanalysis must be opposed and denigrated for theology to assert itself. Along these lines, Phillip Blond claims that psychoanalysis is "an essentially atheistic discourse" that cannot "reconcile a theological conceptuality."[12] Radical Orthodoxy can appropriate phenomenology for its theological ends, but it is forced to suppress or deny psychoanalytic insight. If psychoanalysis is incompatible with Radical Orthodoxy, then the question arises whether it is essentially incompatible with any theological orthodoxy. If this is the case, then what would it mean to construct an image of theological thinking in the context of psychoanalytic theory? Such a theology would necessarily be a radical theology, and it would be opposed to orthodoxy.

In addition to neoorthodox theologies, another important theoretical alternative has emerged — a continental philosophy of religion that directs the tools of continental philosophy to an analysis of religion and religious experience. This continental philosophy of religion is heavily influenced by the thought of Levinas and Derrida and is most notably associated with the work of John D. Caputo. Caputo's work follows the turn toward a conceptual grappling with the phenomenon of religion in Derrida's philosophy, and Caputo—especially in his influential book *The Prayers and Tears of Jacques Derrida*—accentuates the affirmative openness toward religion and religious belief suggested by Derrida's work.[13] Caputo, as a representative of continental philosophy of religion, has kept his distance from theology, suspicious of its status as "onto-theology," following Heidegger's critique. While Caputo favors a religion without religion, an open space for faith that would not be determined by orthodoxy, many representatives of the continental philosophy of religion employ the philosophies of a broad phenomenological tradition from Kierkegaard and Husserl to Heidegger, Levinas, and Derrida for the sake of a faith that in its belief and profession could be considered broadly orthodox, at least in a formal sense.[14]

The contemporary orthodoxy I am working against is not a Platonic orthodoxy—a set of correct opinions—but has to do with right beliefs in a modern and postmodern context. It is not literally a classical theological orthodoxy either, but more accurately a formal neo-orthodoxy. Contemporary orthodoxy in postmodern theology concerns the tremendous effort to affirm a belief in belief itself, above all the rightness of the Christian belief in a broad sense, although it is not fundamentalist in terms of its subscription to particular doctrines and dogmas.[15] The goal is to restore belief in Christianity's rightness, or at least to delineate a theoretical space within which Christian belief has at least as much validity as any other belief. Radical Orthodoxy aims more directly at the former goal, whereas much phenomenology of religion concerns itself with the latter. The problem with any variety of orthodoxy is that it is always Right, no matter how profound its phenomenological voice or how radical its commitment to any social or political theory. From the standpoint of psychoanalytic theory, orthodoxy expresses a powerful desire for faith and justified belief, even if contemporary theologies are sophisticated enough to understand the difficulties of attaining such beliefs in a credible manner, and contemporary orthodox theologies are forced to deploy complicated postmodern methodologies. The forceful expression of desire in itself is not enough to guarantee the object of desire. We can be suspicious of the nature of desire, having been duped by its duplicity before. We are not innocent, though we crave a second naiveté. At the same time, suspicion is not certainty, and to question the object or even the adequacy of desire is not the same thing as denying the possibility of its goal, or disavowing the desire itself.

If continental philosophy of religion itself is neutral, and keeps its distance from theology, this is both an asset and a weakness. The strength is that the phenomenological and philosophical readings are solid and are uncompromised by theological agendas. The weakness is that with the resurgence of orthodox varieties of postmodern theology, a continental philosophy of religion becomes unable to contest these theologies on their own grounds. This abdication forecloses any direct engagement with theological desire and ignores the significance of Freudian and Lacanian thought in postmodern theory. Continental philosophy of religion has ignored or downplayed the importance of psychoanalytic thought within French postmodernism.[16]

Derrida has consistently affirmed the importance of psychoanalytic thinking, even though he has questioned and critiqued both Freud and Lacan in important ways. In a strange non-encounter with Hans-Georg Gadamer, Derrida posed three brief questions, which Gadamer mostly either dismissed or misunderstood. After suggesting that Gadamer appeals to a Kantian notion of a "good will," Derrida asks what happens to good will "if one wants to integrate a psychoanalytic hermeneutic into a general hermeneutic?"[17] This central question is directed against Gadamer's assumption that the overall goal of discourse is understanding. Gadamer interprets Derrida's critical question as indicating a breach or a rupture within the process of understanding, which is what Gadamer is trying to overcome. Gadamer claims that "psychoanalytic interpretation does not seek to understand what someone wants to say, but instead what that person doesn't want to say or even admit to him or herself."[18] For this reason, psychoanalysis must be excluded from hermeneutics. On the other hand, Derrida's question suggests a more radical hermeneutics that involves attending to the ruptures that necessitate a "discontinous re-structuring" of discourse.

This book is an attempt to unsettle contemporary postmodern theology and continental philosophy of religion by taking up psychoanalytic theory and its continuing significance in and for religious thought. This is not a scholarly book "on" Freud, or "on" Lacan, but rather a book that seeks to inscribe Freudian and Lacanian thought into theological thinking in such a way that unsettles both theology and psychoanalysis. My readings follow the opening provided by Paul Ricoeur in *Freud and Philosophy*, which provides an epistemological reading of Freud as opposed to a scientific or a clinical/therapeutic reading.[19] In fact, the issues of reduction and sublimation are at the core of any attempt to think about religion in the context of psychoanalytic theory.[20]

The Sublime From Kant to Freud and Beyond

In *A Theology of the Sublime* I trace a link between the transcendental imagination in the *Critique of Pure Reason* and the notion of the sublime in the *Critique of Judgment*, relying on the insights of Heidegger, Lyotard, Derrida, and Deleuze.[21] At the same time, I argue that this reading is a theological reading by appealing to the thought of Paul Tillich. I suggest that the sublime, broadly understood, constitutes what Tillich calls the depth aspect of existence. In a sense, religion in the modern world can be defined as sublime; that is, what exceeds or resists the modern project of representation even as religion is ever the acknowledged or unacknowledged object of modern representation.

This book reads the Kantian sublime forward into Freud and Lacan, suggesting that psychoanalytic theory represents an elaboration of the Kantian sublime, even as it diffuses and bifurcates it. This reading follows the opening provided by Ricoeur's epistemological reading of Freud, which is essentially a Kantian reading. Ricoeur writes under the pressure of Lacan—although he fails to directly engage Lacan—but Ricoeur does develop a theoretical understanding of what is at stake between a language of force and a language of meaning. At the same time, Ricoeur inscribes teleology into Freud's thinking of sublimation, which allows him to restore Freudian psychoanalysis to meaning in a broadly Hegelian way.[22] I treat Ricoeur's reading of Freud in more detail in chapter 1, "On Sublimation," which also deals with the general question of sublimation and its relevance for understanding religion.

For Kant, the sublime is clearly located within the subject, not within the object. The disorientation provoked by the process of sublime judgment indicates a discord at the heart of the self, and this process prefigures the complexity and disorientation within the self diagnosed by psychoanalysis. In fact, according to Lacan, the psychoanalytic subject is modern and begins with Kant.[23] The Kantian sublime is characterized by an oscillation or trembling that occurs when the human being attempts to represent something that cannot be simply represented within human understanding. This sets off a struggle between imagination and reason to set things aright, and restore representation to its proper place. Imagination loses, but reason declares that its victory is essentially a moral victory and it reflects a human dignity that transcends the might of nature.[24]

The Freudian sublime calls reason's moral victory into question and accelerates the disorientation, suggesting that the self is composed of conflicting drives that can at best constitute an unstable and precarious accord. What I am calling the Freudian sublime indicates two distinct tendencies in Freud's thought: the notion of sublimation on the one hand, and trauma—or the death drive—on the other. These two processes cannot be thought separately, but must be seen as profoundly interrelated. Traumatic events open up holes— interstices that must then become stitched together in a complex process of sublimation that makes us who and what we are. The stitches are what Lacan calls quilting points, and they form knots or folds that open up a window on the Real as they simultaneously weave imaginary and symbolic discourses together.[25] A reading of the Freudian sublime as it is elaborated by Lacan, Kristeva, Žižek, and others, opens up a window to psychoanalytic concepts and conceptions as they pressure religious and theological understandings and self-understandings. Disorientation is necessarily unsettling, but it can also possess a certain revelatory intensity as it forces theological thinking to take into account its own unconscious desires, anxieties, and motivations. The psychoanalytic sublime refers to the uncanny and disorienting feeling of discord at the base of conscious reflection. This uncanny feeling before, behind, or other than conscious intentionality makes all determinate conscious reflection tremble, and this is a religious sensation or experience that demands honest theological reflection and articulation.

This book consists of distinct but related and overlapping readings that cluster around specific themes linked broadly to ideas of sublimation and creation. My goal is not to provide a seamless narrative but to open up spaces for theological reflection under the pressure of psychoanalytic theory from Freud to Lacan and Žižek. In chapter 2, "We Are All Mad: Theology in the Shadow of a Black Sun," I discuss theology and schizophrenia as represented in the image of the black sun, which includes a reading of Freud's case study of Judge Schreber along with insights from R. D. Laing, Gilles Deleuze, and Jacques Derrida. Schizophrenia becomes a problem that demands a broadly theological schizoanalysis, rather than simply a medical condition. Chapter 3, "Desiring the Thing," opens up the question of the ethics of psychoanalysis by considering the desire for the Thing discussed by Lacan in his Seminar VII. The desire for the Thing is beyond good and evil in a conventional moral sense, and indicates a powerful desire for what Lacan calls the Real. Sublimation is necessary because we cannot approach the Real in itself, but it is also problematic because it does not simply overcome the insistence of the Real in ethical and theological discourse. I return to the question of ethics—more explicitly in relation to God and the good—in chapter 8, "God Without Being (God)," which brings in a consideration of Marion's reading of Anselm's proof of God in relation to being. Here I critique Marion's reading in Lacanian terms by suggesting that "greater" cannot simply be assumed to be good in (human) moral terms. More than being, we want God to be good, but psychoanalysis suggests that this is not a simple want, and theology's God may be more subtle and ambivalent than many are prepared to admit.

Chapters 4, 5, and 8 each take up aspects of theological thinking about God, pressured by psychoanalytic insights in the wake of the death of God. Chapter 4, "Foreclosing God," considers the complex topic of foreclosure and combines a reading of Freud and Lacan with a consideration of Heidegger and Julia Kristeva. Foreclosure is not the same as disavowal, and if we foreclose God in a certain way we do not shut down but rather open up theological thinking. Chapter 5, "Anxiety and the S(ub)lime Body of God," considers the topic of anxiety, especially the anxiety of the body in relation to traditional thought about the divine and the human. I attend to Freud's reversal in his understanding of the relationship between anxiety and repression, and Slavoj Žižek's interpretations of Lacan in relation to Kant, to suggest a distinction between repression and anxiety in contemporary theology. Chapter 8, as mentioned above, deals with the relations between God and being and God and the good after Heidegger's critique of ontotheology, and revisits Anselm's proof of God under the pressure of Lacan's seminar on *The Ethics of Psychoanalysis*.

Chapters 4, 5, and 8 are wrapped around chapters 6 and 7, "Ages of the World and Creation *ex Nihilo*," which develops an understanding of creation *ex nihilo* out of a confrontation of Lacan and Tillich. The notion of creation in Lacan's work is introduced in chapter 3, but here it is explicitly related to Tillich and Schelling. A confrontation emerges out of a contrast between Tillich and Žižek in their respective readings of Schelling, and I provide my own reading of the second draft of Schelling's *Ages of the World*. The psycho-theological concept of creation *ex nihilo* rests at the center of the book and functions as an axis around which the other essays partially pivot.

Chapter 9, "Expressing the Real," grapples with the problem of the Real as expressed at the limits of language and possibly captured by a quasi-mathematical formalization in Lacan's later work, and these ideas are in turn related to a story by Herman Melville: *Benito Cereno*. Trying to formalize the Real ties us up in knots in many ways. In some ways, expressing the Real beyond the limits of language is a Platonic method of approaching the Real. A contemporary expression is Alain Badiou's mathematical ontology, which is strongly influenced by Lacan.[26] On the other hand, one can understand the Real more in terms of a process, and in chapter 10, "Processing the Real," I sketch out a trajectory from Aristotle through Spinoza and Whitehead to Deleuze and Lacan. Lacan can be read either in more Platonic or in more Aristotelian terms, but I argue that it is ultimately more fruitful to understand him in an Aristotelian manner. In addition, both chapters 9 and 10 provide distinct perspectives on Lacan's interpretation of the Real in *Seminar XX*.

In this book, then, I inscribe psychoanalytic theory into theology, primarily to unsettle theoretical thinking about religion. This discussion of psychoanalysis focuses around the notion of the sublime as it is expressed by Freud and interpreted by Lacan. The sublime is not a term that Freud uses, but I have reconstructed this idea in psychoanalysis by linking it in particular places in chapters 1, 3, and 5 to Kant's understanding of the sublime. The sublime is the object of sublimation, and the sublime is intrinsically religious. Furthermore, thinking about the sublime theologically is a creative albeit challenging task.

This book proceeds in a progressive although not a linear fashion—themes are developed, then returned to and redeveloped in subsequent chapters. This is not a chronological development, but rather a series of intensive reflections on distinct but overlapping themes. One image for this book could be that of a series of stepping stones that are not contiguous but create deep impressions in a sequential but winding manner. Between the stones, lines of grass, or filaments grow and connect the steps in a rhizomatic manner, to borrow a metaphor from Deleuze and Guattari.

Another way to think about this book is in terms of a circular orbit. Hopefully the circle is not a vicious circle, but rather is open at both ends. In many ways the book is centered on the middle chapters (4–8) that most explicitly deal with God. Furthermore, the book is specifically centered on the interpretation of creation *ex nihilo* that is developed in chapters 6 and 7. In some ways, the earlier chapters are essays or partial attempts that build up to this interpretation, which is an extensive reading of Schelling and Tillich in relation to Žižek and Lacan. In addition, in some ways the last three chapters consist of echoes or aftereffects of this central reading, as creation is implicated in God, the Real, and Substance. Throughout the entire book, the theme of sublimation persists, even if it becomes less obvious, although even sublimation is subordinated to the sublime, which goes by multiple names, including God, the Thing, the Other, the Real, and Substance.

These chapters constitute complex attempts to trace the sublime through Freud and Lacan and beyond, and indicate theological effects. Psychoanalysis resists theology even as theology resists psychoanalytic insights in an analogous way to the contested relationships between philosophy and psychoanalytic theory in France and elsewhere. At the same time, this struggle is necessary and vital to fashion a vital radical theology, a theology that is responsive to the death of God.

Psychotheology After the Death of God

The phrase, "death of God," can be understood in at least two distinct ways. In a metaphysical sense, God dies and in Hegelian fashion becomes immanent in and as the world. This is the viewpoint of Thomas J. J. Altizer's theology from *The Gospel of Christian Atheism* onwards.[27] The death of God is the kenotic self-sacrifice of God to be resurrected otherwise, in an ongoing process that points to a metaphysical end of history that would constitute a radical reconciliation of opposites. On the other hand, the death of God can be assimilated to the linguistic turn, in which the being of God is dissolved into language non-metaphysically. For Charles Winquist, following the linguistic turn means reflexively attending to theological formulations as discourse formations in the fashioning of a "theological tropology" in which "the concept of argument is itself deconstructed by reading the tropes or turns in language that characterize the discourse as levers of intervention."[28] A turn toward psychoanalytic theory—especially that of Lacan, who focuses overwhelmingly on language and integrates linguistics into psychoanalysis—enables one to better understand the theological implications of the linguistic turn.

If the being of God is dissolved into language, and if that is what the "death of God" means, or at least one meaning of the death of God, then the problem that results is the question of desire in language. Following the linguistic turn, along with any and all other "turns," theology must attend to that in which it is implicated, a turn from being—ontology in a Tillichian sense—to language. The question of desire results directly from the twentieth-century formulations of psychoanalysis, which transforms the nineteenth-century preoccupation with will into questions about desires and drives. If theological thinking signifies at least as much about the desire of the theologian (the desire for God) as it does about God in itself, then theology must attend to its expressions and formulations as indicating desire in a secular as well as a religious sense. Freud, Lacan, Kristeva, and Žižek provide theoretical tools to interrogate desire, and this interrogation possesses theological implications. This project is important whether or not the twenty-first century will overcome or transform the problem of desire as well as move beyond the issue of language. Such developments may be prophesied, but their truth remains to be seen.

If the metonymical object of desire is God, but God cannot be expressed as a referential object referred to by language or a concept within language, then in light of the linguistic turn this limit of language is felt as the death of God rather than as an inadequacy of language. Kristeva writes about "the crisis of truth in language," which refers to the interminable (not necessarily infinite) substitutability of words, concepts, and objects, without any ground or foundation. This means that the theological desire for God may function as a mask for other desires—political, psychological, ideological, and economic desires, among others. The substitutability and undecidability of desire, from an epistemological standpoint, converges with the acceleration of these substitutions in both a cultural and technological sense, which leans toward a schizophrenic limit in the interplay of desires and meanings.

Analytic description and prescriptive intervention are necessarily conjoined, and it is an open question whether our awareness of the duplicity of language prevents it from being recharged, or whether we will have to turn elsewhere for our salvation in a desperate grasp for transcendence that—from the standpoint of language—appears rather to be a return to naive realism. We are saturated in multivalent and polyvalent meanings, overwhelmed with "doublespeak" and ambiguity at a personal, social, and political level. These significations mask the "real" workings of the machinery of our global economy, whose engines turn exceedingly fast and grind exceedingly fine. I think we have to refuse any forced choice of either/or, the option of being stuck with language and the danger of its duplicity or thrust into a reality that is over-determined to mask the openness and ambiguity of its significations.

We have life, we have theory, and their interrelations are not simply dialectical. If we have passion in life, we should in no way disavow passion in theory, and this conclusion possesses religious implications.[29] Since science contests the Real, from a psychoanalytic point of view it functions "as a species of theology," whereas psychoanalysis "questions the manner by which its artifacts become real, and through the relation that represents desire, the relation between self and other."[30] We cannot simply or essentially separate theology as a discourse that contests the Real by representing it from psychoanalysis as a discourse that questions the manner and stakes of such representation. We can, however, establish a circuit between psychoanalytic theory and theology in hopes that it will prove to be a productive circuit by working (through) the sublime, which is at once sublimation and deconstruction of the Real, or the religious.

Eric Santner coins the phrase "psychotheology of everyday life" to suggest the link between a psychoanalytically informed view of life and religious experience and expression. According to Santner, Freudian psychoanalysis in its "spiritual" dimension attends to "the constitutive 'too muchness' that characterizes the psyche."[31] Santner claims that both the Jewish tradition in which Freud was steeped as well as Christianity testify that "human life always includes more reality than it can contain and this 'too much' bears witness to a spiritual and moral calling, a pressure toward self-transformation, toward 'goodness.'"[32] This understanding of Judaism and Christianity is fully secular in that it does not locate the "too muchness" above or outside the world in a transcendent way, but rather within it. The fact that we are always "too much" is both a problem and a challenge that spurs self-transformation, despite the resistances that psychoanalysis uncovers that teach us that knowledge is a brutal struggle, because, as Žižek says, "the fundamental desire is the desire *not* to know too much."[33]

Santner reads Franz Rosenzweig along with Freud to draw out this spiritual aspect of Freud's thought. Ultimately, "God is above all the name for the pressure to be alive to the world, to open to the too much of pressure generated in large measure by the uncanny presence of my neighbor."[34] This pressure and this experience occur within the midst of everyday life rather than in an otherworldly realm. Although Santner does not consider the specific violence that takes place between Christianity and Judaism, which are the most uncanny of neighbors, he does point to a way forward for thinking about their affinity within the context of a psychoanalytic space. A psychotheology inscribes a contemporary radical theological thinking after the death of God into the chaos of our postmodern world, without falling for the seductive trappings of orthodoxy. Working through the complex interrelationships of sublimation, creation, and the sublime in this book unfortunately does not reassure us that God loves and cares for us, but it does open a space for serious theological reflection.

1

On Sublimation

The Significance of Psychoanalysis for the Study of Religion

Introduction

Amid the multitudinous variety of historical, ethnographic, and cultural studies taking place within the academy, one can detect a certain crisis or at least confusion regarding theoretical discourse about religion. This confusion refers to the felt discord among heterogeneous languages and incommensurable modes of description and questioning. Such languages include traditional theology, analytic philosophy of religion, hermeneutics and other symbolic-semiotic languages, methodological approaches to the history of religions, and various forms of postmodernism. This confusion is felt at the same time as religion is being taken up by many philosophers and theorists as an important topic for understanding, in part as a response to cultural and political events during the last two decades.

My intention here is to rehabilitate a sometimes marginalized religious discourse—psychoanalysis. Psychoanalytic theory is not marginalized in literary or cultural theory, but it has not had as much influence on religious theorists, including those who study philosophers strongly influenced by Freud and Lacan. Such a proposal and rehabilitation will not "solve" the crisis or end the theoretical confusion that I diagnose, but it provides tools for casting some of the central theoretical issues and stakes differently. In fact, a sophisticated reading of psychoanalytic theory overcomes one of the most persistent problems of theorizing religious discourse—today—that of reductionism, which psychoanalysis is generally seen as necessarily involving. Psychoanalysis participates in the problem or controversy surrounding reductionism in many people's minds because it seems to settle the question of the origin and genesis of religious practices and beliefs in a materialistic way. This situation leads to oppositional conflict, because practitioners of religion experience their beliefs as trivialized, even when people who espouse psychoanalytic and psychological explanations still desire to value the significance of such beliefs and practices.

Intimately connected with this notion of reductionism is the question of sublimation, because sublimation represents the attempt to surmount the material reality, which is viewed as fundamental. Sometimes sublimation is seen as eliminating the most vicious aspects of reductionism by elevating such materiality. Other times opponents of psychoanalytic thinking criticize sublimation based on the idea that sublimation reinscribes the very reductionistic materialism it tries to overcome because it works with a material base. Heuristically, we can consider three schematic alternatives based on a simplified, provisional understanding of psychoanalytic theory: (1) religion is explained materialistically by psychoanalysis, and because it is a complex illusion, religion should be opposed and denigrated; (2) religion is explained materialistically by psychoanalysis, but it is a significant human and/or cultural achievement that should be valued according to a logic of sublimation; and (3) religion cannot be explained by psychoanalysis, and psychoanalysis should be opposed as necessarily denigrating the significance of religion and its spiritual value.

Within these three broad variations, my constructive thesis is that psychoanalytic theory is essential for thinking about religion but not in simple-minded reductionistic terms. This hypothesis depends upon a rethinking of sublimation—which will be undertaken below—as a recasting of position (2). Psychoanalytic thinking is crucial for contemporary cultural theory and postmodernism, but it is sometimes seen as inherently inimical to religious or theological thinking, as noted in (3) above.[1]

Vicissitudes of Theorizing Sublimation

Of course, psychoanalysis can function as a reductive theory that subsumes all others because psychoanalytic libidinal drives "explain" religious impulses and phenomena. The classic example is the beginning of Freud's *Civilization and Its Discontents*, which treats religious feeling or what Romain Rolland calls the oceanic as the result of an illusion brought about by the persistence of infantile ego feeling. Freud claims that our ordinary "present ego feeling is, therefore, only a shrunken residue of a much more—inclusive—indeed, an all-embracing—feeling which corresponded to a more intimate bond between the ego and the world around it."[2] Furthermore, Freud argues that the oceanic is not the true source of religion, which derives rather "from the infant's helplessness and the longing for the father aroused by it."[3] For orthodox Freudianism, religious feeling is an illusion that then becomes a collective delusion when humans objectify and worship the source of this feeling, regardless of whether the actual source is the persistence of an expanded infantile ego-feeling, or the need for the father brought about by the dependency of the infant.

Freud's hostility to standard forms and expressions of religion leads him to devalue religious feeling in relation to artistic and intellectual pursuits which represent a positive sublimation or elevation of primary drives. Later in *Civilization and Its Discontents*, Freud claims that sublimation, "such as the artist's joy in creating, in giving his phantasies body, or a scientist's in solving problems or discovering truths," yields a pleasure which "has a special quality. . . . [such] that such satisfactions seem 'finer and higher.'"[4] At the same time, however, sublimation remains a partial satisfaction because it "is mild compared with that derived from the sating of crude and primary instinctual impulses."[5]

In his book, *The Other Freud*, James J. DiCenso notes Freud's inconsistency regarding art as opposed to religion. "The psychological area that is so problematic when disclosed in religious formations," he writes, "becomes highly significant when channeled into art."[6] DiCenso rehabilitates religion's significance in terms of instinctual renunciation and cultural formation through careful and profound readings of Freud's later works, such as *Civilization and Its Discontents*, *The Future of an Illusion*, and *Moses and Monotheism*. At the same time, DiCenso critiques Freud's materialistic positivism which reduces sublimated expressions to instinctual drives. In his reading of *Moses and Monotheism*, DiCenso articulates a notion of *Geistigkeit* or spirituality as central to psycho-cultural existence, when understood "in a non-hypostatized, de-literalized form, to convey the dynamic relations mutually constitutive of symbolic systems and subjectivity."[7]

The result is a complex revalorization of sublimation which is opposed to Freud's expressly reductionistic mechanistic materialism.

The question of sublimation in some ways goes right to the core of any understanding and evaluation of psychoanalysis in relation to religion. If religion is a human phenomenon—whether understood primarily as feeling, practice, or belief (or all three)—then spirituality is the ability to transcend the material existence which is so empirically incorrigible. Within a materialistic or scientific *Weltanschauung* that characterizes the perception of the modern world, the question of religious transcendence necessitates either a denial of the materiality of the world or an elevation above it. Although psychoanalytic drives can be transfigured into mystical energies and Jungian archetypes, most adherents to psychoanalysis accept the material reality of the world and human existence, along with the irreducible sexual or libidinal quality of such drives.

On the other hand, as Jacques Lacan's interpretation of Freud makes clear, psychoanalysis recognizes an irreducible moment of interpretation that can be expressed under the name of the "talking cure."[8] The claim is that meaning or understanding in language can represent an intervention into the dynamics of force that constitute the libidinal drives. To enter into analysis implies a belief that understanding can alter neurosis, at least partially, and lead to—satisfaction—this is what sublimation is all about. What Freud's pessimism in *Civilization and Its Discontents* claims is that total satisfaction is impossible in society: all we can achieve is the partial satisfaction that sublimation allows.

Psychoanalysis cannot do without either force or meaning; the two are mutually interrelated in such a complex fashion that they cannot be extricated. In his work on *Freud and Philosophy*, Paul Ricoeur has demonstrated this relationship. He claims that Freud's core psychological theory implies that "the language of force can never be overcome by the language of meaning," though meaning is never thereby completely eliminated.[9] Although DiCenso criticizes Freud's reductionism, Ricoeur's work opens up an epistemological reading of Freud and of psychoanalysis as a whole. Here Ricoeur defines symbol and interpretation in terms of each other, and asserts that "very excess of meaning in comparison with the literal expression that puts the interpretation in motion."[10] By reading Freud philosophically and epistemologically, psychoanalysis becomes a mode of interrogation or questioning which raises difficult issues but does not settle them, despite Freud's personal belief in the literal materiality of the drives.

Ricoeur's reading, upon which DiCenso relies in his work on Freud's cultural writings, allows one to read Freud's metapsychological work itself as more *geistig* (spiritual) and less reductive.

Before turning to a (re)reading of sublimation in Freud's metapsychology, I want to note that Ricoeur also returns to Freud's cultural work to reestablish interpretation or capture force in meaning, despite his awareness of the risks involved: "The danger for the philosopher . . . is to arrive too quickly, to lose the tension, to become dissipated in the symbolic richness, in the abundance of meaning."[11] Nevertheless, because Ricoeur understands the task of the philosopher in an essentially Hegelian way, he demands the retrieval of meaning via hermeneutical interpretation. It should be stressed that this philosophical move is also a sublimation, and in fact Ricoeur claims that "sublimation is the symbolic function itself."[12] Here is a repetition of the question of sublimation, a displacement into the realm of theoretical meaning. On the one hand, sublimation has to do with the redemption of material reality, which in itself is seen as fallen, depressing, or meaningless. On the other hand, sublimation is also at stake in a theoretical orientation to reality, which Ricoeur perhaps too quickly assimilates to the essence of philosophy. At a primary level, philosophy or theoretical reflection on religion can be seen as a sublimation of instinctual drives of aggression and sexuality into the individual and cultural desires to know and create models of reality. At a secondary level, sublimation is internal to philosophizing or representing as the retrieval of positive meaning in an affirmation of force either as it is or as transfigured in(to) symbolic interpretation.

Ricoeur, however, recognizes the existence of a philosophy or hermeneutics of suspicion, even if he attempts to contain it with a philosophy of retrieval. Here a suspicious philosophical approach raises troubling questions about both reality (force) and philosophizing itself (the adequacy of meaning), in a way that repeats the disturbing nature of psychoanalysis itself. Psychoanalytic thinking becomes the paradigm of a hermeneutics of suspicion that must be rescued or sublimated in a hermeneutics of retrieval. The question is whether every inquiry and every piece of writing is an exercise in retrieval, and if not, why should it not be? One answer might be that a "retrieval" or sublimation of our experience is dishonest or insincere; that to idealize experience which may be messy, brutal, painful, or even banal into a beautiful philosophical or religious worldview may consist in a distortion that undermines the credibility of sensory experience. Of course, the "faith" in sensory experience may then be seen reductively (by critics) as a materialistic positivism which is ultimately nihilistic; on the other hand, Nietzsche, who is usually singled out as a nihilistic thinker, devotes much of his thinking to an attack on deceptive ideals which devalue sensory experience because self-devaluation of these very ideals of the supersensuous, or ascetic ideals, are precisely what bring about nihilism, or what he calls the death of God.[13]

These difficulties revolve around a reading of sublimation at the center of Freud's work, one which Ricoeur has provided tools to rethink. When entering into Freud's metapsychology, however, it is important to note that what Freud calls the unconscious is not an objectified entity but a dynamic principle of explanation that is testified to only indirectly. Freud does not simply oppose two entities or mechanisms, consciousness and unconsciousness (or later three, id, ego, and superego). Rather, as his masterwork on *The Interpretation of Dreams* demonstrates, it is the slips, breaks, and distortions within consciousness which require the positing of an unconscious mechanism. This mechanism, additionally, is not simply the passive realm of preconscious thought of things which have escaped conscious awareness, but an active force that prevents certain thoughts from becoming conscious. We only know that such a force exists by the resistance which occurs when we attempt to wrest such ideas into conscious awareness. "How are we to arrive at a knowledge of the unconscious?" Freud writes in his 1915 essay, "The Unconscious." "It is of course only as something conscious that we know anything of it, after it has undergone transformation or translation into something conscious."[14] Lacan later elucidates the Freudian unconscious as structural, with the help of structural linguistics based on Saussure, but already in Freud the unconscious is not a static entity or a thing.

What occurs when an instinct or a drive becomes repressed, and then how do sublimation or partial satisfaction and redirection of a drive work? In his 1915 essay, "Instincts and Their Vicissitudes," Freud discusses the events which befall the instincts or drives along their route to a predetermined goal. Although his language reads as extremely technical and scientific, and in fact is made more so by the translation of *Trieben* as "instincts," it is important to follow the argument carefully in terms of what Freud is actually saying. Freud writes about a "stimulus of instinctual origin" which is called a "'need'; that which does away with this need is 'satisfaction.'"[15] So instinctual drives are stimuli which exhibit a need, and the aim or goal of the need is in every case satisfaction, which is the elimination of the need as a need. Freud distinguishes among the aim, the impetus or motor element, the somatic source, and the object through which a drive can achieve its aim.[16] He then spends most of the essay laying out the four major vicissitudes or detours which the drive can undergo: reversal into its opposite, turning round upon the subject, repression, and sublimation. Freud primarily discusses the first two and leaves an extended analysis of repression to the 1915 essay by that name. Significantly, he writes, "I do not intend to treat of sublimation here."[17]

What Freud's essay assumes, in the context of his metapsychology, is a standard or normal paradigm of the stimulation of a drive and its satisfaction in an activity. Humans experience drives which possess a somatic or bodily source, and they express a direct desire or need which immediately calls forth the activity which satisfies them. For instance, if someone becomes conscious of an itch, that expresses itself as a need which is attributed to a drive which demands satisfaction by scratching. The activity of scratching satisfies the need by doing away with it. This simple model is made complex by civilization, which requires that primary drives undergo vicissitudes. These vicissitudes take different forms, and some forms are "better" than others, but every vicissitude or detour implies a deviation from immediate satisfaction, and thus entails a certain amount of dissatisfaction or discontent.

The fundamental question, which Lacan opens up, is whether the existence of language mediates every drive such that it is no longer possible to speak of satisfaction but only of some form of vicissitude. When Lacan claims that the unconscious is structured like a language, he means not only that the unconscious exhibits an uncanny sort of sense, but also that for human beings we cannot isolate purely instinctual drives which necessitate satisfaction from linguistic vicissitudes that mediate satisfaction. In his Rome Discourse on "The Function and Field of Speech and Language in Psychoanalysis," Lacan contrasts language with creative speech that delivers the psychoanalytic symptom from the clutches of language. He reverses Goethe's reversal of speech and deed: "it was certainly the Word that was in the beginning, and we live in its creation, but it is our mental action that continues this creation by constantly renewing it."[18] Satisfaction is a complex state which is evaluated and determined from a point within language rather than a simple determination that a specific neuron fired or not. If satisfaction works purely and directly, then how can one become conscious of it? The immediacy of satisfaction of a need implies that it does not undergo any vicissitudes, and yet consciousness implies the mediation of language, which is already a vicissitude that forces one to negotiate satisfaction rather than instinctually actualize it. Becoming conscious of scratching one's ear institutes a certain detour, and this detour can become more or less complex depending on the social situation and its resonances, or scratching one's ear might be interpreted as a symptom of something else which is going on, but already with language and consciousness the gap or mediation is there in what I am calling a vicissitude, following Freud.

Prior to Lacan, Freud already wrestled with the vicissitudes of language, meditating at the end of "The Unconscious" on the relation between word and thing as the determining characteristic of schizophrenia. His relentless and probing questioning allows him to detect a resemblance between the schizophrenic's inability to master the split between word and thing and his or her abandonment to a world of abstraction, and "the expression and content of our own philosophizing."[19] Freud claims that the schizophrenic "treats concrete things as though they were abstract." The dangers of philosophizing, however, arise from "a danger that we may neglect the relations of words to unconscious concrete ideas."[20] What is incredibly complicated here is the relationship between word and thing at the core of human psychological thinking and functioning. One vicissitude that can result is an extreme inability to dissociate word from thing in schizophrenia, as I consider further in chapter 2. Another closely related vicissitude is the difficulty of using an abstract theoretical language to probe this very relation between thing and word or idea in terms of conscious and unconscious processes.

The question is whether we can delimit the realm of things and the realm of ideas with certainty, and if not, what does this imply for the satisfaction of drives? If satisfaction has to do with material things and not with ideas, then the detour into language implies that drives *necessarily* undergo vicissitudes. Even if we can imagine an action that immediately satisfies a need, in order for it to become conscious, it must be thought, and if it is thought then there is something else that attends to it that affects the evaluation of it as satisfying. Here the implication is that the only drives which do not undergo vicissitudes are those that remain unconscious; or rather, drives that never become conscious (not even to undergo repression; Freud uses the term preconscious in his metapsychological essays). This would consist of purely physiological processes like breathing and heartbeat, with the proviso that they remain unaffected by consciousness. If this is what Freud means by satisfaction, then his theory is at bottom materialistic, but not very interesting, especially in terms of the richness of Freud's own work, which consistently grapples with the effects of the vicissitudes of drives.

Furthermore, sublimation would be a particular form of vicissitude that would be a "partial" satisfaction, but would not all of the other modes of vicissitude be in some way entangled in sublimation? Here one would have to oppose satisfaction in its "ideal" physiological sense, which never even enters into relation with consciousness; and with satisfaction in a complex sense that invokes both unconscious and conscious or primary and secondary processes. The point is that reversal into its opposite, turning round upon the subject, and above all repression all carry along a certain amount of satisfaction, even if such satisfaction is diagnosed to be neurotic or psychotic. Repression would not occur if it did not involve satisfaction at some level, according to the pleasure principle. Here sublimation would have to be expanded to relate to all of the various vicissitudes, because sublimation conveys both partial satisfaction and the impossibility of complete satisfaction. In fact, sublimation becomes the essence of vicissitude itself because no criterion exists to distinguish the two within the interior realm of psychic functioning. This equation of vicissitude with sublimation creates ambivalence regarding the natural aim of the drives, as well as the adequacy of our conception of satisfaction. The ambivalence that makes up sublimation then extends to all of our drives such that even powerful and seemingly immediate drives of aggression and sexuality would have to be understood as mediated in complex ways by language, society, and representations of power, identity, and self-esteem. It is much too simplistic to assume that murderous impulses, for example, are immediate and straightforward, rather than to appreciate the fact that homicidal drives already exist in a state of sublimation, at least at the conscious level. In a sense, one could say that the only pure object of desire that is not sublimated would be God, understood in a certain metonymical way as the totality of the field of primordial desire rather than conceptually as an object or Supreme Being.

Ideality or Materiality of Affects?

What would it mean to think of a drive in itself, a pure drive or desire untainted by any negotiation or compromise, a drive that strives to attain pure satisfaction totally and completely? This pure drive can only be expressed through language, and a basic physiological notion of satisfaction actually brings about no satisfaction to the subject because there is no "sense" of satisfaction. The alternative is the possibility that a drive already possesses a linguistic component in itself; that there exists no possible drive that is not already vicissitude.

In his essay on "The Unconscious," Freud repeats his mental topography already established in "The Project for a Scientific Psychology" and *The Interpretation of Dreams* of conscious-unconscious-preconscious. Again, the major distinction is between conscious and preconscious processes on the one hand and unconscious processes on the other. The phenomenon of repression that takes place in unconscious processes is related to the role and function of censorship, which precludes certain things from entering consciousness. In his essay on "Repression," Freud distinguishes between primary repression, in which something is kept out of consciousness, and repression proper, or after-expulsion, in which something that was at one point conscious is rejected or eliminated from consciousness. What is repressed from consciousness?

Freud makes the striking claim that "the antithesis of conscious and unconscious does not hold for instincts. An instinct can never become an object of consciousness—only the idea that represents the instinct."[21] He goes on to claim that "even in the unconscious, moreover, it can only be represented by an idea." The instinct or drive in itself is a feeling, emotion, or affect. Freud states that "for emotions, feelings, and affects to be unconscious would be out of the question." There are no unconscious affects, only unconscious ideas. To speak of something as unconscious is to refer to "an instinctual impulse the ideational presentation of which is unconscious." Ideas undergo repression, become unconscious, and thus appear to be subject to vicissitudes. Affects, on the other hand, do not appear to undergo vicissitudes. According to Freud, affects always directly express, fulfill, or achieve their aim; he calls an affect "a process of discharge."[22] It is the nature of ideas, however, to undergo detours along the route toward satisfaction.

In "The Unconscious" Freud distinguishes between *Vorstellung* and *Repräsentanz*. A conscious idea or representation is called a *Vorstellung*; this is a concept which can be separated from what it represents and is necessary for conscious thinking to occur. On the other hand, a *Repräsentanz* is the ideational representative of the drive itself. This is what Ricoeur calls a psychical idea, which intimately relates an affect of pure force to a meaning at its most basic level.[23] The notion of *Repräsentanz* or ideational presentation is invoked by Freud to account for what undergoes repression instead of an affect, because "the affect was never unconscious but its ideational presentation had undergone repression."[24] The ideational presentation is a heuristic construct provided by Freud to explain the bare ideational component necessary for repression to occur. Repression needs the resistance of ideas to work. Affects are pure discharges which possess nothing to catch hold of to repress or make unconscious. This is why affects cannot be said to undergo vicissitudes — they lack any friction which would allow their path to satisfaction or discharge to be impeded. Something strange is going on here. Affects are described in tones that make them sound absolutely ideal — they seem to possess no material effects, whereas it is ideas that possess the materiality or resistance (in a psychic sense), which allows redirection. The difficulty is that at this level of psychic functioning a clear distinction between ideality or spirituality and materiality threatens to break down. Is pure energy ideal or material? Is a *Repräsentanz* an ideal or material "representation?" Affects are described almost in terms of the neutrinos which pass through the earth so quickly that until recently it was speculated that they possessed no mass. Recent scientific experiments, however, have established a minute mass for the neutrino. What about affects?

Ricoeur assimilates Freud's discussion of affects to a pure economics of force, which must be described in quantitative terms, but then he relates the "vicissitudes of quantity" to "vicissitudes of affects," including the absence of affect and anxiety.[25] So perhaps affects are not so pure after all, and do indeed undergo displacement, even if we cannot describe such displacements except in ideational terms. The conclusion Ricoeur draws, however, is that the irreducible character of affects implies a splitting of ideas and energies at the basic core situation of repression. The conscious concept or *Vorstellung* is split into the word and thing referred to. The unconscious "something" is split, however, into an ideational and an affective component. This splitting implies that "the language of force can never be overcome by the language of meaning," even if meaning is never completely eliminated.[26]

Ricoeur stresses the negative conclusion because he wants philosophical hermeneutics to retrieve meaning from the jaws of psychoanalytic force, but I am suggesting that we think of psychoanalysis and theoretical reflection much more intimately. Is not religion always already implicated in relations of force and relations of meaning? And is this not necessarily so? Finally, what if these two relations are not set up, one on top of the other, in a repetition of a two-tiered world of nature and supernature, but rather combined into a single-swirled phenomenon or discourse? In this situation, psychoanalytic inquiry raises powerful and even disturbing questions regarding the disruption of conscious intentions by processes of deceit, disguise, and distortion that cannot simply be settled by a sublation which is a leap to a higher level. Such an understanding is a simplification of sublimation thought as an inevitable vicissitude that human drives and desires undergo. Such vicissitudes may be de-meaning, uncomfortable, and embarrassing, such as the scapegoating of certain peoples or adherents of another religion due to strategies of compensation, inferiority, and greed, or they may be poignant, profound, and inspiring, such as transfigurations of material existence, which allow ethical gestures of benevolence and mercy. I am suggesting that sublimation be thought of more broadly as a redirection or repetition of a primary drive. The primary drive as primary drive, which Freud calls pure affect, is inaccessible as such. Even when primary processes are thought as primary processes, they are also inevitably thought through the mediation of secondary processes. If the primary drive represents a limit, then the whole field of human activity and understanding has to be figured as sublimation. This is what DiCenso is working toward in *The Other Freud*, although he fails to conduct a more complex, nonreductive, and *geistig* reading of the central metapsychology. Ricoeur provides many resources for such a reading, but he too-consistently separates a philosophical appropriation of the insights of Freudian epistemology to a broadly Hegelian philosophical retrieval of meaning as positive interpretation of symbols, which allows room for a valorization of cultural myth and religious faith. Ricoeur assimilates the "empty concept of sublimation" to "the symbolic function itself," but he holds tightly to the priority of the disclosure of what symbols reveal over the concealment of what they disguise.[27]

Sublimation as Repetition of Difference: Deleuze

What are the possibilities of a reinterpretation of sublimation that does not eliminate either the integrity of what is sublimated or the authenticity of the sublimation itself as a creative process and a profound achievement? Can we do anything other than sublimate insofar as we exist as conscious human beings and do not nostalgically hold out the possibility of living in a pure utopian state? Or rather, we may still possess hope for such a state, but its realization as such may seem incredible given the situation of the world we inhabit, especially in light of the history of the twentieth century as well as the violence that has inaugurated the twenty-first.

Sublimation remains "uncanny," however, because its ability to distort or disguise messy power dynamics and "reality" may lend it an aura of inauthenticity. According to DiCenso, "Freud sees the emergence of cultural ideals as akin to neurotic repression and the return of the repressed. However, . . . this analysis also shows that linguistic and ideational forms take on a life of their own, becoming independent of material sources and forces."[28] In other words, DiCenso critiques the notion of the return of the repressed as a sublimation and renunciation that is merely a material repetition of neurotic identity, but he opens up the possibility of a cultural sublimation that is creative and productive of genuine difference. I am suggesting that sublimation at the individual level of identity can be understood already as creative in both linguistic and ideational forms.

In *Difference and Repetition*, Gilles Deleuze criticizes Freud in similar terms. According to Freud, the compulsion to repeat is the result of a profound repression, which is analyzed in *Beyond the Pleasure Principle*. In contrasting a repetition of identity that is a bare repetition of the same to a repetition of difference, Deleuze develops a notion of repetition that is more fundamental, such that repression is secondary to repetition. He reverses Freud's formula, "we repeat because we repress," and instead claims "we repress because we repeat."[29] Deleuze criticizes Freud's speculative conception of the death instinct because it is "understood as a return to inanimate matter, [it] remains inseparable from the positing of an ultimate term, the model of a material and bare repetition and the conflictual dualism between life and death."[30]

Repetition must be thought here in terms of sublimation. A psychoanalytic model of repetition that anchors repetition in a realist or materialist identity that is then "repeated" in various ways with varying amounts of success or satisfaction remains caught within the logic of a repetition of identity that denies difference. On the other hand, the understanding of a repetition of difference that Deleuze develops does not posit an original essence to be repeated, but rather conceives identity as constructed out of the different repetitions or iterations. What Deleuze calls "the traditional theory of the compulsion to repeat in psychoanalysis" conceives sublimation as a repetition of identity, whereas in this chapter I am trying to reconceptualize sublimation as a repetition of difference.[31] Traces of such an understanding already exist in the Freudian corpus (I have suggested) because of the impossibility of circumscribing or containing the vicissitudes of the drives along with the entanglements of language and representation, which can be neither pinned down within the psychic apparatus nor exorcised from its essential functioning.

Understanding sublimation as a repetition of difference allows a valuation of the repetitions as redirections of psychic drives, which deconstructs the opposition of lower material and higher spiritual reality. At the same time, Deleuze utilizes a more complex and nuanced understanding of affect that takes into account its internal division, already inchoately intimated in Freud. As I will discuss further in chapter 8, Deleuze introduces the notion of the virtual to overcome the opposition between potential and actual. For Deleuze, affects are virtual, rather than simply or purely potential. As Brian Massumi puts it, "affect is the virtual as point of view," or "affects are virtual synesthetic perspectives anchored in (functionally limited by) the actually existing, particular things that embody them."[32] The repetition of difference distributes affects as virtualities, and affect is the "material" of sublimation.

The problem with a straightforward materialism is not primarily that it threatens to undermine the lofty conceptions of spirituality that we desire to cling to, but that it simplifies and reduces the significance of a complex and important material reality, which in certain ways is always already spiritual, just as spirit is always already material, and this imbrication of material and spiritual coalesces around the notion of affect. These two "realities" are heuristic devices, which function to make provisional value determinations. But they are in fact entangled or swirled together to such an extent that it is impossible to separate them.

If sublimations are repetitions of difference that are productive of creative effects, this notion introduces a destabilization into any thinking that is concerned with segregating material and spiritual reality. The reason Freud insists upon a return of the repressed is that these forces or drives cannot be completely contained or pinned down; they always threaten to break out anew in a disturbing fashion. Again, there are two distinct conceptions here. A material return of the repressed implies that libidinal drives that cannot be socially expressed in a direct fashion "return" or break out in socially disruptive ways at a "higher" level. Here the resistance to such a notion might imply the sophisticated critique of mechanistic materialism developed here, or it might simply express repugnance toward explaining sublime spiritual desires in terms of base drives of aggression and sexuality. On the other hand, a return of the repressed understood in terms of the logic of sublimation understood as a repetition of difference implies that meanings and drives do not necessarily stay put—they wander, and this confusion can also be felt as extremely threatening. This latter theory should not imply that we are delivered from aggressive and sexual motivations—what Nietzsche would call the egoistic expressions of will to power—but rather that such motivations themselves are extremely complex phenomena which necessarily involve "spiritual" considerations. The point is not to reduce one level to another, or to do away with "positive" or reassuring feelings by converting them to negative and discomforting ones or vice versa, but to attend honestly to the complexities of thinking human desires and to possess the strength to raise difficult and disturbing psychoanalytic questions without necessarily believing that asking the question is the same as answering it.

Theologisms

Psychoanalysis provides a tool for thinking about religion as a complex (at least) human phenomenon, although it does not exhaust or explain it. A nonreductive theory of Freudian psychoanalysis and sublimation can enrich our conceptual understandings of religion, especially when augmented by the work of later thinkers such as Lacan, Deleuze, Kristeva, Derrida, and Žižek. The elaboration of a sophisticated psychoanalytic theoretical discourse can contribute to a complex theoretical discourse about religion that combines continental philosophy, theology, and theoretical issues concerning the history of religions.[33] As a conclusion to this chapter, however, I want to sketch a theological trajectory from Descartes to Freud and beyond to raise the stakes of crossing psychoanalytic and theological thinking. This reading is tentative and experimental, but it is suggestive of a general sense of modern historical experience, and will provide context for some of the more specific themes considered in later chapters.

In his essay, "Descartes and Onto-theology," Jean-Luc Marion explains that Descartes refashions the world in terms of the thinking subject, or *cogito*. Although in his *Meditations on First Philosophy* Descartes offers proofs for the existence of God, Marion explains that God is thought negatively as the source of a power that limits the subject. This situation expresses a separation of intellect and power, which were previously united in medieval and Thomistic speculations about God. In defining the *cogito* as a thinking being par excellence, Descartes removes thinking from God and subsequently is able to think of God only in terms of unthinking power. Marion writes, "God does not so much cogitate as He cannot cogitate. The exercise of *cogitatio* neither reaches Him nor defines Him as much as does the exercise of power."[34] The result is that God becomes "radically incomprehensible" except as power. Hereafter in modernity, for the most sophisticated philosophical understanding, God can be thought but cannot be conceived as thinking.

The separation of thinking from power in God leads to what the theologians of Radical Orthodoxy such as John Milbank and Phillip Blond call modern sublimity, which in Kant takes the form of "the final denial of the transcendent."[35] The Kantian sublime represents the epitome of modern aporias concerning God because the sublime is thought of as a power that threatens to overwhelm reason. In the *Critique of Judgment*, Kant treats the analytic of the sublime as an appendage to his theory of taste or beauty. The sublime represents a contra-purposiveness that occurs when a natural object prompts the mind to attempt to make a presentation of infinity in a single intuition.

In the *Critique of Pure Reason*, Kant elaborates how human faculties of imagination and understanding work together to produce determinate, objective knowledge. Reason does not play a direct role in the first *Critique*, but supplies merely regulative ideas to guide the production of knowledge. The important point is that imagination is consistently subordinated to understanding in the subsumption of sensible intuitions under conceptual categories. In the third *Critique*, however, understanding and imagination work together in a free accord to produce aesthetic knowledge. Judgments of taste are necessarily subjective, even though they can be universally referred to any rational being. What distinguishes the sublime, however, is that imagination outstrips the ability of the understanding to conceptualize it in a linear presentation. To "save" knowledge, reason is forced to directly intervene, to demand that the imagination perform a role that previously in the third *Critique* and also in the *Critique of Pure Reason* was the responsibility of the understanding. Reason is forced to show the limits of imagination to preserve its ultimate interests.[36]

This demand by reason placed upon the imagination sets off a struggle that produces a negative pleasure within the subject. Even though reason is ultimately able to contain the disturbing power of imagination, according to Kant, "if a thing is excessive for the imagination and the imagination is driven to such excess as it apprehends the thing in intuition, then the thing is, as it were, an abyss in which the imagination is afraid to lose itself."[37]

The abyss that the imagination fears—and to which it is inadequate—characterizes modern sublimity for Radical Orthodoxy. This situation can be understood as a consequence and further development of Descartes's thinking. According to Blond, the result of the Kantian sublime "is that God becomes both unknowable and yet deeply feared."[38] The response of Radical Orthodoxy as well as Marion is to try to mend the break and rehabilitate a notion of transcendent deity that is conceptualized as both powerful and thinking. If God is thought as rational then God would not be seen as fearful or negative, and transcendence can be viewed in continuity with human existence rather than as a radical break. What these more orthodox postmodern theologians miss, however, is the elaboration of the Kantian sublime into the Freudian unconscious, which locates God at the heart of the subject as a dislocation of power and thinking within the human being.

For Kant, "sublime is what even to be able to think proves that the mind has a power surpassing any standard of sense."[39] This power, which lies at the core of heterogeneous faculties of human thinking, becomes elaborated in the hermeneutics of suspicion by Nietzsche, Marx, and Freud. The hermeneutics of suspicion, which is Ricoeur's term, introduces disguise, distortion, and relations of power, egoism, and sexuality into the gap Kant opens up within human representation. To raise these disturbing questions, and to take seriously the hermeneutics of suspicion, is not simply to accept their descriptions and explanations unthinkingly, but taking such difficult questions seriously remains far from a strategy of containment or reassurance that seeks to allow such questions only to dismiss them. In the case of Freud, and following Ricoeur's epistemological—that is, basically Kantian—reading, the dynamic notion of the unconscious at the base of human desire and thinking testifies to a further permutation of Descartes's separation.

What the Radical Orthodox theologians miss is that already in Kant sublimity disrupts thinking not as external limit, as in Descartes, but internally to subjective consciousness. Freud then develops his notion of the unconscious to explain processes of displacement, condensation, secondary revision, and conditions of representativeness that occur in the dreamwork. The truly radical notion that Freud introduces into this philosophical process is that the thinking that was formerly attributed to God is not simply attributed to the human subject; in the idea of the unconscious a notion of power is reunited with a process of thinking that takes place before, behind, or beneath the conscious subject. This thinking, however, is not a conscious thinking, but it does exhibit a different logic or sense that can be known only indirectly. One way to describe this unconscious logic would be with the term "uncanny." In his essay on "The Uncanny," Freud identifies the source of the Kantian sublime as the estrangement of the ego from itself at its most basic and familiar level. The uncanny perception or feeling produces a negative pleasure, just like the Kantian sublime. The purposiveness refers to a felt sense of familiarity, almost a *déja vu*, while the negativity inherent in the feeling attests to the radical disorientation it introduces because such a feeling cannot quite be possessed or owned. Freud explicitly identifies the source of the uncanny judgment with the compulsion to repeat, which later constitutes the death drive in *Beyond the Pleasure Principle* when he writes that "whatever reminds us of this inner 'compulsion to repeat' is perceived as uncanny."[40] Deleuze has critiqued the compulsion to repeat as a materialistic assumption tied to a notion of repetition of a bare identity, and thus called into question the location of the source of this feeling. On the other hand, to question of where the uncanny feeling comes from is different from denying its existence. For Freud, the feeling of the uncanny is an analogue of the Kantian sublime and testifies to the force of unconscious or primary processes. If the uncanny feeling is the result of a complex primary process thinking, then such a feeling also testifies to the thinking that was previously characterized as divine, according to this speculative genealogy.

The Kantian sublime thus passes into the Freudian unconscious, and reappears, most explicitly and powerfully, in the sense of the uncanny that disturbs conscious thinking from inside. A theology that attends to psychoanalytic reality, then, must interrogate such traces of divinity that are expressed in primary processes, following Lacan's famous claim that "God is unconscious."[41] One of the tasks of such theological thinking, then, would be to explicate the conclusion of *The Four Fundamental Concepts of Psychoanalysis*, where Lacan juxtaposes the "dark God" of Nazism that evidences "the presence of the desire of this Other," to Spinoza's *Amor intellectualis Dei*, or intellectual love of God.[42] Lacan evokes Spinoza, however, only to disqualify his "transcendent love" from our contemporary experience. Our experience of the world is closer to Kant's; that is, it carries along with it the extreme dangers of moral law and (religious) sacrifice and murder that attend to the grappling with human desire, which is always the desire of the Other. The Other is not God; it is rather the required locus of symbolic discourse, but this desire may detect alternately brighter and darker shards of a broken divinity.

For theology, the question is whether psychoanalytic tools can be used to interrogate and conceptualize notions of divinity. I am suggesting that a constructive theological thinking can understand itself as a creative sublimation of tradition and/or religious experience. Such sublimation would be a repetition of difference rather than a repetition anchored in a fundamental identity, to which more orthodox theologies desire to return. My nonreductive interpretation of sublimation differs from the alternatives present in most readings of religion and psychoanalysis, as explained at the beginning of the chapter. An understanding of theology in a broad sense as a sublimation of religious experience means that theological discourse can be interrogated for its repressive and liberating aspects, based on how it interprets religious experience, which I would call (the) sublime.

The sublime is uncanny, and while it is always caught up in a complex process of sublimation, it is also disturbing. And if it is thought apart from sublimation, it is akin to madness. Religion in its extreme form verges on madness if it cannot be contained within the limits of reason. In chapter 2, I will consider schizophrenia as a fruitful term of psychoanalysis to stimulate theological thinking, and the image of the black sun will be offered as a trope under which to read this psychotic sign.

2

We Are All Mad

Theology in the Shadow of a Black Sun

Almost everywhere it was madness which prepared the way for the new idea, which broke the spell of a venerated usage and superstition.
— **Phillipe Lacoue-Labarthe,** *Typography*

Varieties of Schizophrenic Language: The Case of Schreber

Schizophrenia usually refers to the most representative case of psychoanalytic or psychiatric pathology or psychosis. Taken as a problem, however, schizophrenia concerns not simply a medical diagnosis but a condition that implicates all of human culture and signification.[1] In this chapter I do not want to settle the question of schizophrenia by locating it or attributing it to a particular and determinate region of discourse, be it political, cosmological, or psychological. I want rather to write schizophrenia large as a profound problem that is ultimately a theological problem. In this effort I want to resist any simple assimilation of theological discourse as a realm of discourse that corresponds to what I am calling cosmic or cosmological. What I am approaching, however obliquely, is the question of schizophrenia in and as language itself, and it is this question that is to be understood as theological.

Freud's famous case study, *Psycho-analytic Notes on an Autobiographical Account of a Case of Paranoia (Dementia Paranoides)*, grapples with the *Memoirs of My Nervous Illness*, by Daniel Paul Schreber, an unsettling and compelling account of a former judge attempting to come to terms with his illness.[2] Judge Schreber recounts his delusions and hallucinations, including his persecution by his physician, Flechsig, which he calls soul murder. This persecution develops into persecution by God, which includes the transformation of Schreber from a man into a woman. In his diagnosis, Freud allows space for Schreber's elaboration on the conditions of his illness, particularly Schreber's division of the creative powers of the human soul and God respectively into nerves and rays. Schreber's relation to God is complex and ambivalent because God both torments and needs Schreber, and also because God is not omnipotent; God is constrained by what Schreber calls the Order of Things.[3] Freud focuses on Schreber's transformation into a woman, and eventually reduces the complexity of Schreber's discourse to an Oedipal relation between Schreber and his father, where God occupies the role of Schreber's father in the psychotic symptoms.[4] Freud simplifies a complex discourse with individual psychological, social-political, and cosmic-theological registers, into a straightforward genetic explanation based on the Oedipus complex.

The basic question is on what level Schreber's struggle plays itself out. Is Schreber's madness an individual problem or a social one? Are the causes of his mental illness primarily biological or discursive? Freud's texts pose profound discursive problems, and such problems are compatible with psychological investigations. Freud's writings raise profound interpretive problems, precisely because they open up dense psychological and psychoanalytic domains. At the same time, we may seriously question Freud's confidence in his own conclusions, although that does not mean that we should dismiss the significance of his theoretical investigations.[5]

In *Écrits*, Lacan describes psychosis as a "foreclosure of the Name-of-the-Father." For Lacan, Freud's term *Verwerfung*, or foreclosure, refers to "a hole excavated in the field of the signifier by the foreclosure of the Name-of-the-Father," where the Name-of-the-Father represents the Law as well as the symbolic realm.[6] Madness is a problem that deals with a failure of socialization, and one way to understand this reading by Lacan is to suggest that psychotic schizophrenia remains an individual problem because the individual is unable to make the transition to the realm of the symbolic. And this implicit ascription of individual responsibility, even if schizophrenia is ultimately an unfortunate and tragic situation, is most problematic in contemporary understandings of psychosis as well as neurosis in psychology and psychoanalysis.

I want to briefly reread Freud's exfoliation of Schreber's condition. The settling of Schreber's illness by attributing it to his relation to the father belies the suggestive possibilities he opens up in connection with the rays of God. "In their creative capacity," Freud writes of the nerves of God, "that is, their power of turning themselves into every imaginable object in the created world—they are known as *rays*. There is an intimate relation between God and the starry heaven and the sun."[7] Freud affirms in a footnote the essential connection of nerves and rays, "based on the linear extension of what they have in common. — The ray-nerves, by the way, are no less creative than the spermatozoon-nerves."[8] What do the nerves and the rays have in common? They are both creative; that is, they have the power to turn themselves into any imaginable object in the world. This creativity refers in turn to the origin of the rays of God in a "basic language." "The 'rays of God,'" Freud states, "are identical with the voices which talked the 'basic language.'"[9]

This "basic language," which, according to Freud, Schreber learned—but not well or sanely enough—from his father, is the source of Schreber's psychosis. Schizophrenia has to do with not learning a language in a certain way, but schizophrenia is also marked by its own phantasmagoric language, which is a substitution for so-called normal language. At the end of his essay on "The Unconscious," Freud explains that schizophrenia is "a primitive object-less condition of narcissism," but what is extremely suggestive is that its description is characterized by "a number of changes in *speech*."[10] Freud desires to explain the "meaning and genesis of speech-formation in schizophrenia," which he names as "hypochondriac language or 'organ-speech.'"[11] Once again, Freud allows a hermeneutic or discursive element into play, although, just as in the Schreber case, he then overdetermines the meaning of this language practice.[12]

Varieties of Schizophrenic Language: Black-Head Boy

Freud uses the example of an adolescent who withdraws from life because he "declares that he has blackheads on his face which everyone notices. Analysis shows that he is working out his castration complex upon his skin."[13] This means that the adolescent experiences both loathing and pleasure regarding his condition, and that he squeezes out the blackheads to create a cavity or a void, which then horrifies him. "Pressing out the content of the blackhead is clearly a substitute for onanism," and the black holes, like every hole, is "a symbol of the female genital aperture."[14] I want to trouble Freud's overconfidence in his conclusion without rejecting the entire process of his analytic method.

What is important here is that Freud acknowledges that the resemblance between pores on the face and the vagina is not literally true, and he explains schizophrenic language in terms of this substitution which confuses the two. The confusion is not a confusion of objects, however, but of words. "The identity of the two when expressed in words, not the resemblance of the objects designated, has dictated the substitution," and the substitution takes place in such a way that word and thing do not coincide.[15] Schizophrenia is then defined as the confusion or non-coincidence of the division of the conscious idea of the object into "the idea of the word (verbal idea) and the idea of the thing (concrete idea)," and also a radical flight of the ego, which "consists in withdrawal of instinctual cathexis from those points which represent the unconscious idea of the object."[16] The flight of the ego, or the schizophrenic's flight from the ego and from reality, is based on an extreme confusion of words and things, verbal ideas and concrete ideas. In calling both words and things ideas (*Repräsentanz*), however, and in assimilating both to the "conscious idea of the object," is there not already a problematic confusion of words and things? How is there a clear separation between concrete and verbal ideas, and is an idea itself more a word or a thing?

Freud is not ignorant of the dangers of this thinking. The conclusion of the essay warns that

> when we think in abstractions there is a danger that we may neglect the relations of word to unconscious, concrete ideas, and it must be confessed that the expression and content of our philosophizing begins to acquire an unwelcome resemblance to the schizophrenic's way of thinking. We may, on the other hand, attempt a characterization of the schizophrenic's mode of thought by saying that he treats concrete things as though they were abstract.[17]

The schizophrenic mode of thought "treats concrete things as though they were abstract." Is this not the definition of philosophy, and therefore also philosophical theology? If the fundamental explanation of schizophrenia is a confusion of concrete and abstract terms, how does one approach the history of philosophy and theology, with its obsession with abstract words like being, substance, mind, God, etc., and its desperate attempt to render these terms in a concrete manner?[18] But if philosophers and theologians are schizophrenic, what becomes of the specificity of the term, used to demarcate mad and sane? Is the word schizophrenia being used here in a merely analogical way?

So for Freud, as well as for Lacan, schizophrenia comes down to an approach to language. Julia Kristeva, following both Freud and Lacan, claims that "psychosis is the crisis of truth in language." In her essay, "The True-Real," Kristeva demonstrates how, in the history of western thinking, the progressive loss of the Real to linguistic symbolization is matched by a corresponding loss or disappearance of a stable truth in discourse. She uses psychoanalytic language to illuminate this philosophical situation, and considers various approaches to the situation of a generalized psychosis, or "certain kinds of foreclosure" of either truth or reality.[19] Kristeva accepts neither a straightforward neurotic approach, which holds onto conventional truth in everyday discourse, thereby disavowing any reality that lies beyond such "truth," nor a literal psychosis, which consists of clinging to a Real beyond signification or expressing a desire for a pure signifier in the Lacanian sense. To these alternatives Kristeva develops a notion of artistic discourse, which combines elements of neurosis and psychosis into a hallucinatory hysterical discourse, which she claims becomes "a microscopic expansion of the 'true-real,'" because it creates truth and reality together by means of a revolutionary poetic language.[20] Kristeva enacts or creates a language that is a genuine response to, rather than a disavowal of, a situation of generalized psychosis or schizophrenia. This language "obliterates [conventional] reality and makes the Real loom forth as a jubilant enigma."[21] I will return to Kristeva's ideas in this important essay in the context of Lacan and Heidegger in chapter 4.

Is the situation in which we find ourselves schizophrenic, or is the language that we must develop to respond to that situation necessarily a schizophrenic language, or both? Kristeva does not call either the condition of psychosis or the language that responds to it schizophrenic, but her combination of neurotic and psychotic moments reproduces Freud's aligning of hysterical elements of a narcissistic, hypochondriac language with the inability to dissociate the abstract from the concrete, or the inability to master the split between word and thing, which uniquely marks schizophrenia. Kristeva's emphasis on the splitting of the subject is also indicative of a preoccupation with schizophrenic realities; she attempts to value and retain the position of the subject or the thetic position even as she puts the subject in *en procés* (in process/on trial).[22] The splitting of the self in its irreducible multiplicity requires a language complicated and supple enough to be adequate to such a multiplicity. Such a schizophrenic language would not merely, simply, or literally be psychotic but would combine elements of neurosis and psychosis in a constructive or productive way to avoid disavowing the complexities of experience, life, and subjectivity.

Varieties of Schizophrenic Language: The Other Julie

"A child had been murdered." More disturbing than "A Child is Being Beaten," and resonating with Schreber's charge of "Soul Murder," R. D. Laing's description of a schizophrenic woman in *The Divided Self* remains relevant and haunting. In fact, the last chapter of his book wrecks Laing's whole project for an existential and ontological "foundation for a science of persons," divided into true and false, embodied versus disembodied selves.[23] For the young woman, Julie, the "basic psychotic statement she made was that 'a child had been murdered.'" Here madness is equated with murder, in a loss of selfhood and identity that is particularly tragic. There remains, however, a fundamental ambiguity regarding the perpetrator and victim of the crime. "The child could have been herself. She had been murdered either by herself or by her mother, she was not sure" (179).

Laing recounts the three stages that characterize a schizophrenic child such as Julie. "These three stages in the evolution of a psychosis in members of a family occur very commonly," he writes, "Good—bad—mad," (184). Initially, the child is presumed innocent, until her behavior begins to become antisocial, upon which she is punished. Finally, however, her actions reach such a state of extremity that they evade simple attributions of blame and naughtiness, and she is considered mad. According to Laing's analysis, at some point Julie interiorizes the accusations of her mother that she is blameful and bad, and her illness is the result of a failure to blame her mother for tormenting her.[24] Laing is forced by the severity of the situation to problematize any simple resolution, but for him the central problem of schizophrenia is the failure to achieve autonomy, and the blame for such a situation is placed squarely on the mother. Laing repeats Freud's Oedipal move in his book on Schreber, but merely shifts the blame from the father to the mother. Thus in this instance, murder is simply "the negation of any autonomous point of view on her part" (193).

This diagnosis lends poignancy to the final section, entitled "The Ghost of the Weed Garden," which illustrates the extreme fragmentation of Julie's identity beyond any possible rescue. Laing relates that "Julie's self-being had become so fragmented that she could best be described as living *a death-in-life existence in a state approaching chaotic nonentity*," (195). Her condition consisted of a "word-salad" with both molecular and molar splits:

> The overall unity of her being had broken up into several 'partial assemblies' or 'partial systems,' each of which had its own little stereotyped 'personality' (molar splitting). In addition, any actual sequence of behavior was fragmented in a much more minute manner (molecular splitting). Even the integrity of words, for instance, would be disrupted. (196)

Recall that for Kristeva psychosis is the crisis of truth in language, and note that much of contemporary philosophy consists of tracing the splitting of identity and language, in what could be considered a generalized schizophrenia. What is fascinating is that Kristeva combines a neurotic hysteria with a psychotic hallucination in "The True-Real" in a similar way to Julie's combination of molar and molecular splitting.[25] The autonomy and integrity of selfhood and language is what is at stake in this discourse. One response would be to marginalize Julie's situation and discourse, no matter how tragic it may be, in order to hold onto the autonomy and integrity of "normal" nonschizophrenic persons. In this way, one can dismiss both sufferers of mental illness *and* contemporary philosophers as beyond bad; that is, mad. Another approach would be to rehabilitate Julie and philosophy—to recuperate their insights at the edge of our experience to translate them into "sane" discourse. In this way, we cannot accept them on their own terms, but they can provide relevance for our lives.

Finally, what if our contemporary situation is already one of "a death-in-life existence in a state approaching chaotic nonentity?" Laing explains that Julie "would sometimes marvelously come together again and display a most pathetic realization of her plight." These "moments of integration" were a source of terror and anxiety.[26] What if our precious sanity consists of what Laing calls Julie's periods of madness; that is, deadness, unrealness, and numbness, whereas what we might value as moments of integration consists of a terrifyingly lucid appraisal of our psychotic situation precisely in the forging of language to adequately express such insights?[27] Such an appraisal implies, in a Nietzschean sense, that the honesty required to face truth is necessarily painful, because fundamentally, "we knowers are unknown to ourselves," and every effort at self-knowledge comes at a terrible price.[28] What if such an attempt at self-knowledge brings a person into the unsettling proximity of a black sun?

We are approaching the "really mad kernal of her being, that central aspect of her which, so it seemed, had to be maintained chaotic and dead lest she be killed."[29] Laing is faithful to Julie's vision and Julie's witness, but once again in the last pages he attempts to "paraphrase her schizophrenia into sane speech" to understand it. This translation is really a reduction, because Julie's most profound utterances are assigned an all-too-determinate meaning rather than allowing Julie's language to pressure his own directly and allowing the resonances and attributions of her statements to resound on multiple registers.

> She was born under a black sun.
> She's the occidental sun.[30]

For Laing, Julie's schizophrenic speech simply and completely refers to her state as an unwanted daughter. Her mother had desired a son, but instead Julie arrived. "She was 'an occidental sun,' i.e. an accidental son whom her mother out of hate had turned into a girl."[31] The black sun itself is simply the mother, a powerful symbol of the cruelty and destructiveness wrought by a vengeful mother who, in the natural order of things, desires a male child and takes out her revenge upon a daughter with the audacity to be born. I do not mean to discount the "reality" of Julie's familial situation, but I do want to question the meaning of this symbol, at least in terms of its implications.

What if Julie were a prophet instead of a victim? Western intellectuals cannot accept as credible the cosmic and cosmological references of such a discourse about a black sun or even a Tree of Life. But what do such powerful symbolic statements mean, anyway? Is Julie making an indictment, not merely of her mother, but of the whole society, species or universe that created her? "She was born under a black sun. She's the occidental sun." The sun that gave her life did not provide light and nourishment. Julie is not simply making up her own private language; she expresses poetic and political insights out of the extremity of her situation of chaotic nonentity. If one thinks politically and historically about her context and condition in mid-twentieth-century England, one notices the reference to an eclipse of an occidental or western sun. This insight may not be merely idiosyncratic or symbolic. "She's the occidental sun," Laing writes, but who or what is responsible for its eclipse, and is there a difference between the two suns, the black sun, and the occidental sun; or is it simply a question of a sunset or twilight, perhaps in a Heideggerian sense of a sunset of Being?

Laing writes that "She's just one of those girls who live in the world."[32] Nothing distinguishes Julie ontologically from anyone else, despite her experience of herself as being dead in life. Why does Julie represent a certain abyss for western culture and rationality? And how can such a situation be considered theological?

Black Sun of Theology

In *Anti-Oedipus*, Deleuze and Guattari articulate a task of schizoanalysis that expands psychological language outward into political language. This project reverses the Oedipal reductionism operating in Freud's texts. In fact the Real and practical effects of psychoanalytic language operate in social and political terms. Schreber's reaction to his persecution by Dr. Flechsig is an important attack upon a powerful representative of a repressive psychiatric institution. "But when we replace the doctor with the father and commission the father to explain the God of delirium, we ourselves have trouble following this ascension."[33] Deleuze and Guattari view schizophrenic language as immediately productive and effective in a political world charged with desire and power: "all paranoiac deliriums stir up similar historical, geographic, and racial masses" which are then supposed to be tamed by a virulent familialism (89). Oedipalization and familialism, or a reduction to individual-parent issues to explain madness, repress an explosive desire that "is revolutionary in its essence," (116).

The therapeutic task of schizoanalysis is the liberation of desire that "goes by way of destruction" in the articulation of a libidinal economy (311). This is not strictly speaking a political program, although Deleuze and Guattari do not want to sanitize language and desire from messy political implication and effects, but rather an absolute deterritorialization, "the decoding of flows," which brings about a "new earth" beyond "the neurotic and perverse reterritorializations that arrest the process or assign it goals," (381–82).

Deleuze and Guattari take their inspiration for schizophrenia from Antonin Artaud, who explicates "The Rite of the Black Sun" in his last work, *To Have Done with the Judgment of God*.[34] Artaud explains that this is the Mexican dance of the Tutuguri:

> the Rite is that the new sun passes through seven points before
> blazing in the orifice of the earth.
> And there are six men,
> one for each sun.
> and a seventh man
> who is the sun
>   in the raw
> dressed in black and in raw flesh.

Artaud goes on to explain that "the essence of the Rite is precisely THE ABOLITION OF THE CROSS."[35] To be done with the judgment of God is not necessarily to be done with God, and the question one immediately asks, "what does this language mean?" has less to do with a cosmological referent somewhere in the universe or with an anthropological description of a Native American ritual, than with a profound theological tension in language that is attempting to find expression out of the power of Artaud's suffering.[36]

The real power of this revolutionary book, *Anti-Oedipus*, resides in the language it creates in the experimental first chapter, on the "body without organs," which is another image borrowed from Artaud. Once again Deleuze and Guattari's constructive notion of schizophrenia has less to do with what is literally considered insane than with the creation of a language that is theological in essence. But this very creation of language—of desire as it moves language and creates reality in a practical manner—rebounds upon our conceptions of literal insanity and undermines the status of all our concepts and categories, precisely because language is steeped in desire or is schizophrenic. Language is schizophrenic insofar as it cannot precisely or consistently demarcate the split between word and thing in its attempt to speak truth, but in its attempt it continually gives rise to further splits, or schizzes. Again, as Kristeva asserts, "psychosis is the crisis of truth in language," and this is a general crisis or condition.

Deleuze and Guattari emphasize a certain political register, but the question here is not simply the attribution of schizophrenia to a certain region or domain of language. The question of schizophrenia is the question of the black sun, or the destabilizing effects exerted on language by the Real, which creates a schizophrenic condition and necessitates the articulation of a schizophrenic language in response. The place of theology is envisioned not as a particular domain among others but as a formal preoccupation with language and signification in general. In this sense a theological investigation has less to do with settling questions at the level of content once our concepts are already established and given: "God," "world," "salvation" and so on, but with the intensive interrogation of the formation of our terms and the tracing of the point of connection (or joint) at which a transference among and between words and things occurs.

This split between the "idea of the word" and the "idea of the thing," which Freud attends to in "The Unconscious," cuts across both conscious and unconscious ideas.[37] This is a crossing that doubles both word and thing as conscious and unconscious, and provides a category—the idea or *Repräsentanz*, as I discussed in chapter 1—that enables us to subsume the two, but that remains in itself extremely problematical. Is an idea in this sense a word or a thing? Can an unconscious idea be called a word? Can it any more credibly be considered a thing? And what masters the metaphors and substitutions of words and things for themselves and for each other? Finally, if one could devise a language to "represent" the interchange of such schizophrenic substitutability, how could it fail to be theological, whether as a modern expression of the consequences of the reality involved in thinking through the idea of the essence of God that necessitates God's existence, or as the principle of existence or materiality that governs abstraction and idealization in a more Spinozist fashion?

In his essay, "White Mythology: Metaphor in the Text of Philosophy," Derrida traces the origins of metaphor to the founding distinction between literal and metaphorical—or proper and improper—to the beginnings of philosophical attempts to explain and master the world in terms of language. By asking, "What is the metaphor of metaphor?" he deconstructs the simple opposition between metaphorical and literal language and calls into question the "white mythology" of western philosophy. Metaphor is determined to be an analogy, but this analogy is thought to be anchored by a proper name or literal designation of reality, and Derrida takes the use of the sun as a master metaphor from Aristotle's *Metaphysics*.

The sun and its generative rays becomes the central analogy that is "the nonmetaphorical prime mover of metaphor, the father of all figures. Everything turns around it, everything turns toward it."[38]

Derrida, of course, takes the sun both in its metaphorical and its supposedly literal or cosmological aspects. The sun, in its turn as the site of the mastery of metaphorization, gives way to metaphoricity, especially when Aristotle multiplies the sun into a determinate number of stars after using the sun to illustrate his definition of God or the prime mover in *Metaphysics*, Book X. "As soon as one admits that all the terms in an analogical relation already are caught up, one by one, in a metaphorical relation," Derrida writes, "everything begins to function no longer as a sun, but as a star, the punctual source of truth or properness remaining invisible or nocturnal."[39] He then turns to the metaphorical nature of the heliotrope, which complicates any simple distinction between sensory, natural, and artificial or metaphorical. If "the sun is the sensory object par excellence," it cannot be completely known or properly mastered because what is sensible can always be hidden or absent. It shares this quality, however, with metaphor, whose metaphorical nature can either be explicitly visible or else hidden, or even seemingly absent altogether.

Finally, Derrida plunges metaphor itself into an abyss (*en abyme*) in which the detour of metaphor as a path from the literal or proper back to itself is challenged by a notion of an unfolding of metaphor without limit and a wresting of borders of propriety from itself, which "explode[s] the reassuring opposition of metaphoric and proper."[40] The image of this abyss is Derrida's conclusion that asserts that "heliotrope also names a stone,"; that sun as metaphor carries death within itself of generative metaphors that can then be reappropriated by conceptual philosophy.[41] This image of the sun or heliotrope raises questions about the relation of an image to the notions of idea, word, and thing discussed earlier in connection with Freud. Providing an image of thought—in this essay an image of a black sun—has certain effects upon words and things because it pressures our thinking, even to the extent of distorting it, especially an image of such extreme connotations as that of a black sun.

Derrida does not use the image or the concept of a black sun in his essay on "White Mythology," but his deconstruction of sunny metaphors provides an opening for considering such an image, used explicitly by Julia Kristeva in her important book on depression and melancholia. In contrast with Kristeva, however, I associate the image of the black sun more closely with schizophrenia than with melancholia. I want to keep the connection expressed by Laing's patient, Julie, between a black sun and schizophrenia, as well as hold onto Freud's analysis of schizophrenia in terms of language as an inability to master the split between word and thing in his essay, "The Unconscious," which also contains the striking example of an adolescent's blackheads. This assemblage of an image in terms of its interconnections and conceptual manifestations and ramifications is then mined for its theological significance in an aesthetic or formal sense.

The black sun warps traditional theological discourse, and the challenge of schizophrenia as the "crisis of truth in language" necessitates theological thinking as a response; that is, any response to such a crisis cannot ultimately be other than theological. The proper sun of theology is usually called God, and subsequently God sends another Son in Christian theology, which the Gospel of John calls *Logos*. Theology urgently needs an interrogation of the epistemic nature and status of its language, as well as attention to the powerful effects of such language in terms of images, ideas, words, and things. Theology needs to question its own complicity in a general schizophrenic situation, as well as any possible response to such a situation, especially considering the dizziness and disorientation that results when we are told that theology itself is God's thinking of God (Augustine) or that speaking the Word of God is both necessary as a demand and impossible for a finite, sinful human being (Karl Barth).

Unfortunately much of contemporary theology is mired in an obsessive concern with content, understood as the objective status of the referent(s) of theological language. I want to invoke Freud's distinction between the manifest and the latent content of dreams as an interpretive principle.[42] If theology remains in the light of manifest content, it disavows attending to the "heart of darkness" of the black sun, understood as power and intensity, deception and difficulty of perception, as well as the effects of negativity, whether human, subhuman, or superhuman. A turn toward latent content (which I am calling theological form, or a formal theology that is more concerned with raising questions of ultimacy than with settling them) is a lesson theology can learn from psychoanalytic theory. Such a borrowing, however, does not indebt theology to psychoanalysis to such an extent that the black sun becomes a black hole, or that such a hole cannot be explained in terms other than female genitalia, or what can be more generally considered the normative masculine model of sexuality, which has governed psychoanalysis through most if not all of its official history.[43] In fact the same problem that inhabits Freud and Lacan haunts most theology; that is, the need to attribute a proper and determinate meaning or referent to theological or psychological language that represents a reductive explanation. And the most harmful view is the obsessive need to consider a discourse to be theology or psychology only if it results in such an explanation.

In "White Mythology," Derrida adopts Fontanier's notion of catachresis to challenge the philosophical mastery of metaphoric substitution. Derrida explains that "there is no substitution here, no transport of proper signs, but rather the irruptive extension of a sign proper to an idea, a meaning, deprived of their signifier. A 'secondary origin.'"[44] This "irruptive extension" of metaphor in its essence means that every substitution is not natural but rather forced, and that every metaphor is intermediate between a proper and a figurative sense. A catachresis is also a mistake, and this implies that every natural or proper ascription of a concept or term to an objective referent or content consists of a mistake.

According to Derrida, catachresis (or metaphorization) is inevitable, but we can inquire into the conditions of thinking reality as both metaphoric and proper, and we can avoid a certain alarming naiveté (even if it is called secondary naiveté) regarding our assumptions of theological content. "Thus all species of words can be employed, or in effect are employed, *metaphorically*, if not as *figures*, as least as *catachreses*."[45] Of course, a pure form without content is impossible, and every form carries with it its own content, which it distributes as effects. I am proposing, however, that attention to the form (or *aesthesis*) of theological discourse opens up a more intense and important region of theological inquiry than more conventional treatments of theological content. The black sun of theology institutes a destabilizing catachresis that affects and infects all of our concepts, setting up a disorienting oscillation—between proper and figural, word and thing, latent and manifest, finite and infinite, etc.—that can best be described as schizophrenic.

Recognition of the essentially schizophrenic nature of language does not constitute a complete break with traditional theological ideas, but it does challenge, distort, and pervert notions of God, creation *ex nihilo*, etc. This challenge is akin to the challenge that Lacan poses to traditional ethics in his seminar on "The Ethics of Psychoanalysis." According to Lacan, desire is desire for the Thing as it encapsulates the Real. In chapter 3, and then later in chapters 6, 7, and 8, I will perform an extended theological reading of Lacan's famous seminar as it touches upon other thinkers and themes, including Schelling, Freud, Heidegger, Tillich, Kristeva, Mark C. Taylor, Edith Wyschogrod, and Slavoj Žižek, before turning to Seminar XX in chapters 9 and 10.

3

Desiring the Thing

The Ethics of Psychoanalysis

The psychoanalyst is a detective; his or her cases are always detective stories. In the eyes of the analyst, surfaces are never explanatory but are always symptomatic of the psychic underground.
—**Mark C. Taylor**, *Hiding*

Prelude: A Detective Story

In this chapter I suggest that conventional ethics, which is oriented toward the good, is challenged by psychoanalytic theory. Lacan's work allows us to distinguish between desire for the Other, which is limited to symbolic language, and desire for the Thing, which lies beyond the symbolic in the Real. Primarily by reading Lacan's discussion of the Thing in *The Ethics of Psychoanalysis*, I relate the idea of the Thing to the idea of God, which later becomes the focus of chapter 8, where I contrast Lacan with Jean-Luc Marion's understanding of God as Good rather than as Being. The desire for the Thing implies a complex and ambivalent understanding of sublimation that Lacan draws out in his reading of *Antigone*. In conclusion, I construct three alternative graphs of desire according to three distinct understandings of the nature of ethical desire.

According to Lacan, Freud's claim, "Where it was, there I should be" (*wo es war, soll Ich werden*), is an ethical demand. In his essay on "The Freudian Thing," Lacan reformulates Freud's statement away from its standard reading as a demand that the unconscious id should transform itself into ego and consciousness. Rather, Lacan translates Freud's phrase as "There where it was . . . it is my duty that I should come into being."[1] For Lacan, the I is the subject, which cannot be identified with the ego, or with any stable, self-subsisting entity. If it is my duty to bring about subjectivity at the heart of the unconscious, however, then the mystery concerns what or where it (id) is.

In a more classically Freudian sense, the psychoanalyst as detective relentlessly seeks out and uncovers the unconscious by following the symptoms of repressed drives that testify to primary processes at work in the body. Yet in Lacan's reconstruction of Freudian psychoanalysis the problem is not simply unconscious as missing (presumed dead, murdered, castrated?) body, but the fundamental question of the Real, which lies before or beyond the imaginary and the symbolic realms. According to Lacan's famous typology, we can thematize three realms or registers: the Real, the imaginary, and the symbolic. The Real is that which precedes and resists symbolization. The imaginary is the natural human egoism and narcissism that Freud calls the Pleasure Principle and Lacan elaborates in his early essay on the Mirror Stage. The symbolic is the intersubjective order of meaning and signification, and this is also the realm of ethical desire.

These three registers consistently reappear throughout Lacan's career, although his work does betray a shift in emphasis. In his early work, including his article "The Mirror Stage as Formative of the *I* Function as Revealed in Psychoanalytic Experience," his famous Rome Discourse, and his early seminars, Lacan seems to set the imaginary and the symbolic in opposition to stress the importance of coming to terms with the dangerous and distorted nature of imaginary drives. In his later work, including Seminar XX: *Encore*, Lacan seems more suspicious of the duplicitous nature of symbolic language and desire. Here Lacan attempts somewhat quixotically to mathematically formalize the Real. In some ways, *The Ethics of Psychoanalysis* can be read as a hinge between these two emphases, and it evinces a foregrounding of the problem of the Real as it can be accessed via the Thing. That is, the Real in Lacan's early work is mostly pre-symbolic, mute, and thereby inaccessible to symbolization; it is what escapes signification. But, from the late 1950s on, the Real takes on a more privileged focus—that which is still inaccessible—but the Real is the object of symbolic representation. I return to the question of the real in Lacan's *Seminar XX* in chapter 9.[2]

At the height of his intellectual powers, in his 1959–60 seminar on *The Ethics of Psychoanalysis*, Lacan formulates the question of the Real in terms of the Thing (*das Ding*). The ethics of psychoanalysis centers around the detection of the desire for the Real as it manifests itself in its orientation toward the Thing. In chapter 8, I will return to *The Ethics of Psychoanalysis* and its significance to the good in more explicit relation to the desire for God. In this context, to be an ethical subject, one would presumably have to penetrate this mystery surrounding the Thing and find the body, not of the unconscious psyche, but of materiality itself.

According to Mark C. Taylor, the postmodern theorist of religion and cultural studies the body is irretrievably lost, and reality thereby becomes virtuality, particularly in theoretical conceptions of cyberspace and information technology. "Language, it seems, is the appearance of the disappearance of the body. If the word is the death of the thing, the mystery of language *always* involves a missing body."[3] Taylor goes on to declare that "if the body cannot be found, the mystery cannot be solved," but he does provide a solution, claiming that the body cannot be found, and what is more, it has always already been missing. Such a solution—that mediated symbolic language reveals that immediate, non-symbolic reality never existed—cuts the tensed knot that sustains ethical desire and leaves us floating adrift along a field of signifiers. From a certain standpoint, a reading of Taylor's virtual reality as virtual nihilism calls into question the possibility of a postmodern ethics in a radical way.

For Taylor, the Thing cannot be reached, and reality will reveal itself as always already virtual. Lacan, on the other hand, articulates a different conception of the Real in relation to an ethical structure of desire that remains ethical, but in a radically different way from traditional ethics. For Lacan, we can just barely conceptualize the Thing. At first glance, however, the Thing severs or undoes all conventional ethical relations because it lies beyond good and evil.

Beyond Good and Evil (Das Ding)

For Freud, the Thing is the primary object of desire, originally the mother's breast. Lacan situates Freud's discourse about the Thing in relation to the history of philosophy, particularly Kant and Heidegger. For Lacan, *das Ding* refers to the immediate object of desire, but as such it remains completely inaccessible from the standpoint of symbolic language. *"Das Ding* is that which I will call the beyond-of-the-signified,"* Lacan writes, "and is constituted in a kind of relationship characterized by primary affect, prior to any representation."[4] The German word *Ding* is contrasted with the German *Sache*, which indicates an object within the purview of symbolic representation.

The *Sache*, which can be represented, structures symbolic discourse around the loss of *das Ding*, or the Real. Lacan claims that "it is precisely as we shift into discourse that *das Ding*, the Thing, is resolved into a series of effects—in the sense that one can say *meine Sache*." At the level of symbolic representation, however, "the Thing is not nothing, but literally it is not. It is characterized by its absence, its strangeness," (63). In this seminar on ethics, Lacan is tracing the boundary of the Real in relation to the symbolic, and he is suggesting that this conception of the Real as beyond the network of symbolic discourse has profound consequences for ethics.

According to Lacan, the Freudian conception of *das Ding* dislocates traditional ethical discourse, understood as a meditation on human goods. Tracing a line of continuity from Aristotle to Jeremy Bentham, Lacan casts traditional ethics as a species of utilitarianism because in some way ethics revolves around a system of human goods in relation to a highest good, happiness. As far as it takes its task as the articulation of the good, this utilitarian ethics, broadly conceived, functions in relation to the pleasure principle, which refers to the interaction of what Lacan calls the imaginary and the symbolic. Even though in his *Nicomachean Ethics* Aristotle contrasts rational happiness with sensual pleasure, he understands happiness as the highest good in the sense that it brings about a greater amount of satisfaction. Lacan explains that on the contrary, "the question of ethics is to be articulated from the point of view of the location of man in relation to the real" (11).

In a profound sense, *das Ding*, which metonymically refers to the Real as that which resists representation, lies beyond good and evil. In the symbolic realm, humans can deliberate and decide about the Good so long as goods and the Good conform to representation. The Real as that which eludes symbolization, however, challenges rational utilitarian ethics. According to Lacan, Freud turns moral law on its head with his formulation of the principle of incest, which testifies to an ethical "beyond the pleasure principle." From the standpoint of human desire, the mother represents the Supreme Good—the primary object of desire. But the notion of incest proclaims that this "is a forbidden good, and that there is no other good," (70). Freud's conception of the Thing as that which is both desired and forbidden undermines an ethics of conventional good and evil, because the Thing lies before or beyond any ethical determination. Lacan extends Freud's object of desire—the mother—into the question of the Real. This expansion then allows the notion of *das Ding* to refer to the real that avoids representation but also makes it possible and necessary. Lacan writes, "There is not a good and bad object; there is good and bad, and then there is the Thing. The good and bad already belong to the order of the *Vorstellung* [representation]," (63).

The universal law of incest that brings about the Oedipal complex revolves around the object or the Thing as the Mother, which is both desired and forbidden. For Lacan, the law of incest becomes a structural relationship, organized around the *vel* of alienation. The term *vel* refers to a forced choice in relation to the symbolic, where the subject must "choose" to enter into discourse, and this choice forecloses the Real as Real. Bruce Fink explains that an uneven struggle takes place between the child and the Other. By "losing and submitting to the Other, the child nevertheless gains something: he or she becomes . . . a subject 'of language.'"[5] To hold out against the Other and "win" is to become psychotic. The Thing is that within the symbolic that refers to the "beyond-of-signification," and thus lies beyond good and evil.

Although Lacan uses the terms good and bad to refer to the order of symbolic representation, I am using the Nietzschean terms good and evil to show the similarity of Lacan's claim regarding Freud with Nietzsche's critique of conventional morality. Nietzsche sought an extra-moral vantage point, and that view is articulated in Lacan's notion of the Thing. Lacan does not discuss Nietzsche in his discussion of "the great revolutionary crisis of morality," but he foreshadows Freud's breakthrough by combining Kant and Sade.[6] Parenthetically, one might reasonably inquire whether a combination of Kant and Sade produces a Nietzsche?

The reading of Kant with Sade raises the possibility of radical evil because Kant, in a theoretical manner, posits a motivation to do evil for its own sake, which had previously seemed unthinkable. Kant prescribes duty as the supreme moral law and argues that one must follow a deontological ethic for its own sake without any consideration of gain or loss. The flip side of duty as pure good would be a radical evil in which someone does evil for its own sake and not for anything that would benefit them. Sade attempts in his extreme writings to work out the practical possibilities of carrying out such a radical evil. Kant's imperative to do one's duty becomes a reverse (or perverse) moral imperative to perform one's sadistic duty to seek pleasure and power no matter what.[7] This combination foreshadows Freud's breakthrough because it is Freud who achieves the insight that the Thing lies fundamentally beyond good and evil. The fundamental object of desire is what is forbidden as such. The good and the evil coalesce and deconstruct, and the Thing is the remainder. The Thing then inhabits language in a negative way as that which manifests desire for the Real. Lacan's reading of Freud in the context of the history of philosophy challenges ethics because it raises the question of the Thing as a powerful and extramoral matter.

The Thing, the Other, and God

The relevance of the Thing for religious ethics raises two related questions about the connection between the Thing and the Other, on the one hand, and God. Contemporary postmodern religious ethics swirls around readings and appropriations of Jacques Derrida and Emmanuel Levinas. Such postmodern versions of ethics celebrate an ethics of alterity, where "the Other" is a positive ethical term. Examples include the work of John D. Caputo, Edith Wyschogrod, and Wendy Farley.[8] Sometimes the question of God is bracketed or subordinated to the ethical demand of the other person. Other times God is identified, either implicitly or explicitly, with the claim of the Other, and posited as an absolute Other. Caputo, for example, repeats Derrida's formula, *"tout autre est tout autre"* [every other is completely other], and goes on to suggest that "God is the exemplar of every 'other,' the other is the exemplar of God."[9] Caputo goes on to contend that the exact relationship of otherness and divinity is undecidable, but he does make a profound connection.

For Lacan, however, the Thing is profoundly different from the Other because the Thing is associated with the realm of the Real, while the Other mainly refers to the symbolic realm. From the viewpoint of *The Ethics of Psychoanalysis*, to simply make the Other a Supreme Good that then organizes others as goods is to remain within a traditional ethical framework. On the other hand, to equate the Other with divinity, and to place it beyond good and evil, is to conflate the symbolic with the Real. According to Lacan, "man's desire is the desire of the other," which means that to be a subject, one must negotiate a relationship with language—the symbolic order—which structures desire and makes it social.[10] Humans are shot through with otherness, but this is a social relation, not a spiritual one. In fact the Other can take on a sinister aspect because it means that desire is not your own—your desire is structured by the desire of the Other, the desires of language, social representation, citizenship, and even things like capitalism and advertising. To become a subject, one must sacrifice the radical uniqueness of one's primary desire and negotiate a representational order that structures desire along other lines. To become an authentic individual, one must take on an inauthenticating and possibly even "evil" desire, the desire of the Other.

The Other is a metonym for the social field, or the symbolic order, both linguistic and political. This is both investing of a subject's desire as well as divesting of original desire for the Real; that is, *das Ding*. You sacrifice your desire for the Thing in its primary form to take on the substitutions of language that structure desires in a secondary manner around goods. To refuse to compromise your desire is to become psychotic because for Lacan psychosis is defined socially, not organically. Psychosis is the refusal to enter into the symbolic order, to cling to the Real, and, since this is impossible, it results in hallucinations. Your desire is not your own, and this otherness can be reassuring (desire is shared, in common) or disturbing (your desires are at least partially created for you). Otherness is the condition of having the possibility to have a social relation to oneself (to be a subject) and with another (to be a moral being or a good citizen). At the level of the symbolic, the question of ethics is fundamentally related to otherness, to the negotiation of the desires and the partial satisfactions that are possible along with the sacrifice of the satisfaction of desires that are necessary to have a civilization.

Lacan, however, situates ethics in relation to the Thing; that is, the Real. Since the Real is inaccessible as that which originates desire, as well as that which is forbidden to be a thinking human being, can the Thing be taken to represent God, albeit in a negative manner? The Thing cannot be equated with God thought as the Supreme Good (Being), because that would merely recall the Sovereign Good of utilitarian ethics, which the Thing dislocates. God as the Supreme Good, which organizes all the human goods, is a product of the symbolic order of linguistic representation.

The Other actually functions as a hinge for Lacan because it allows the passage to the symbolic, but it is also the threshold to penetrate the desire for the Real. So there are at least two ways of thinking about and conceptualizing the Other: the Other as symbolic good and the Other as strange Thing. Finally, desire *for* the Other and desire *of* the Other might be two very different things. The Other as relation to the Real could simply be the condition of possibility for talking about what lies beyond the symbolic, as opposed to the more substantial and differentiated Other that functions as the medium of social relations. On the other hand, in his 1965 essay "On Freud's *'Trieb'* and the Psychoanalyst's Desire," Lacan shifts toward a more defensive understanding of desire, associating it with the Other, whereas the drive is intimately related to the Thing.[11] This viewpoint is also reflected in *The Ethics of Psychoanalysis*.

For Lacan, the Thing is not God, because after both Nietzsche and Freud, God is dead or unconscious. In his reading of Freud's *Moses and Monotheism*, Lacan argues that Freud's myth of the murder of the father, Moses, testifies to the death of God. "The myth of the murder of the father is the myth of a time for which God is dead."[12] Lacan goes on to say that "if for us God is dead, it is because he has always been dead, and that's what Freud says."[13] Lacan makes the claim that Mark C. Taylor structurally repeats: the death of God reveals that God has always already been dead. In the same way, the disappearance of reality reveals that reality has always already been virtuality. The objective here is not to deliberate about the status of an objective entity, God, who exists in some representational cosmic realm, but to perceive the similarity of a certain conception of divinity with an attempt to think of the Real by means of the Thing. The Thing is not God, but God can also be a thing. God can metonymically represent the Real, which resists symbolization, which must be present as an absence to symbolize or represent anything. And this Thing cannot simply be absorbed into symbolic discourse without remainder, as Taylor implies. The question of the Thing poses a profound challenge for ethics and for theology.

The Question of Sublimation

As the primary object of desire, God is a Thing; that is, a metonym for the Real. *Das Ding* is not God, however, which attests to a radical dislocation of theology. Because access to the Thing is foreclosed in symbolic discourse, the complete satisfaction of desire is impossible. The most important question of both ethics and religion in a psychoanalytic register, then, is the question of sublimation, as I suggested in chapter 1. Ethics traditionally addresses the necessity and possibility of sublimating one's base desires into noble but partial satisfactions. Many theoretical understandings of religion organize themselves around some conception of spirit, which is seen as a sublimation of material reality.

The Thing is beyond symbolization. To speak of desire is to be always already to sublimate. For Lacan language in its broadest sense structures desire so totally that it makes no sense to imagine that our drives or instincts can be satisfied directly. To speak of desire in any meaningful way is to be enmeshed in the symbolic in such a way that satisfaction is sublimation. Everything is sublimation; there is no Real that admits satisfaction. To be a human being is to sublimate or substitute for one's primary desires.

God as Thing is a metonym for the Real, or the object of primary desire. God as such is completely inaccessible. To think of sex or murder as immediate desires that are then sublimated in cultural or socially acceptable ways is to fail to understand that even such seemingly simple or intense desires are symbolically mediated in complex ways. It is not simply that one sublimates one's fundamental drives of sexuality and aggression to negotiate them and to achieve partial satisfaction. To have sex is itself sublimation. To kill an annoying insect, parent, or even oneself is already a symbolic sublimation because these seemingly primary desires and their satisfaction are necessarily mediated through language, as I discussed in chapter 1. There is no simple outside of sublimation because there is no place outside of signification or symbolization.

In another way, however, sublimation does not work. According to Freud, there is always a return of the repressed. In a Lacanian sense, the return of the Real as a Thing signifies a beyond of the pleasure principle. This insight is developed by Julia Kristeva in *Revolution in Poetic Language*, where poetic language represents a "return" of the semiotic that disrupts the symbolic, and again in a slightly different way in *Powers of Horror*, where the abject returns to threaten the boundaries of the moral subject.[14]

The question of sublimation revolves around the question of elevation. In the history of philosophy, one can trace a trajectory from the Kantian (dynamical) sublime to Hegelian sublation (*Aufhebung*) to Freudian sublimation. The question is whether sublimation raises one above a base to a more refined or spiritual place or plane while preserving the essence of desire itself. As the attempt to elevate oneself from a lower (material) to a higher (spiritual) plane, the sublimation of desire does not work.

Why? As I mentioned in chapter 1, psychoanalysis is viewed with hostility by many vested representatives of religion because it is seen as materialistic and reductionistic because psychoanalysis reduces spiritual and religious questions, values, and ideas to a material level of base desires that function in a quasi-scientific and positivistic sense. It reduces the higher and more noble—the spiritual—to the lower and baser. Some adherents of psychoanalysis, of course, value this very debasement and enjoy seeing lofty religious ideas reduced to more immediate, bodily, and even embarrassingly sexual needs and wants. The problem with the issue of reductionism and materialism is that from the standpoint of Lacan, there is no materialistic anchor for sublimation, except possibly in a radically negative sense. Furthermore, as I argue in chapter 1, Deleuze critiques a materialistic understanding of Freud in *Difference and Repetition*, which claims that we repeat (repetition compulsion) because we repress primary desires. On the other hand, every repetition or substitution is a different substitution or arrangement on the same plane, which is conceived horizontally rather than vertically. We repress because we repeat, but the primary repetition, substitution, or sublimation is a repetition of difference that results in a completely new circumstance of concepts and things. Deleuze transforms Henri Bergson's distinction between a difference in degree and a difference in kind by claiming that every difference in degree is ultimately a difference in kind.[15] Every repetition is a rearrangement. Every sublimation is a substitution, but not at a higher level; rather in a different combination and at a different location. Deleuze concludes that "repetition is thus in essence symbolic, spiritual, and intersubjective or monadological."[16] Desires or drives are always already in a state of sublimation or substitution, but we cannot segregate primary desires from secondary desires, or higher from lower desires, within symbolic representation. Original desire is for God as Thing, metonym for the Real beyond signification.

The Ethical Structure of Desire

In what sense is an understanding of the Thing a sublimation? How is ethical desire for the Thing related to desire of and for the Other? Here we reach the core of Lacan's thought regarding the ethical structure of desire. *The Ethics of Psychoanalysis* is a profound inquiry into the question of sublimation that centers around the concept of creation *ex nihilo*.

In the central section, "On Creation *ex nihilo*," Lacan claims that the Thing is fundamentally veiled. According to Lacan, "the Thing is that which in the Real, the primordial Real, I will say, suffers from the signifier."[17] The Thing represents a creation out of nothing because it is a signifier of signifying as such. Lacan builds upon Heidegger's analysis of a vase in his essay, "Das Ding." For Heidegger, influenced by Daoism, it is the emptiness of a vase that makes it a thing and allows it to function. Lacan brings Heidegger together with structural linguistics, equating the Thing with the signifying function as such, not within symbolic discourse, but the process of signifying the Real.

Creation of a signifier is out of nothing because the vase is "an object made to represent the existence of the emptiness at the center of the Real that is called the Thing, this emptiness as represented in the representation presents itself as a *nihil*, as nothing," (121). The Thing is not the object (the vase) but the emptiness that is represented by the object in order for it to function in symbolic discourse. Lacan equates the necessity for a vase to be empty in order for it to function—so someone can fill it with water—with the necessity for signifying speech to be empty to fill it with meaning. This emptiness is a hole that marks the Real.

Lacan writes that "the fashioning of the signifier and the introduction of a gap or hole in the real is identical," (121). He refers to the Gnostic medieval sect of the Cathars who believed that matter is evil, to suggest that the matter that composes the Thing can be thought of as evil—"evil may be in the Thing," (124). Here again is a foreshadowing of radical evil—the dislocation of traditional morality definitively accomplished by Freud. The Thing expresses evil because it is resistant to signification, even though it is what allows signification to take place. According to Lacan, "man" fashions the signifier "in the image of the Thing, whereas the Thing is characterized by the fact that it is impossible for us to imagine it," (125). The possibility of creation, that is, of fashioning a signifier out of nothing or the Real, which leaves a remainder—the Thing—is the possibility of sublimation for Lacan.[18] The work of sublimation resides in giving representation to the Thing, which is generally given a feminine form. Lacan's interest in medieval troubadours and courtly love in Seminar VII stems from this insight into the possibility of having a Lady represent the Thing, or the hole in the Real, which is also a form of creation—the creation of a signifier. I will return more explicitly to Lacan's conception of creation *ex nihilo* in chapter 7 in the context of a discussion between Tillich and Žižek about Schelling.

Any valorization of such sublimation as specifically feminine must also grapple with the reading of *Antigone* at the end of the seminar, where it is precisely Antigone's refusal to submit to the good of human or divine law that allows her to incarnate "the pure and simple desire of death as such."[19] For Lacan, Antigone desires the Thing—her brother's burial—not the social, human, or divine good. Antigone's rejection of morality is a radical sublimation that nevertheless induces a certain dazzling "beauty effect."[20] The key issue is the incompatibility of beauty (and sublimation understood in terms of beauty) with all articulations of the Good. The Thing is beyond good and evil, although it is usually figured as evil by conventional morality. Authentic sublimation relates to a terrifying beauty associated with the death drive, not a sublime moral beauty that supports traditional ethics.

And yet, this articulation of sublimation in relation to the Thing is still an ethical articulation. It expresses an ethical relationship of desire. Ethical desire is for the Thing, not the Good. This is the meaning of Lacan's ethical law at the end of the seminar: "Have you acted in conformity with the desire that is in you?"[21] That is, have you acted in conformity with the desire for the Thing, which aims at death and beauty, and not in conformity with the Other's desire, which aims at the rational good?

I am developing a contrast between desire for the Other, which is ultimately the Other's desire, and desire for the Thing. The desire for the Other establishes the symbolic order and structures conventional morality around the Good, defined as what the Other wants. This is a slight distortion of Lacan because in his work the Other is a more ambivalent and complex term, associated with both the Real and the symbolic in certain ways, but I am exaggerating this tendency to sharpen the contrast between the Other and the Thing. The desire for the Thing manifests a profound desire for the Real, which cannot exist outside of the symbolic order without any reference to the Other, but it is this desire that Lacan identifies as ethical. The Thing, a manifestation of creation *ex nihilo*, metonymically represents the Real and functions as a death drive within symbolic discourse, taking it to the limit of symbolic representation. An extreme or total death drive ends in death because a complete rejection of the symbolic devastates the ability to signify and results in destruction, as Antigone shows. A partial death drive, however, can transform or restructure the symbolic by means of a sublimation, which Lacan calls ethical.

There is also a profound difference between literal psychosis and sublimation, despite their structural similarity. Psychosis in a Lacanian sense manifests itself as a refusal of the symbolic and a savage clinging to the Real. Insofar as the *vel* is refused, which is not fully possible, the child cleaves to the Real and negotiates a relationship to the symbolic marked by tragedy and hallucination. Since the *vel* is a forced choice, it cannot be refused, and so psychosis in an absolute sense is impossible. We consider behavior more or less psychotic as it manifests desire for the Real as Real, or what Kristeva calls the attempt to return completely to the semiotic. Sublimation, however, is the desire not for the Real as Real, but for the Real as Thing. It is a reinscription of the semiotic in the symbolic, and a refusal of the self-sufficiency of the symbolic that nevertheless acknowledges the entanglement of the semiotic and the symbolic.

In a practical sense, desire for the Thing and desire for the Other (the Other's desire) are practically impossible to disentangle or separate. There exists only the minutest possible difference between "your" desire and the Other's desire. This is not an actual difference because it does not refer to a different desire, but it is a virtual interval in a Deleuzian sense.[22] The virtual interval between the desire for the Thing as the Real and the Other's desire as the symbolic is a gap that sets off an oscillation and creates anxiety when it is recognized, because one cannot determine the limits of each to distinguish them. This gap or interval is the hole in the Real that Lacan calls *das Ding*. The Thing burns a hole in the Real, and it is the nothing organized in the work of art or creation of a signifier that enables "authentic" signification to occur.

The Thing is not God, but it can encapsulate the desire for God. At the same time, it can also foreclose access to God. In chapter 4 I will consider God in terms of the important Freudian concept of foreclosure (*Verwerfung*), as it occurs in Freud, Lacan, and Kristeva, and also in terms of how it converges with Heidegger's notion of refusal (*Verweigerung*) in his *Contributions to Philosophy*. The foreclosure of God is a desperate theological move, but it is the response to a general situation of psychosis, which Heidegger details as the refusal of Being, and on which Kristeva elaborates in her essay on "The True-Real."

Appendix: The Graphs of Desire

To demonstrate the nature of properly ethical desire, we can construct three representative graphs of desire. It must be remembered that the supreme object or goal of desire is God, but the attainment of this goal is also death. For this reason, a graph of pure desire would show two axes (an inverted simple xy graph), with an arc of desire crossing the upper limit of the x axis. Here the subject carries her efforts to achieve satisfaction to the extreme and, crossing the limit, achieves obliteration and what Alfred North Whitehead calls perpetual perishing, which is also an objective immortality.[23] The subject is immortalized in her death because she achieves her ultimate *telos*, her end.

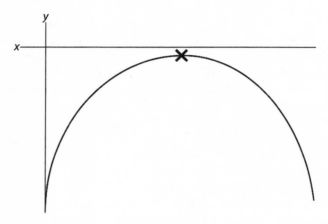

The second graph is that of ideal desire, which is, strictly speaking, impossible. Here the arc of desire is asymptotic in its approximation of the limit, God or death. This is the ideal form of desire, which sustains an unbelievable and impossible tension in its approach of its goal or telos.

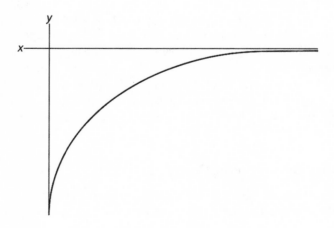

Finally, the third graph represents practical or ethical desire. Here the arc of desire takes the form of a parabola, which is also what Pynchon calls gravity's rainbow, because desire peaks and then falls to undertake the flight again. Here is the possibility of a repetition of desire, which exists always already because to formulate graphs or laws of desire those graphs or laws must have been repeated or experienced before many times. The flight of desire is Whitehead's airplane, which takes off from the Aristotelian field of goods. The x marks the point of descent or reentry, which is what I have analyzed as Lacanian ethical desire for the Real in terms of the Thing.

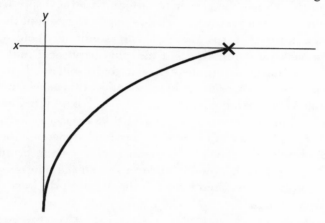

To flesh out this representation, I will briefly consider a short story and a film. In *Flowers for Algernon*, a short story by Daniel Keyes that later became a movie and then a novel, the main character, Charlie, a mentally retarded adult, takes an experimental drug to become smart. The novel demonstrates how Charlie develops his intelligence and language as he becomes smarter and more aware of himself and his life. Of course, the tragic outcome is that the miracle drug wears off, and Charlie then descends slowly back into stupidity, and this process is even more poignant because Charlie is fully aware of what is occurring. In fact it is Charlie who makes the scientific discovery that the drug will wear off. The passage from stupidity to brilliance and back is also marked by Charlie's anger, unhappiness, and bitterness in relation to his intelligence, and his naive happiness when he is retarded and does not know any better.

The novel, published in 1966 (the short story was published in 1959), epitomizes a certain era and a certain attitude regarding Anglo-American psychology, even while it questions and protests certain aspects of it. The most interesting dilemma in relation to the ethics of psychoanalysis, however, is the impossibility of untangling Charlie's desire to be smart from the Others'—his teacher, doctors, the scientists, society as a whole—desire that he become smart. In relation to my conclusion that ethical desire is for the Thing, not the Other, one could say that the difference is nothing. Charlie does not possess an authentic ethical desire to be smart and is happier as a retarded person. At the same time, however, there is a virtual difference, which must be posited but cannot be located anywhere with any definiteness: Charlie does possess a desire for the Thing, for the Real, and this allows the reader to differentiate his desire from that of the Others', but it is only in Charlie's uncertainty about the origins of his own desire that it is manifested. It is only just before Charlie descends back into stupidity that he splits between I and Charlie, objectifying Charlie as an alien person, and oscillates between the two poles, unsure where to settle his identity. It is at this moment of descent along the parabolic arc that the "gap" between Charlie and the smarter I that is returning to Charlie that an ethical desire can be posited—not the desire to hold onto his intelligence, or the understandable hatred of who he is becoming, or even the brute will of Charlie to return to his own complacence and happiness (which is perhaps a myth perpetrated by the author), but in the very question that he approaches:

> I wait, and leave myself open, passive, to whatever this experience means. Charlie doesn't want me to pierce the upper curtain of the mind. Charlie doesn't want to know what lies beyond.
> Does he fear seeing God?
> Or seeing nothing?[24]

The formulation of this question attests to an ethical desire, one without the urgency of Antigone, but a desire nonetheless in relation to death and productive of a certain aesthetic beauty. The main point here is that the moment of ethical desire or recognition occurs as Charlie descends back into stupidity, along the arc of desire that has been graphed.

In the 1998 film *Pi*, the main character, Maximillian Cohen, searches incessantly for the numerical pattern which underlies the universe, the stock market, and God. He reaches a paroxysm at the apex of desire, formulated as a 216 digit number, which is the secret Hebrew Kabbalah name for God, and which only he understands but cannot sustain. The metaphor that appears throughout is one of staring at the sun. In the end, Max almost kills himself but pulls back from literal death to reenter the world of human community. The reach for God is a reach for ultimate death—a nihilism—but as a detour it is productive of life when redirected downward in a parabolic arc that admits of repetition. Tellingly, at the end of the movie Max loses his savant ability to multiply complex numbers, which he would perform for the amusement of a little Chinese girl with a calculator. The final scene is one of the sun, but now framed and buffered by trees. Max's moment of recognition occurs after he learns the secret number, and he is able to pull away from its ultimate embrace before it destroys him. The "gap" is the difference between Max's profound desire to know the truth and his latent desire to be a human being in community. Here the disorienting, black and white postmodern film repeats a similar representation of the structure and complications of ethical desire to the out-of-date romantic story.

┌─────┐
│ **4** │
└─────┘

Foreclosing God

Heidegger, Lacan, and Kristeva

Heidegger's Refusal and Psychoanalysis

Despite his explicit separation of the concepts of God and Being, Martin Heidegger, in his later philosophy, treats them with a certain structural similarity.[1] That is, both God and Being lie beyond the calculating attempts to possess and wield them by a technological society bent on mastery. At the same time, however, this very technological epoch is a determination of Being, or in the *Beiträge zur Philosophie*, a result of the "flight of the last God."[2] The *Beiträge*, unpublished until 1989, lays out a foundation for Heidegger's later thought, and provides the connection upon which the "turning" (*Kehre*) from *Dasein* in *Being and Time* to being itself in his later philosophy hinges. In the *Beiträge*, Heidegger develops six interlocking themes, or joinings, which sketch the situation or event of being: echo, playing-forth, leaping, grounding, those to come, and the last god.[3] In a brief but provocative chapter on "the last god," Heidegger demonstrates the interconnection of god and Being. The flight of the last god is also "the truth of be-ing as refusal," which indicates a turning away from humanity on the part of God and Being.[4] Being and God recede together from a metaphysical tradition consumed with scientism and calculative grasping, or what he calls onto-theology. And the condition for any contact with the Being of beings or the god becomes a completely self-abandoning thinking of *Gelassenheit*.[5]

Heidegger, then, does not subscribe to the simple position that some of the theologians who have appropriated him have taken: that one can simply rescue God from metaphysical or philosophical being and restore theology to a pure access of God unmediated by philosophical categories. Gods do not have being—they need being, and therefore they actualize temporally, but we live in the time of the passing of the last god(s), or the refusal of God, which is no less a refusal of Being. Heidegger uses the German word *Verweigerung* to discuss God, which he translates as "refusal."

> What if that domain of decision as a whole, flight or arrival of gods, were itself the end? What if, beyond that, be-ing in its truth would have to be grasped for the first time as enownment [*Ereignis*], as that which enowns which we call *refusal*?[6]

Being, as the flight or passing of the last god or God, or as be-ing or coming to pass, demonstrates an originary alterity, or a refusal to submit to demands for human rationality and control. Heidegger claims that rather than a simple rejection, refusal "is the highest nobility of gifting . . . which makes up the originary essential sway [*wesen*] of the truth of be-ing."[7] The turning away from humanity by Being that occurs in the flight of the last god represents an abandonment that is at the same time an opportunity to think of Being and God more profoundly precisely in its turning, abandoning, and refusal. The calling of being calls for responsibility and *Gelassenheit*— letting the Being of beings be rather than attempting to master and control Being through the manipulation of beings.

What does the refusal of God or Being have to do with psychoanalysis? I want to undertake a different thinking of both God and Being by reading Heidegger along with Freud, Lacan, and Kristeva. In my reading, a convergence occurs between Heidegger's term "refusal" (*Verweigerung*) and the Freudian "foreclosure" (*Verwerfung*). Foreclosure is a specific form of refusal, as developed by Lacan and later Kristeva. For Heidegger, the proper response to the refusal of Being to presence directly is letting go or letting be (*Gelassenheit*). On the other hand, from a psychoanalytic viewpoint, a foreclosure of this refusal represents a different, more desperate response to a situation in which Being refuses or withdraws. Foreclosure is not simply a negative response, a rejection of Being (or God); it is also a productive response that possesses important artistic and theological implications. In this chapter I read Heidegger's notion of the refusal of Being (and/or God) from the perspective of Lacan and Kristeva's

conception of foreclosure, and this reading challenges the more conventional and faithful interpretation of Heidegger that issues from
Gelassenheit. Such a reading of Heideggerian refusal and psychoanalytic foreclosure constitutes a distortion of Heidegger, to be sure, and
perhaps also a distortion of Lacan and Kristeva, but perhaps produces an uncanny distortion that is revelatory for theological thinking.

In his essay "On the Possible Treatment of Psychosis," Lacan
identifies psychosis with the Freudian term *Verwerfung*, or foreclosure. "I will thus take *Verwerfung*," Lacan writes, "to be *'foreclosure'* of
the signifier."[8] Foreclosure represents what Freud calls primal repression, which prevents a mental ideational presentation from entering consciousness at all. Primal repression is contrasted by Freud
with "repression proper," which is an after-expulsion of the ideational
presentation or psychical representative (*Repräsentanz*) from consciousness.[9] What is barred from entering into consciousness in the
first place cannot be properly called repression because there occurs
a short circuit at the level of the unconscious that refuses to allow
such an idea entry into the topography of systems of preconscious-
conscious or even explicitly into the system unconscious. We cannot
properly consider primal repression to be either a repression or unconscious, since "it is of course only as something conscious that we
know anything" of the unconscious, and an object of primal repression is foreclosed from ever achieving consciousness.[10]

As we saw in chapter 2, Lacan calls psychosis a kind of foreclosure, specifically a foreclosure of signification that he dubs the
"Name-of-the-Father." He claims that in psychosis, "at the point at
which the Name-of-the-Father is summoned . . . a pure and simple
hole may thus answer in the Other; due to the lack of the metaphoric
effect, this hole will give rise to a corresponding hole in the place of
phallic signification."[11] This hole in the Other caused by foreclosure
of the "Name-of-the-Father" corresponds to a hole in signification,
which is "a disturbance that [has] occurred at the inmost juncture of
the subject's sense of life."[12] The "Name-of-the-Father" is simply the
passage into the realm of the symbolic, which is also an entry into a
community governed by social rules and norms. Such a refusal or
foreclosure undertaken by the subject at the very formation or constitution of that subject represents a profound rejection of human
society.

And yet this foreclosure expresses more than a simple voluntary
refusal to join the tribe of humanity because such a radical foreclosure either creates, or responds to, a hole in the Other. And Lacan's

notion of the Other has deep affinities with Heideggerian Being. In *The Four Fundamental Concepts of Psychoanalysis*, Lacan discusses the opening that the concept of transference represents. The Other is identified as the locus of speech and truth. Transference represents "the moment of the closing up of the unconscious, a temporal pulsation that makes it disappear at a certain point of its statement (*énoncé*)."[13] Lacan affirms that "the Other, the capital Other, is already there in every opening, however fleeting it may be, of the unconscious."[14] He continues by relating the opportunity for interpretation present in transference to a process of revealing and concealing on the part of the Other:

> It is precisely this part that is concerned in the transference, that it is this part that closes the door, or the window, or the shutters, or whatever—and that the beauty with whom one wishes to speak is there, behind, only too willing to open the shutters again. That is why it is at this moment that interpretation becomes decisive, for it is to beauty one must speak.[15]

Here the movement of closure represents an opening for interpretation, and one speaks to the beauty behind the shutters. Lacan next reaffirms that "the unconscious is the discourse of the other."[16] Although he characterizes the relation of unconscious and Other as a "knot," Lacan reproduces here the structure of Heideggerian Being, except here the relation is doubled. For Heidegger, Being conceals itself as it reveals beings.[17] For Lacan, one can say not only that the unconscious conceals itself in the revealing of consciousness, but also that the Other, which structurally approximates what Heidegger calls Being, conceals itself in revealing the unconscious.

This comparison of Lacan with Heidegger indicates a convergence of Heidegger's term *Verweigerung*, "refusal," and Freud's term, *Verwerfung*, "foreclosure." Foreclosure is a kind of refusal, but it involves a more active role on the part of the subject. Heidegger's language is more ontological and cosmological, describing an event (*Ereignis*) of Being that refuses to deliver itself to human understanding, and Heidegger prescribes a passive response of *Gelassenheit*. Lacan's language is psychological and also social, and refers to an act on the part of the individual, who refuses to enter into the realm of signification. This refusal of foreclosure takes a more active form. The similarity, however, between Lacan's Other and Heidegger's Being, allows one to interrogate one with the other, and to ask questions. The question to Lacan is whether foreclosure does not have an epochal aspect, being not simply an act, the responsibility for which rests with the individual psychotic, but rather indicates a much larger phenomenon on the part of the Other as a situation of reality. And the question to Heidegger is whether refusal of God or Being does not possess a psychotic component, or at least if the reception of the refusal on the part of the human should not take the form of a foreclosure of this refusal. A foreclosure of refusal is not a refusal to accept what has been refused and cling to God and Being, but a radical rejection of that which has refused itself, that is, a rejection of God and Being. Surely such a rejection consists of madness, but is it any more psychotic than an original or originary psychosis on the part of God or Being itself? And would not such madness possess an uncanny quality, much like Nietzsche's Madman who announces the death of God?[18]

Freud's Death Drive

To provide more specificity for this reading of refusal and foreclosure, I turn to Kristeva's notion of rejection, which she develops out of Freud and Lacan. Kristeva uses the term rejection to understand *Verwerfung*, although she modifies and goes beyond Lacan's use of the term. First, however, I want to step back and look at Freud's elaboration of the death drive in *Beyond the Pleasure Principle*, because it is an interpretation of the death drive upon which Kristeva relies to assemble her concept of *Verwerfung*.

Beyond the Pleasure Principle represents a powerful reappraisal of Freud's earlier work, as well as a profound challenge to contemporary thinking. It is well-known that in this book Freud opposes two fundamental drives, death drives and life or sexual drives, and that this dichotomy replaces his earlier opposition of sex drives and ego drives because now the death drive is posited as the most basic drive, from which the life drive is derived. The phenomenon of "repetition-compulsion," which determines that one act out a repressed trauma instead of understand and remember it, testifies indirectly to a drive that lies outside the purview of the pleasure principle. Freud speculates, in the climax of the book, that a drive "is an urge inherent in organic life to restore an earlier state of things." This statement applies to all drives or instincts in their very nature, and expresses "the *conservative* nature of living substance."[19] Freud is compelled by his own logic and by his experience with trauma dreams of veterans of

World War I, to recognize that fundamentally, "the aim of all life is death," (46).

Freud resorts to the myth presented by Aristophanes in Plato's *Symposium*, where humans are originally composed of a combination of two people who are then split apart by Zeus in a fit of rage and therefore spend their time seeking their other half. Freud formulates the speculative hypothesis that living substance comes to exist by means of division, that coming into life means being "torn apart into small particles," and that the death drive, as the drive par excellence, aims to restore the earlier inorganic unity (70). So-called life drives are secondary because they also aim to restore this inorganic unity, but in their own way; that is, via a detour through life that wards off external dangers so that the organism can "die only in its own fashion." Here, writes Freud, "the living organism struggles most energetically against events . . . which might help it attain life's aim rapidly—by a kind of short circuit," (47).

Aristotle bases his philosophy on the principle that all humans desire to know the good as the goal, end, or *telos*. For Aristotle, and a traditional Aristotelian understanding that Lacan critiques in Seminar VII, as I will show in chapter 8, the good is identified as God, and knowing God as the good is happiness. In *Civilization and Its Discontents*, Freud argues that the goal of life is happiness, but this happiness is defined as the absence of suffering.[20] Existence is stimulation, which is necessarily suffering. For Freud, the end of all human desire is death, inorganic unity, and cessation of tension. Is such knowledge of death, then, the fundamental insight into the good for human beings? Can one worship the Supreme God of Death? According to Heidegger, Being refuses to reveal itself; it withdraws, concealing itself as it reveals beings. God becomes radically absent as the condition for any possible return. According to a Freudian logic, God and Being as a static end or goal can be best represented as death, and Heidegger's meditative philosophy is a submissive resignation to this reality. According to Heidegger, Freud's logic reveals an epochal situation that is marked by a desire for death (being-unto-death) along with a corresponding foreclosure or short circuit of this desire, which is what allows life to continue. What is at stake is the question of a proper (or improper) response.

Kant provides a different way to think about desire in the *Critique of Judgment*, because for him beauty is characterized by purposiveness without an objective purpose, or finality without end.[21] If the ultimate end is death, then that is the ultimate purpose, but life consists of the finality or purposiveness in its striving. In this way one can return to Freud and reread the sexual drives with an eye to the detour they make along the path of desire. For Freud, the only true life drives are the sexual drives because although they too are conservative, their effect is to delay or defer the end by means of a division that is a repetition of the original coming into life. The paradigmatic life drives are the germ cells, "which work against the death of the living substance and succeed in winning for it what we can only regard as potential immortality, though that may mean no more than a lengthening of the road to death."[22]

Death drives and life or sexual drives are not opposed to each other because both have the same end, and both are inherently conservative, but the division of the germ cell represents a detour in the journey toward death—a detour that makes all the difference. One should not mistake Freud for a physiological reductionist, especially here at his most speculative moment, and think that the germ cell narrowly represents only a certain natural organic phenomenon. It is helpful to compare Freud's discussion of the germ cells with Kant's description of Enlightenment, where human ability to think freely and exercise reason is called a "germ on which nature has lavished most care," which develops within the external social and political constraints of what Kant calls a hard shell.[23] Kant intends the hard shell to nourish the germ of rational thinking, but his deep respect for authority leads him to enclose the germ almost wholly within the shell so as not to expose it to subversive elements. The hard shell may also refer to the words of our language as a reified Word, and the ideality they represent as static representations, such that the germ cells attest to a profound division already at work in each word, whose force shatters any unified signification. One cannot possess a germ without any shell, just as one cannot isolate a pure life drive apart from the death drive(s), but one can value precisely this germ of radical thinking amid the encrustations of traditional theologizing that threaten to harden it so it cannot divide, be fruitful, and multiply.

According to my reading of *Beyond the Pleasure Principle*, Freud uses the notion of a short circuit, or foreclosure, to explain how the death drive converts into life drives. Another way to say this is life drives can continue to exist by short circuiting their essential goal to fulfill their basic function. Foreclosure, or rejection, is necessary for life in both a physiological and a metaphorical sense.[24]

Kristeva's Rejection

Kristeva builds upon Freud in articulating an understanding of *Verwerfung* that is theoretically sophisticated and practically productive. In her book, *Revolution in Poetic Language*, Kristeva develops her notion of rejection out of an engagement with Freud's essay on negation, *"Verneinung."* In Freud's article, according to Kristeva, "expulsion (*Ausstossung*) is what constitutes the real object as such; it also constitutes it as lost, thus setting up the symbolic function."[25] Every expression of negation, Freud claims, ultimately rests upon an expulsion of an object from the ego-image into an external reality. Negation as a judgment is secondary to, and derivative of, expulsion.[26] Expulsion, Kristeva claims, "establishes an outside that is never definitely separate—one that is always in the process of being posited."[27] Expulsion represents a powerful eruption of pleasure that is constitutive of the symbolic, but that nevertheless disrupts or subverts the symbolic. Following Lacan, Kristeva explicitly connects the term expulsion with *Verwerfung* or foreclosure in Freud's work.[28] The pleasure of expulsion refers to the pleasure of the anal drive and constitutes a *"jouissance* of destruction" that, when directed inward toward a person's own ego, puts the subject *en procès* (in process/on trial) (150). Rejection is Kristeva's term to represent this fundamental aggressiveness and pleasure. In her description of the pleasure of expulsion, she writes that

> these drives move through the sphincters and arouse pleasure at the very moment substances belonging to the body are separated and rejected from the body. This acute pleasure therefore coincides with a loss, a separation from the body, and the isolating of objects outside it. . . . This expulsion of objects is the subject's fundamental experience of separation—a separation which is not a lack, but a discharge, and which, although primitive, arouses pleasure. (151)

Rejection is a pleasure that operates beyond the reach of the pleasure principle. As expulsion or foreclosure, rejection represents a powerful option for the expression of a process of subjectivity that is not a lack, or a "mere" hole, but also a discharge. "Although it is destructive," Kristeva writes, "rejection is the very mechanism of reactivation, tension, life; aiming toward the equalization of tension, toward a state of inertia and death, it *perpetuates* tension and life," (150). Thus anal rejection is an expression of the death drive, which when turned upon the subject itself represents a primary masochism.

In *Beyond the Pleasure Principle*, as we have seen, Freud argues that "the aim of all life is death," but that the compulsion to repeat means that each organism desires to "die only in its own fashion."[29] The death drive is primary, but the sexual drives perpetuate life by means of a certain division, which is a detour on the path of desire in its journey toward death. Rejection as aggressiveness is death, but, on the other hand, the tension it sets up and keeps in motion contributes to life. Freud claims that the living organism perpetuates life by short circuiting impending mortal situations to die on its own terms, in its own way. This short circuit, or foreclosure of death, which is the aim of all life by means of an aggressive separation or division, is a radical rejection of being and a refusal of the symbolic order. Does this rejection, then, lead simply to madness or psychotic schizophrenia?

Earlier in *Revolution in Poetic Language*, Kristeva sets up her dichotomy of semiotic and symbolic realms. The semiotic refers to a region of pulsing drives that precedes or underlies the realm of linguistic signification. Rejection in the form of poetic language represents a return of the semiotic within the symbolic, which subverts the symbolic as such. This function of poetic language, which is not simply semiotic, allows an echoing of semiotic rhythm at the symbolic level. Kristeva claims that "rejection therefore constitutes the return of expulsion—*Ausstossung* or *Verwerfung*—within the domain of the constituted subject."[30] At the level of psychic drives and ego formation, rejection must be overcome in the individual by placing oneself "under the law of the father," which means to enter the realm of the symbolic, of language, which means to be(come) sane. On the other hand, the constant return to rejection by the subject constitutes "the schizoid moment of scission."[31] Kristeva understands the precarious position of the subject, which she calls the thetic position, and she does not want to dispense with it to attempt a psychotic return to the semiotic, which is impossible in any case. The challenge is rather to see a return of rejection or a "surplus of rejection that puts in process/on trial the symbolic already instituted by *Verwerfung*—represented in discourse," or poetic language.[32] This would be a negativity of text, or a poetic negativity that is "third-degree rejection" and does not thereby elide or forget the importance of the drives but evokes them in heterogeneous textual practices.[33]

Foreclosure of the True-Real

Kristeva returns to the topic of foreclosure in a later essay, "The True-Real" ("*Le vréel*"). In this essay she describes the flight of truth

from the realm of human signification in the course of western theoretical discourse, claiming that "the *true* has lost its former logical and
ontological security, and is now expressed instead as the *true-real.*"[34]
This convergence of the true with the Real is understood as a profound absence because Kristeva uses the term Real to mean "that
impossible element which henceforth can only be designated by the
Lacanian category of the *real,*" (217). Lacan's typology of the imaginary, the symbolic, and the Real, in which the category of the Real
is the most inaccessible to human understanding, testifies to a felt
sense of the disappearance of reality, or that which is ultimately significant, from the realm of human interaction and communication.
This loss of the Real is followed by a flight of truth, and Kristeva is
insistent about specifying this mutual convergence of truth and reality as utterly absent.

This state of affairs resembles that of Heideggerian being because,
for the later Heidegger, being is characterized primarily by its withdrawal or refusal to show itself to a grasping technological civilization. Instead of a response of radical passivity, Kristeva turns to
psychoanalysis as a means of intervention, specifically the language
of foreclosure, to understand "the crisis of truth in language," (218).
Foreclosure, according to Kristeva, "decapitates the Name of the
Father and snatches the subject away, into the real," but now she
explicitly states that one must "envisage certain *kinds* of foreclosure,"
(218). The crisis of truth in language is a general situation of psychosis, as we saw in chapter 2, because the Real is foreclosed to signification. In Kristeva's essay, however, one confronts different versions
of psychosis, which also represent diverse responses to this psychotic
situation. The crisis of truth in language, or the disappearance of the
Real, is also the refusal of Being and the bypassing of God, in a Heideggerian sense. This crisis or refusal necessarily brings about a general psychosis: "psychosis is the crisis of truth in language," (218).

Kristeva goes on to consider, in Freud's writings, the various aspects "by which truth is always already 'falsified,'" (225). She fas-
tens on disavowal, or *Verleugnung*, which is a defense on the part of
the ego introduced by the mechanism of language. Disavowal is a
mode of foreclosure, and it takes two main forms: neurosis and psychosis (proper). Neurosis "operates through the disavowal of desire
and/or of the signifier," while psychosis "proceeds by the disavowal
of [conventional, historical] reality and demands that the signifier be
real to be true," (226). In other words, neurosis attempts to cope
with the loss of the Real by adapting language to conventional norms

through substitutions and transferences, forgetting that the signifiers express desire for something beyond language. Psychosis, on the other hand, obsessively clings to the Lacanian linguistic signifier in all of its purity and rejects all human conventional "truth." Both forms of disavowal are problematic because neurosis clings to truth at the expense of the Real, and psychosis remains obsessed with the impossible Real, thereby losing touch with communicable truth.

Kristeva articulates a third form of disavowal, although she hesitates to call it disavowal, because of her antipathy toward the term:[35] "I feel more and more that a separate place must be set aside for so-called artistic discourse. If there is any disavowal in it . . ."[36] Artistic discourse refuses to disavow either desire or reality and therefore represents "a microscopic expansion of the 'true-real,'" (227). Rather than accepting the bifurcation of the true and the Real, or the irrevocable loss in the convergence of both that marks the historical condition of western intellectual discourse, artistic discourse creates the true-real, but under very specific conditions.

Kristeva turns to what she calls hallucinatory hysterical discourse to express her vision of artistic discourse.

> In hysterical discourse, truth . . . often assumes the obsessive, unsayable, and emotionally charged weft of visual representation. Floating in isolation, this vision of an unnamed real rejects all nomination and any possible narrative. Instead it remains enigmatic, setting the field of speech ablaze only in order to reduce it to cold ashes, fixing in this way a hallucinatory and untouchable *jouissance*.[37]

This form of discourse combines a hysterical element taken from neurosis with a hallucinatory element borrowed from psychosis, and it represents a positive discharge dependent on the anal drive, which recalls her description of rejection in *Desire in Poetic Language*. "In the hysterical hallucination," she continues, "we therefore find ourselves in a border zone where the Real, to burst on the scene as truth, leaves a hole in the subject's discourse, but is none the less taken up by that very discourse in a repetitive representation that produces meaning . . . without creating signification."[38] This hole, which the Real makes to burst out as truth in artistic discourse, must be productive, but it should not become clogged by static significations or fixed representations.

The aim of such hysterical discourse is the production of an icon.[39]

> This heterogeneous semiotic encounter . . . is a hallucination that marks the insistence of the *true-real*, an archaic and salutary

attempt to elaborate the irruption of the real that leaves a hole in the symbolic weft of hysterical discourse. This hallucination recurs periodically, in order to indicate, like an icon, an unutterable jouissance that endangers the symbolic resources of the speaking being. The hallucinatory icon, which becomes obsessive by virtue of its repetition, challenges what may be structured as a language: it obliterates reality and makes the real loom forth as a jubilant enigma.[40]

Even if such a hole in the subject is ultimately psychotic, it represents a response to the refusal of Being as a psychosis, rather than a simple catatonic disavowal. Kristeva does not want to celebrate a literal psychosis as such, but desires to exploit the openings of subjectivity and language for their access to reality and revolutionary transformation. Kristeva's notion of artistic discourse in "The True-Real" must be understood in continuity with what she calls poetic language in *Revolution in Poetic Language*. Similarly, her description of hallucinatory hysterical discourse in the former provides a nuanced application of her central notion of rejection in the latter, as well as a more sophisticated engagement with Freudian and Lacanian foreclosure.

Conclusion

Returning to Heidegger, if he is correct in claiming that we live in a time of the passing of the last god(s), which is at the same time a default or refusal of Being, this conclusion can be heard in at least two ways. On the one hand, in a more properly Heideggerian manner, the nihilism that characterizes our time is also a triumph of Being because humans need to learn the lesson that an instrumental approach to reality does not work, and that Being recedes the more we try to grasp at it. On this reading, a meditative thinking of Being, or that which presences, represents a spiritual discipline of *Gelassenheit* that is the only option that could prove salvific. If humans learn the proper awe and humility before Being, perhaps Being and God(s) will turn toward us anew.

I do not want to simply discount such an understanding, but I want to challenge it by juxtaposing against it the reading I have developed in this essay. Heidegger delineates an objective situation of refusal or withdrawal, and his subjective response is one of passivity and self-abandonment. On the other hand, for Kristeva, the foreclosure or short circuit of God and Being creates a psychological condition of psychosis, which calls for a more productive, if also a more desperate, response. This response is suggested by Kristeva's notion of artistic or poetic language, but it also should be no less a theological language. One of the claims of this book, in fact, is that the psychoanalytic language of Freud, Lacan, and Kristeva is already deeply theological, even if one must read it with a great deal of subtlety and sensitivity to discern these theological elements.

In addition, one must revise one's understanding of what theology, and especially theological language, is and can be. According to Kristeva, foreclosure or rejection involves the production of an icon — both an artistic and a religious process. Language is inherently theological because it is the creation of sense and meaning. But, at the same time, language forecloses our access to body as body in its depths to create signifying effects because it involves the production of sense, according to Deleuze in *The Logic of Sense*, despite the extraordinary parallelism of language and body.[41]

What are the possibilities of a psycho-theological language in an epoch of refusal on the part of both gods and Being? Can we envision a productive short circuit that would not simply be a disavowal, but rather a radically living theological thinking? Most orthodox theology is repressive because it forecloses or disavows the body. Even if we have to think about the body through language, if we forget the body it threatens to reappear in a return of the repressed. The possibility of the return of the repressed produces enormous anxiety, and this is nowhere more evident theologically than with the body of God, which most theology desperately attempts to deny. In chapter 5 I will read Freud's revision of his understanding of anxiety with the help of Lacan and Žižek and set out an alternative understanding of theology as anxiety in manner that is productive rather than repressive.

Language is theological because it creates a signifier *ex nihilo* — out of nothing. This is not the orthodox dogma of *creatio ex nihilo* because nothing does not precede creation temporally; rather, nothingness is the substance of the creation of meaning, as Lacan argues in *The Ethics of Psychoanalysis*. In chapter 6, to work out a psycho-theological interpretation of creation *ex nihilo*, I turn to Tillich, who provides resources for reunderstanding theology and creation *ex nihilo* along the lines of Lacan, specifically through Tillich's reading of Schelling. Then, in chapter 7, I directly engage Schelling's thought in his drafts on the "Ages of the World," distinguishing my reading from Žižek's. Finally, I confront Tillich and Schelling directly with Lacan on the concept of creation at the conclusion of chapter 7.

5

Anxiety and the S(ub)lime Body of God

But let us imagine what would take place in a patient who saw in his analyst an exact replica of himself. . . . To take an extreme case, if experienced in the form of strangeness proper to apprehensions of the double, this situation would set up an uncontrollable anxiety on the part of the analysand.

— Jaques Lacan, *Écrits*

Introduction

In his early career, Freud understood anxiety as a response to repression, but in a later work he reversed himself, arguing that anxiety is primary. In this chapter I argue that anxiety is fundamentally related to the body as well as to *jouissance*, which refers to a fascination with the process of expelling body to create a subject or *cogito*. This bodily remainder, which sometimes takes the form of slime, generates enormous anxiety, at the individual, social, and theological levels. Following Lacan's formulas of sexuation distinguishing between the exception (man) and the not-all (woman), Slavoj Žižek applies this distinction to Kant's dynamical and mathematical versions of the sublime in *Tarrying with the Negative*. According to a logic of exceptionality, the (masculine) exception lies beyond the limit, and this model accords with Freud's earlier understanding of anxiety. Žižek explains, however, that the exception paradoxically reproduces or reinscribes the limit, and thus it is limited. On the other hand, the (feminine) not-all functions as an unlimited excess because it does not seek to simply project itself beyond limits, but works along the limit with more creativity and freedom, and this understanding coincides with a modified reading of Freud's later theory of anxiety.

In light of these differences among repression and anxiety, exception and not-all, and mathematical and dynamical sublime, I sketch out two alternatives for understanding theology. Following Freud's early view that subordinates anxiety to repression, theological repression of the body, or the body of God, is what makes theology intrinsically repressive and requires critique, because it misplaces the body and thereby generates anxiety. On the other hand, a theology associated with the not-all paradoxically preserves a richer field because here theology is anxiety, following Freud's later reversal, and both anxiety and theology work at a primary level below or before repression. This theology of anxiety would be a s(ub)lime theology, and would attend to the slime nature sloughed off by God as traces of divinity. Anxiety traces the construction and deconstruction of the subject in its constitution (of itself as thinking immaterial spirit) and its disavowal (as formless matter).

The Jouissance of the Other

In his seminar on *The Four Fundamental Concepts of Psycho-Analysis*, Jacques Lacan provocatively claims that "man's desire is the desire of the Other."[1] The Other (*Autre*) represents the social unconscious, but in a structural or functional sense, rather than an ontological sense. Socially, human beings are constructed in their subjectivity by social pressures and demands. There exists within individuals an opening toward the social field as a whole, which is evoked in every action or desire of the individual.

One can also think of this situation in a Kantian way: the Other stands for the universal, which is never encountered as an object of experience, but is rather a social a priori evoked by the particular objects and intuitions. In the *Critique of Pure Reason*, universal or a priori knowledge is defined as "knowledge absolutely independent of all experience."[2] Furthermore, "we can conclude from the universal to the particular, only so far as universal properties are ascribed to things as being the foundation upon which the particular properties rest."[3] The universal Other is the basis of the particular, but the universal is never directly or immediately intuited, only the particular other object. The Other is the universal or transcendental ideal encountered both in and beyond every particular other, which Lacan calls an *objet petit a(utre)*. This is Lacan's distinction between Other (*Autre*) and other (*objet petit a*), which is structurally similar to Kant's distinction between universal knowledge a priori and particular determinate knowledge.

The particular object is a manifestation or encapsulation of the Other as a whole. In this way the Other is a limit concept because the Other only appears in others/objects, but it is a concept that refers to what is ultimately real and important about human sociality and intersubjectivity. Every time you desire a soft drink such as a Diet Pepsi, in some ways you conform to the desire of the social Other that you purchase and consume, that you affiliate yourself with a certain image and product, and that you integrate yourself into the social order in a particular way. Your desire is not simply your own but manifests the desire of the Other, which expresses itself through you, sometimes in a manipulative and sinister way. Advertising in a commodity-oriented culture intentionally creates or evokes desires, and it attempts to connect with the desire of an individual consumer to sell not simply a product but also an image.

In a similar way, to desire another person sexually or romantically is not only to desire that particular person in his or her uniqueness and singularity, but it is also to buy into what that person represents socially and symbolically, even if only as a rebellion against prevailing tastes and norms. Whom someone is attracted to expresses both a personal taste but also a desired social status, and muscled hunks and skinny, clear-skinned models also assist in the construction of this desire. At a fundamental level your desire is not your own, and this realization can be the cause of enormous anxiety.

The term *jouissance* as used by Lacan is not simply an outpouring of sexual passion, and it does not mean what we normally think of as joy. *Jouissance* is desire carried to the extreme, or the absolute limit of desire, which of course is death. In *The Ethics of Psychoanalysis*, Lacan refers to the power of "a sexual *jouissance* that is not sublimated," but the figure Lacan primarily associates with *jouissance* is Sade.[4] So *jouissance* is certainly sexual or libidinal in nature, but it is also destructive and ultimately self-destructive passion. This extremity of desire in its destructive capacity evokes horror because it is unwilling to compromise or negotiate its drive for satisfaction. Socialized humans react with terror or disgust to an eruption of pure enjoyment, which is precisely the unleashing of absolute desire without any constraint or law. Lacan also characterizes *jouissance* as the exemplary manifestation of the Freudian death drive.

According to Lacan, *"jouissance* appears not purely and simply as the satisfaction of a need but as the satisfaction of a drive."[5] A need refers to an animal need, a purely instinctual affair that has no relation to language, symbolic substitution, or speech, while a drive does possess such a social relation. The relationship between drive and desire is more complicated, but a drive is relatively more immediate and closer to a need, whereas desire is more explicitly related to language. In some ways one can understand the distinction between drive and desire along the lines of Freud's distinction in his essay "The Unconscious" between the idea of an instinct, its ideational presentation (*Repräsentanz*), and a more conventional, conscious representation (*Vorstellung*), as described in relation to Ricoeur in chapter 1.[6] Desire concerns *Vorstellungen*, while the *Repräsentanz* is more directly associated with the drive (*Trieb*). *Jouissance* is not simply an unleashing of nature, or instinctive animal passions, but it represents, even if as a limit, an option within the social field.

Another aspect of *jouissance* that is often overlooked is that human beings are not prime movers of *jouissance*, upsetting the social order to fulfill their own satisfactions. "Desire is the desire of the Other," and the *jouissance* of the Other refers to the Other's destructiveness, which threatens the individual. Even though it is an abstraction, the effects of the *jouissance* of the Other are all too real. An example would be a mob lynching, where the participants are not primarily motivated by individual concerns or passions, but driven to seek their collective version of justice. This represents an outbreak of *jouissance*, which sacrifices an individual to satisfy the Other as a social group, and on some level even the initiators of the act can be thought of as playthings of the Other. Of course, *jouissance* is rarely expressed, but usually rather intimated, where the threat of an outbreak of *jouissance* serves to curb the individual subject's actions and beliefs.

Danielle Bergeron suggests another way to think about the *jouissance* of the Other in her essay, "Aliens and the Psychotic Experience." She claims that the movie *Aliens* "scripts a psychotic fantasy—the position of a subject who has become an object delivered up to the all-powerful Other that demands entire satisfaction of its needs."[7] *Aliens* (1986), is the sequel to *Alien* (1979), in which a crew comes upon an alien spaceship that harbors a deadly creature, and Ripley, played by Sigourney Weaver, finally kills the alien and is the only person to survive. In the sequel, Ripley visits a colony of humans that aliens have infiltrated, and she and a little girl, Newt, engage in a dramatic showdown with the alien queen. Finally Ripley utilizes a loader vehicle to eject the queen into space. According to Bergeron, the Alien is a xenomorph, or a radically unfamiliar form that signifies the absence of a father, or any meaningful symbolic order, and therefore the imaginary confrontation with "the real of the Thing."[8] Significantly, all of the men are killed before Ripley confronts the feminized queen while protecting the little girl.

A psychotic is a person who has been completely delivered up to the *jouissance* of the Other, represented in the movie by the little girl, Newt, who has been captured by the aliens. Ripley's therapeutic task is to free her, that is, to restore her to the position of a subject. Bergeron claims that to free oneself from the *jouissance* of the Other, one must externalize the Other as an object that is "the determinative step in the process of separation securing the psychotic's treatment."[9] In the case of *Aliens*, the externalization of the Other is the loader, or the steel beast that Ripley uses to destroy the "real" beast, which frees Newt (and also Ripley herself, although not completely, as we discover in the third movie) from being a "plaything of the Other."[10]

Within the realm of symbolic meaning, a narrative conflict is set up in *Aliens* that casts the Other in a demonic and threatening role, whereas the individual subject armed with the Name or Law of the Father becomes the protagonist. The Other, in this case the alien, is feminized in its representation to demonstrate the absence of a father, that is, a signifying relation. Usually the subject is correspondingly masculinized; although this is not literally the case in *Aliens*, Ripley is portrayed in very masculine as opposed to feminine ways (for example, she is not referred to by her first name, Ellen). For Lacan, psychosis is a disavowal of the Name of the Father, as we saw in chapter 2, because the acceptance of the Name or Law of the Father is what ensures passage into social discourse and signification. In Bergeron's essay the Other is nearly equated with the Real, or the Thing, beyond all symbolic relation, but it is important to remember that this representation of the limit of representation and of the Real takes place within symbolic discourse and signification.

The Slimy Subject

I have set up a false opposition, following Bergeron's Lacanian reading of *Aliens*, between a *jouissance* of the Other, experienced as psychotic-demonic, and an individual subject characterized as a protagonist. Bergeron's therapeutic task is to free psychotics from their (mis)understanding of themselves and their situation as that of a plaything in relation to the Other as Real and beyond signification. A sane person presumably negotiates a more healthy relation to the social and symbolic Other. The problem with Bergeron's account is that it valorizes the ego, and thus it is strongly influenced by the ego-psychology that Lacan criticizes.

I am suggesting, following Slavoj Žižek, that *jouissance* is not so easily overcome. Ripley, who accomplishes the healing in the little girl, discovers in the third movie that her dream of being invaded by the alien is not merely a dream. When her ship crashes into a prison planet, battles with the aliens break out anew, but at the end of *Alien 3* Ripley discovers that she is impregnated with an alien, and she immolates herself in dramatic fashion. Furthermore, the Law of the Father is compromised by the fact that we discover that Ripley and her crew are in fact playthings of the corporations that want to capture aliens for scientific research. This means that we are all inhabited by the Other, whether we want to disavow the horror of that insight or not. Or in other words, to quote Kristeva, "psychosis is the crisis of truth in language."[11]

Furthermore, this relation between the subject and the *jouissance* of the Other is not simply an external relation, but an intimate one that constitutes the subject as a subject. Žižek claims that the subject or *cogito* appears in the rejection of an absolute formlessness that later horrifies him. Writing about the movie *Alien* in *Tarrying With the Negative*, Žižek claims that "here we encounter *cogito* at its purest when (what will become) the subject constitutes itself by rejecting the slimy substance of *jouissance*."[12] In other words, the condition of the emergence of subjectivity involves the rejection of a formless slime that (re)emerges elsewhere as matter. This slimy substance, which was intimate to the embodied human, then exerts a powerful horror but also fascination on him or her. In addition, the emergent and victorious *cogito* is masculinized while the slimy *jouissance* is feminized. Žižek argues that the subject is a pure form, a Kantian "I think" that cannot be filled out with a determinate content, and that Kant and Hegel draw out the conclusions that Descartes left undeveloped. Žižek here follows Lacan, whose formula for subjectivity implies that "at the very moment of my reduction to a pure cogito qua impossible gaze, a formless slime of the substance of *jouissance* had to emerge somewhere else."[13] In other words, subjectivity is constituted in the process of sloughing off one's body—which is perceived as slime—

and this externalized body encountered as substance provokes horror and sublimity. Kristeva also describes this process in *Powers of Horror*, and she calls expulsion of this slimy *jouissance* an abjection that constantly threatens the boundaries of the ethical subject.[14]

Lacan demonstrates a similar insight in his *Seminar II* when he describes Freud's reaction to his dream, Irma's Injection. In the dream Freud looks deeply into the back of his patient's throat and is horrified by what he sees there.

> There's a horrendous discovery here, that of the flesh one never sees, the foundation of things, the other side of the face, the secretory glands *par excellence*, the flesh from which everything exudes, at the very heart of the mystery, the flesh in as much as it is suffering, is formless, in as much as it is something which provokes anxiety. Spectre of anxiety, identification of anxiety, the final revelation of *you are this — You are this, which is so far from you, this which is the ultimate formlessness.*[15]

This dream represents Freud's famous and first successful self-analysis. His reaction testifies to the enormous anxiety that results when one recognizes oneself in the substance of the *jouissance* of the Other in an uncanny way after the rejection of the body as other. One experiences not simply the determinate form of the human being, but body as body — body as pure substance and absolute formlessness.

Freud's Anxiety

In his late work, *Inhibitions, Symptoms, and Anxiety*, Freud revises his previous understanding of anxiety. For most of his professional life, he believed that anxiety was transformed libido, and that it was produced by repression. In his 1915 essay, "The Unconscious," Freud claims that primal repression consists of an *"anticathexis*, by means of which the system Pcs [preconscious] guards itself against the intrusion of the unconscious idea."[16] This anticathexis prevents an unconscious idea from becoming preconscious or conscious, and this process of repression generates "anxiety-hysteria," in which anxiety appears "without the subject knowing what he is afraid of."[17]

In 1928, however, Freud states that he "can no longer maintain this view." Rather, "it was anxiety which produced repression" and not the other way around.[18] This shift in the understanding of anxiety takes place in the context of two important developments in Freud's later years. The first consists of an emphasis on a more literal explanation of castration, which is elaborated in essays such as "The Infantile Genital Organization" and "Anatomical Sex-Distinction." In these essays the basic difference between boys and girls hinges on a girl's lack of a penis, which is experienced by the girl as a profound lack or wound. The little boy, on the other hand, not only compares his own penis to that of his father, and feels a sense of inferiority regarding size, but more importantly a boy experiences tremendous anxiety when confronted with the absence of a penis in a girl or woman. The little boy reacts by denying or disavowing the reality he sees because to admit that girls do not possess a penis is to admit the contingency of his own, and the possibility of losing it. The little girl, on the other hand, presumably knows exactly what she sees and exactly what she wants, as opposed to Freud, who elsewhere supposedly claims that he cannot understand what women want. "A little girl behaves differently," Freud writes, "She makes her judgment and her decision in a flash. She has seen it and knows that she is without it and wants to have it."[19] This anatomical sex-distinction underlies Freud's conclusion in *Inhibitions, Symptoms and Anxiety* that "the anxiety felt in animal phobias is the ego's fear of castration."[20]

The other feature of Freud's later work, which also manifests itself in the last sentence, is a turn toward the ego as a protagonist in its defenses against a primal id and a punitive superego. It is the ego's fear of castration that prompts anxiety, and this anxiety must be repressed, sublimated, diverted, or otherwise defended against to survive amid civilization's discontents. Both of these characteristics of Freud's late work—the single-minded focus on the ego as well as the obsessive concern to ground anxiety in a literal concern with castration—are open to criticism. In fact the overriding theme of Lacan's *Seminar II, The Ego in Freud's Theory and in the Technique of Psychoanalysis*, constitutes a critique of ego psychology along with any restriction of psychoanalysis to this practice. Lacan also precludes any identification of the subject (I) with the ego (me). He concludes that the ego is by nature resistant, reactive, and inertial, and it attempts to thwart the irruption of insistent speech that marks the truth of the subject.[21] To focus on the ego, Lacan claims, is to obliterate the revolutionary power of the problematic Freud opens up.

Furthermore, feminist criticism—both psychoanalytic and anti-psychoanalytic—has challenged Freud's essentialization of biological sex and gender categories, primarily in terms of the universalization of Freud's speculations on the reactions of little boys and girls to the discovery of their respective genitalia.[22] Freud transfers the value his Viennese culture placed on the virile penis to the formation of every human person, and he presupposes rather than locates the trauma of anxiety in the observation of the other sex's genitals. *There is nothing in itself about female genitals that suggests a lack*, even in relation to a penis, but rather this meaning or value is brought in from elsewhere.

One can question, therefore, the basis of Freud's shift in the explanation of anxiety. Many interpreters overlook this late development in Freud's thought for this and other reasons. To call into question the assertion that "the anxiety felt in animal phobias is the ego's fear of castration," however, is not the same thing as to consider what it might mean if "it is always the ego's attitude of anxiety which is the primary thing and which sets repression going," especially if one brackets the term ego in the latter phrase.[23] Here I am reading Freud against Freud by taking up his later understanding of anxiety in which anxiety precedes and causes repression, rather than vice versa. At the same time I am critical of the other two developments in Freud's later thought that are connected with this transformed understanding of anxiety: the focus on the ego as protagonist and the adoption of an essentialist masculine model of sexuality.

What if anxiety were the cause of repression rather than an after-effect? How would such an understanding of anxiety transform the rest of the corpus of Freudian (and post-Freudian) psychoanalysis?[24] And more importantly, how would such a transformation affect theology, however implicitly? What if theology were characterized as a discourse of repression or defense set in motion by an uncontrollable anxiety? Finally, what if theology were to understand how it is implicated in that anxiety by thinking the anxiety itself as God?

God's Body

To bring together a notion of theology as a discourse of anxiety—or possibly a discourse that responds to anxiety—along with Lacan and Žižek's understanding of the constitution of subjectivity as a rejection of the substance of the *jouissance* of the Other, is to ask about the body of God. One can read the history of theology as an uncontrollable anxiety regarding God's body, which theologians often attempt to cover over or contain. One the one hand, the incredible significance of the incarnation of Christ, which Christian theology affirmed to shift Jesus's identity from Messiah to God, represents an important affirmation of the body of God. At the same time, difficult questions remain concerning this body, especially its disappearance from the tomb and its transformation into a resurrection body. Christ's body is temporary—a unique occasion never to be repeated. God's body is nonexistent, but functions to stimulate enormous anxiety about sexuality and gender in human beings, as well as nature in general.

Most theologians deny that God has a physical body and yet affirm that God created humanity in God's image. Does this image refer to the form of the human body, or solely the existence of a conscious mind? Is God male? Most theologians would say no, but traditional theological language still refers to God with masculine pronouns. If God does have a body, how can God escape sexual difference? If God does not have a body, how then can theology avoid an insidious dualism between spirit and body? If the incarnation of the second person of the trinity is supposed to resolve this dualism, why was God incarnated as a male human being? Would any Christian theologian deny that Jesus had a penis?

The point is that issues of body and sexuality are problematic for traditional and orthodox theological thinking, and they potentially generate anxiety. Martin Luther's writings, for example, illustrate a tremendous theological anxiety regarding justification. In his treatise on *The Freedom of a Christian*, Luther claims that "the moment you begin to have faith you learn that all things in you are sinful and damnable."[25] Justification occurs only in the context of extreme anxiety, and the psychologist Erik Erikson has speculated on some of the psychological roots of Luther's anxiety, which is rooted in the body.[26] Luther writes at length how "savage and destructive a beast is a guilty conscience," that whips or tortures the individual soul "as if it were in hell."[27] On this reading of anxiety, one could understand Luther's discourse as connected to a profound horror of the body of God, understood as substance or *jouissance*. Luther can be seen as an extreme example of how orthodox theologians attempt to deny God any materiality or capriciousness, representing divinity as pure, self-transparent thinking—a *cogito* writ large. At the same time, this disavowal of the body of God by many theologians leads to a return of the repressed, understood as an experience of absolute sinfulness or damnation.

In addition, anxiety about the body is not unrelated to theological questions about nature, toward which Christian theology has shown great ambivalence. Nature that cannot be harnessed under divine providence and purpose becomes demonized as a source of profound horror. I am thinking of nature "red in tooth and claw," which is experienced as slimy, gooey, oozing, primordial, insect-like, reptilian, voracious, etc. Although some of the resonances of this description of nature are Darwinian, in a classical sense nature can be understood as unformed matter, which in some Neoplatonic, Christian, and Gnostic thinking is viewed with profound antipathy if not horror. Nature at its most hideous takes on the aspects of absolute formlessness that characterize the substance of the *jouissance* of the Other as a sublime Thing. This vision is encapsulated, as Žižek points out, by the alien, which can also be understood as reflecting a modern and humanistic horror of a certain understanding of postmodernism, because postmodernism signifies in different, monstrous ways, not respecting clear and clean borders of logic and being.

In the context of anxiety concerning the body of God, traditional theology evinces desperate attempts to "save" God's comprehensibility, while condemning nature as nature or body as body. This situation is a return of the repressed because both the hyperrationality of God and the formless body or nature are seen psychoanalytically as referring to the same subjectivity of God. God's body is repressed to affirm God's rationality and goodness as pure spirit, but the body of God returns as slime in a threatening and destabilizing way: as disgusting natural or bodily processes.

Not-All versus the Exception: Anxiously Writing the Body of God

We can understand this description of sublime nature in the history of theology as a return of the repressed. By ignoring or avoiding questions concerning the embodiment and/or sexuality of God, theology enacts a repression that later erupts in the form of a sublime *jouissance*, which creates more powerful anxiety. This is a reading of theology in the light of Freud's earlier version of anxiety, where anxiety is a reaction or response to repression. To grasp an alternative reading, where theology would understand itself as a repressive response to anxiety, I want to return to Žižek and read his dichotomy between the mathematical and the dynamical sublime.

According to Žižek's Lacanian reading of Kant, "the split of the Sublime itself . . . into 'mathematical' and 'dynamical' Sublime, is far from negligible since it directly concerns sexual difference."[28] In other words, although the distinction between beauty and sublime in Kant and others is commonly seen in terms of a feminine beauty and a masculine sublime, Žižek argues that sexual difference is more primordially inscribed into the split of the sublime into mathematical and dynamical. Žižek continues by associating the mathematical sublime with the feminine, while the dynamical sublime is inherently masculine. He then relates Kant's distinctions of the sublime back to the *Critique of Pure Reason*, where Kant divides the antinomies into mathematical and dynamical. Finally Žižek combines this Kantian philosophical logic with Lacan's sexual distinction of the feminine as "not-all" and the masculine as universality constituted through exception.[29]

"The first two ('mathematical') antinomies are 'feminine' and reproduce the paradoxes of the Lacanian logic of 'not-all,'" Žižek writes, "whereas the last two ('dynamical') antinomies are 'masculine' and reproduce the paradoxes of universality constituted through exception."[30] For Žižek, "not-all" refers to the priority of the limit over what lies beyond the limit. Woman is "not-all" because she does not exhaust the possibilities of gender expressions. This logic implies that any particular determination remains one of a finite but incalculable number of possibilities. This situation represents a limit because keeping within a limit does not cut off the exfoliation or enumeration of alternative expressions. In fact Žižek claims that the limit is what gives a "beyond-the-limit." In the case of Kant, the split between phenomena and noumena creates a noumenon; that is, the barrier that renders the "thing-in-itself" unknowable is what provides certainty that there is a "thing-in-itself". Exceptionality, however, gives priority to the beyond the limit and posits the limit as already overcome, at least in principle.[31] A Lacanian understanding of the masculine as the exception posits a limit that man is an exception because he has passed beyond the limit. This cuts off the alternative possibilities as circumscribed by the limit and privileges the one unique exception. In a more strictly theological sense, God is usually constituted not only as male but also according to this logic of exceptionality.

On the one hand, we could critique Žižek's interpretation of the constitution of subjectivity as a masculine privilege of exceptionality, whereby the cogito determines itself as pure thought by rejecting embodiment and then being repulsed by its externalization in a *jouissance* of substance. Superficially, as Žižek admits, Lacan's characterization of "woman" as limit or "not-all" and "man" as universality constituted through an exception beyond the limit is ripe for feminist criticism.[32] On the other hand, Žižek affirms the importance of the mathematical, feminine sublime, or the "not-all" over the masculine, dynamical exceptionality, just as Lacan affirms that "I believe in the jouissance of woman insofar as it is extra."[33] Rather than settle the issue, however, I want to map Žižek's dichotomy or polarity onto my reading of Freudian anxiety and its respective theological counterpart.

I have suggested that an understanding of anxiety as a response to repression can lead to an anxious theology that must defensively struggle with the return of the repressed. This relationship of repression to anxiety can also be thought in terms of Žižek's logic of exceptionality, the dynamical sublime, and a priority of beyond over limit. Such a theology is constrained to think of God solely in terms of exceptionality and paradoxical universality that mirrors the Cartesian exceptional subject. God is the exception that proves or upholds the rule, and God's beyond or divine sphere establishes the finite world as limit. This very exceptionality, however, provokes tremendous anxiety because the intimate or "extimate" relation between God and the world remains problematic, and finite humans must always already exist beyond the limit to which they are consigned to think of God; that is, to think theologically.

In terms of the dynamical sublime—the elevation of human dignity or moral worth over the raging power of nature that is felt as an exceptional connection to divinity—Žižek points out the intimate and unsettling relation between the dynamical sublime and the superego by examining the logic of the experience:

> True, I may be a tiny particle of dust thrown around by wind and sea, powerless in face of the raging forces of nature, *yet all this fury of nature pales in comparison with the absolute pressure exerted on me by the superego, which humiliates me and compels me to act against my fundamental interests!*[34]

The structure of the dynamical sublime is here understood in terms of logic of exceptionality—that is, an exception to the forces of nature. A transcendent dignity taken from beyond (usually God) raises humanity above the nature that threatens to destroy it. The logic of this sublimity recoils into the psychoanalytic notion of the superego, however, because the inherent dignity cannot be separated from one's own conscience, and (as we saw in Luther) this guilty conscience flays the human soul more powerfully than the external might of nature.

If we think of anxiety as a limiting or fixing of attention from the beyond to the limit, then the attempt to surmount the limit and reach the beyond inevitably fails, which is another form of the logic of the return of the repressed. According to the neuroscientist Jean-Pierre Changeux, the difficulties of schizophrenics with thought and language can be "interpreted as defects in attention, involving both poor selectivity . . . and excessive fixation of attention."[35] The fixation on a beyond effectively limits access to the beyond and bars it, which prompts a further eruption of anxiety. Of what, then, does the alternate understanding of anxiety consist? Following the later Freud, and taking anxiety to be the source of repression, we could think about repression less in terms of its widespread negative connotations than in terms of a Nietzschean active forgetting.

Nietzsche asserts that "it will be immediately obvious how there could be no happiness, no cheerfulness, no hope, no pride, no present, without forgetfulness."[36] Any total memory or complete recall would be paralyzing because one could not act affirmatively without "forgetting" that every argument has at least two sides, that every position and point of view is from a certain perspective, etc. Such a forgetting would not necessarily be solely conscious—that is, undertaken by the ego—but it would be a genuine response to anxiety. In this vein, we could petition Freud's notion of an "evenly hovering attention" to describe an initial response to anxiety, and this state would lie closer to the situation of "not-all" described by Žižek. This dispersion of attention would not preclude, but rather function as the precondition for repression. Here the limiting of attention does not create anxiety because *anxiety exists prior to such a limiting*. Limiting is not the restriction of a beyond to a limit but rather a selection in the sense of an image or thought that selects an alternative and "forgets" the other possibilities.[37] It is that very process of selection, however, that distributes the other possibilities in the constitution of a beyond. Every selection is "not-all," the limit precedes the beyond, and this situation is repressive only to the extent that any choice or selection is repressive or forgetful of other choices, but they only become real choices in the determination of the choice itself.

In the *Critique of Judgment*, the mathematical sublime attests to the struggle or "discordant accord" between imagination's attempt to show and comprehend the infinite, and reason's demand that imagination be able to do just that.[38] Such a task is impossible for the imagination under the strict pressure of reason's demand, but that very tension allows for the appearance of beauty by means of the sublime.

The limit traced out by the struggle between reason and imagination in their profound finitude produces the beyond of the limit, which is the thought of the supersensible.[39] Similarly, in the *Critique of Pure Reason*, the "not-all" of the mathematical antinomies generates the beyond of the world of things as they are in themselves as a product of our intuitions and concepts of phenomenal experience. Here again the limit precedes the beyond and gives rise to it, which is the true meaning of finitude in Kant, Freud, and Žižek.[40]

A repressive or forgetful theology would be a theology of finitude, but not in the sense that it restricts itself from progressing beyond some imaginary line. The "beyond" is neither prohibited nor nonexistent, but it does not lie elsewhere than the limit, which is also a bounds or a boundary, as in Kant's "Religion Within the Bounds of Reason Alone." The limit gives or generates the beyond; finitude generates the "in-finite." Such a theology represents a selective response to a generalized anxiety, which would be prepared by the approximation of an attitude of evenly hovering attention. In this way, constructive theological discourse traces or constitutes the limit, which is the only way to get at or talk about any beyond. In addition, this constructive theological thinking should be distinguished from a clinical or more classically psychoanalytical therapeutic discourse that attempts to analyze the effects of anxiety produced by the return of the repressed in more traditional theological writings.

The aim of a truly constructive theological thinking is to write the body of God. Here theology does not disavow the anxiety that issues from the splitting of reality into *cogito* and slime. Anxiety takes the form of *jouissance*. Writing the body of God is a repressive response to anxiety in a positive way, a selection that "forgets" the other possibilities. Here the anxiety "is" God, and theological thinking incorporates body and God without repressing (in a negative sense) one or the other. If repression precedes anxiety, it is negative, and issues a repressive theology that remains in denial and is constantly threatened by an anxiety that it cannot contain, which takes the form of a return of the repressed. If anxiety precedes repression, then theology is constructively repressive in a self-aware manner because it attends to the anxiety, writing it large in and as the body of God. This distinction is difficult to fully clarify because there are two different understandings of anxiety and repression operating here. The constructive theology that I see and affirm here follows Freud in his later work in thinking anxiety as primary and repression as secondary. Furthermore, such a theology is not-all in the sense that Žižek explains in terms of Kant and Lacan. Finally theology as anxiety thinks and writes the body of God because it attends to *jouissance* as the sublime itself, the sublime split or fold between body as body expelled and rejected, and mind as mind embraced and assimilated into identity to form a self-conscious subject.

Despite the attractiveness of this second model, I cannot deny that theology remains repression, and this is at the same time a tragic fact and a liberating possibility related to our condition as thinking human beings. As Charles Winquist puts it, "Writing is repression. Theology is writing. Theology is repression ."[41] In addition, both views (theology as anxiety and theology as repression) are necessary to think about theology and psychoanalysis at a general level. In fact and in practice, this distinction is extremely fluid, such that theology transforms itself from anxiety to repression and back again within any single work of theology. My wager, however, is that theological thinking is ultimately more creative when understood as repression as a response to anxiety in this specific sense, rather than as understanding theology as anxiety, which leads to the return of the repressed. The task for such a theology is to write the body of God but not as a theological limit to or of a God that lies unreachably transcendent and beyond. God is rather the limit, the beyond within the limit; that is, anxiety itself, and theology is productive/repressive with it. In the next chapter, we will see how an anxious theology of not-all is not only a creative theology, but also a theology of creation, following Tillich, Schelling, Žižek, and Lacan.

6

Ages of the World and Creation *ex Nihilo*, Part I

Tillich and Schelling

Introduction: Theology's Return to Tillich

> That really is the last straw! Where can such a crack in the edifice
> have come from?
> Such a terrifying leaking away of meaning? Vigilance must have been
> relaxed . . . God? No really! Anything but that!
> —**Louis Althusser**, *Women*

According to Lacan, Freud described the reception of psychoanalysis
in the United States by stating, "they don't realize we're bringing
them the plague."[1] This statement refers to the simple-minded embrace of Freudian psychoanalysis by many of its American adherents
(which Lacan attacked), although Freud knew full well that many
opponents of psychoanalysis did treat it like a destructive plague.
This description of the reception of psychoanalysis could also refer
to the contemporary American reception of postmodernism. On the
one hand, many scholars dismiss recent French philosophy as irrational, nihilistic, or irresponsible—that is, as a plague—whereas many
proponents of postmodernism embrace it uncritically and pronounce
its slogans without fully grasping their theoretical significance.

   If postmodernism is perceived as a threat, then it can be tremen-
dously threatening to traditional theology. Derridean deconstruction
disallows the functioning of any transcendental signified, or God,

which would master or control the events of the world or the meanings of human signification. At the same time, Derrida and Levinas have written passionately about religion in positive ways, and some theologians view postmodernism as an important opportunity for an authentic theology because postmodernism deconstructs modernity, and its post-critical theory eliminates the epistemological and scientific difficulties surrounding belief in God and theological thinking. In fact, in France, postmodern thinking has resulted in a *"retour du religieux,"* which is now influencing philosophy in the United States and elsewhere.[2]

If Lacan is correct, however, then perhaps both of these orientations toward postmodernism are problematic, insufficient, or even unhealthy. Lacan's notion of psychoanalysis implies that simpleminded embrace (with its concomitant distortion) is just as dangerous as close-minded rejection (which as repression may lead to a return of the repressed). A genuine theological reaction to postmodernism may actually refer to the possibility to think of both the resources and the shortcomings of postmodern thinking, and at the same time to understand that postmodernism itself has an extremely complex relation to religion. In terms of theological thinking, an encounter with postmodern thinking can be healthy in a transformative way, but only if what occurs is an actual encounter rather than a naive appropriation or a superstitious disavowal.

How can theology orient itself to postmodernism? My first contention is that Lacan represents a central figure in what has come to be called postmodernism, and that his reading of the philosophical tradition through Freud scrambles it, makes it other than it is, and provides a genetic force that marks French thought as it grapples to assimilate and appropriate the significance of what Lacan has accomplished. Unfortunately many contemporary thinkers overlook or marginalize Lacan's contribution to the difference that postmodernism represents in and for thinking.

My second contention is that a substantial theological encounter with postmodernism can involve a return to Tillich. This return is analogous to Lacan's return to Freud, but it is not a simple return because a theological return to Tillich must detour through Lacan's return to Freud and read Tillich via Lacan. Tillich is exceptional in relation to theology, although his radicality and significance have been muted, just as orthodox Freudian psychoanalysis systematized and contained the radical import of Freud's speculative work.

I want to sketch out a rough outline of how Tillich's work is relevant to contemporary theological thinking—and this is intended as both an agenda and a challenge. Then I will put Tillich's thought to work in relation to Žižek and Lacan in terms of a reading of Schelling, which will be continued in the next chapter. First of all, Tillich insists on the importance of culture and cultural expressions, as well as the mutual imbrication of culture and theology. In his 1919 essay "On the Idea of a Theology of Culture," Tillich emphasizes that cultural theology is more radical and revolutionary than church theology: "In this relationship the church theologian is the more conservative."[3] Cultural theology is inherently more radical than church theology in its ability to take risks and ask questions without already knowing the answers. This is not a simple-minded correlation of question and answer; we need to understand the relationship in a far more complex way (we could think of culture studies, semiotics, and hermeneutics), but thinking religion as a cultural manifestation implicates the theologian in culture and its theoretical and philosophical expressions.[4]

The German Protestant theologian Friedrich Schleiermacher addressed his influential speeches *On Religion* (1799) to contemporary cultured despisers of religion. Ironically, many contemporary theologians are cultured despisers of religion because it reminds them of their inextricable implication in contemporary culture. Many orthodox theologians desire to use philosophical and/or cultural theories (phenomenology, deconstruction, semiotics) to get beyond or get rid of culture and philosophy as autonomous entities. Tillich has no patience with such efforts; he targets Barthian theologians because "It is infuriating to see how biblical theologians . . . use most of the terms created by the toil of philosophers and the ingenuity of the speculative mind and then dismiss, with cheap denunciations, the work from which their language has been immensely enriched."[5]

The second major way in which Tillich is useful is his profound emphasis on honesty. Tillich claims that he is addressing those who doubt and ask questions: "I consider the attitude of those people who are in doubt or estrangement or opposition to everything ecclesiastical and religious, including Christianity. And I have to speak to them. My work is with those who ask questions, and for them I am here."[6] Tillich values sincere questioning and doubting, and his "answers" do not involve simple-minded piety and comforting consolation.

If theology is going to matter, it must be prepared to risk its traditional form and even perhaps its very existence. The consolation of theology is certainly efficacious for many, but the price paid for replacing thinking with piety is too steep. Externally, theology sacrifices its professional integrity from the standpoint of other academic disciplines. Internally, theology, configured essentially as confession, inevitably becomes defensive and even reactionary. Theology's estrangement is not estrangement from the world, the market, or contemporary society but primarily from *itself*. Radical theology risks such estrangement without the *assurance* that estrangement will be redeemed, whether provisionally or finally. For Tillich, faith is "the state of being ultimately concerned,"[7] and this is simply a way to describe human existence or being-in-the-world, not a special mode of allegiance, conformity to specific social practices, or an assent to certain propositions.

The third major issue to which Tillich is helpful is in relation to the "Death of God." Perhaps this is a tired and well-worn phrase, but from a certain vantage point Tillich first accomplishes the death of God within theology itself. This is neither the traditional notion of God dying kenotically on the cross, nor the absurd notion of the expiration of deity in the modern world, but signifies a detachment or freeing of theology from the language of cosmology. This is a loosening of thinking God from a limited spatial perspective as some entity out in the universe. Rather, talk of God or theological language is inherently symbolic. Every statement about God is symbolic, and we need to think about this in reference to Lacan's distinction among Real, symbolic, and imaginary realms. For Tillich, the only nonsymbolic statement is "God is being-itself." Now this statement can be viewed as a naive ontological assertion in which Tillich withdraws from the radicality of his theological position, or perhaps as an exceptional affirmation—but this is not the case. This statement must be understood in reference to Lacan's statement that "God is Unconscious." In this light it can be seen that Tillich's phrase, "God is being-itself," does not refer to the symbolic, but rather to the Real, being-itself, which is necessarily unconscious because it is inaccessible as such to linguistic conceptuality. "God is being-itself" refers to a primary process thinking that can only be expressed or interrogated in a secondary process thinking, which is necessarily symbolic.

Tillich's emphasis on metaphors of depth—depth of reason, depth of being—points toward a psychoanalytic thinking that deals with primary processes. God as unconscious, or primary process, implies that God is not simply available to human consciousness and language. This severing frees theological thinking from a naive literalism wedded to fixed symbolic concepts such as goodness, truth, existence, omnipotence, etc., and opens up important lines of theoretical inquiry into theology as a discursive practice. Theology is a secondary process thinking that occurs after primary process thinking. If God is the proper object of theological thinking, then the major contribution of Freud's thought is that there is a fundamental fissure between primary and secondary process thinking. The dreamwork is marked by elements of condensation, displacement, conditions of representability, and secondary revision, and this primary process thinking actively distorts symbolic conscious thinking. Importantly, God resists theological thinking, which attempts to wrest God out of the Real. Tillich does not explicitly develop a psychoanalytic theology, but he provides tools to cast theology differently so a return to the probity of Tillich's thought is at the same time a way forward.

I want to consider briefly two moments in Tillich's work: one European, and one American. It is the passage, but also the tension between the two, that is instructive here.

Tillich in Europe

A careful reading of *The System of the Sciences* (1923) shows that psychology occupies a privileged place as a hinge between the natural and the human sciences: "The placement of psychology is thus the criterion for defining both positions."[8] In fact, Tillich appeals to a *gestalt* methodology to solve the contemporary Neo-Kantian dispute between law and sequence. By translating *gestalt* as "structure," we can read Tillich as providing a structuralist solution to the arrangement of the sciences or the modes of academic discipline.[9] At the same time, Tillich's use of *gestalt* is a sort of post-structuralism *avant le lettre* because the creativity of spirit overflows its containment in both thought and being.

Psychology provides the form for the so-called spirit sciences, which produces an entire psychology of culture. Psychology occupies a problematic position, however, because it can be understood as the extension and culmination of the natural sciences as well as the foundation of the human sciences, and this overlap is neither an overlay nor a smooth transition. Tillich's preoccupation with psychology as a science shows both the significance of structure or *gestalt*, as well as a deconstruction of the very notion of *gestalt*, because "psychology is science of the existential form of thought," but not the thought itself.[10] Yet this post-structuralism is still occupied with the problem of the sciences, which the contemporary humanities have largely delimited, ignored, or else they have taken refuge in a naive positivistic view of science, rejecting the important theoretical issues at stake. Tillich's overview of the diversity, and the complex and contested status of the sciences in Germany in the early 20s helps lead beyond the simple distinction between human (or spirit— *Geistwissenschaften*) and natural sciences traced back to Dilthey. Lacan also rejects this distinction, dividing the areas of academic discourse into "exact" and "inexact" sciences, and Lacan argues for a conception of psychoanalysis as an inexact science. Perhaps we can follow Tillich and Lacan and think of theology and the academic study of religion as inexact sciences, absolving them of the futile opposition to and estrangement from the "hard" sciences. More importantly, such thinking helps liberate the study of religion from its enslavement to the methods of the "social sciences," and allows it to develop its own theories and methodologies.

Tillich in America

Upon his immigration to America, Tillich elaborates structure into a system, a *Systematic Theology*, but we need to free ourselves from a single-minded evaluation of his reified system as object and pay more attention to the rigors of systematic thinking in itself. The other fundamental change in Tillich's theology in America is his appreciation of our stress upon practice and pragmatics in relation to theory. This does not mean an abandonment of theoretical pursuits, and attention to Tillich's transition to America should not efface the German cultural theorist. On the other hand, the transition to America is an encounter with pragmatism, just as European postmodernism's passage across the ocean involves an engagement with American pragmatism and the spirit of thinkers such as Charles Peirce, William James, and John Dewey. A postmodern theology that acknowledges its roots in Tillich must affirm the pragmatic nature of concepts, but such pragmatism is not a straightforward instrumentalism because we lack sufficient determination of a standard or device to measure what works. A radical pragmatism does not simply swallow continental philosophy, and it should admit that a simple affirmation of practice leaves unconsidered both the presupposition of a goal as well as the possibility of measuring progress toward that goal in any precise way. Such pragmatic considerations affect not only the specific concepts we use but also the disciplinary, inter- and extra-disciplinary contexts in which we wield them.

In conclusion, Tillich's passage to America has inspired many radical, cultural, and postmodern theologies, including Death of God theology. Therefore, a return to Tillich is a return to the roots of radical theology in the United States. At the same time, the honest and self-critical theologian or theorist of religion cannot disavow the contemporary significance of continental philosophy for the study of religion. Finally, I am proposing that a sophisticated understanding of psychoanalytic theory can provide a medium to relate American and continental thought and theology, focused around a consideration of God as unconscious.[11]

To flesh out the significance of Tillich's theology for postmodern thought and psychoanalytic theory, in this chapter I will develop Tillich's reading of Schelling and begin to read Schelling's *Ages of the World* draft. In the next chapter I will develop Žižek's reading of Schelling as a contrast with Tillich's about the issue of creation *ex nihilo*. Finally, at the end of chapter 7, I will bring Lacan back in, in what is ultimately an encounter between Tillich, Žižek, and Lacan around a reading of Schelling.

Schelling and Tillich

Slavoj Žižek has rehabilitated German Idealism by reading thinkers like Kant, Hegel, and Schelling from the viewpoint of Lacanian psychoanalysis. Following the awakening of scholarly interest in Schelling prompted by Manfred Frank, Andrew Bowie, and others, Žižek has conducted his own highly original interpretation of Schelling. Žižek has focused on Schelling's *Ages of the World* drafts in *The Indivisible Remainder* and *The Abyss of Freedom* to articulate a thinking of humanity and divinity that is intimately related to the unconscious. The recovery of Schelling for a sophisticated psychoanalytic discourse is significant for philosophy and theology, and it raises contested questions of subjectivity, irrationality, and postmodernism, especially considering the growing awareness of Schelling's influence on Heidegger.[12] Furthermore, the problem that Schelling grapples with in his *Ages of the World* concerns the problem of beginning or the creation of the world.

I want to insert the theology of Paul Tillich into this circuit set up by Žižek between psychoanalysis and Schelling, to fashion an encounter between Tillich and Lacan around the notion of creation.

Tillich wrote two dissertations on Schelling in 1910 and 1912, and Schelling's influence remained significant throughout his theological work, especially in his *Systematic Theology*. Furthermore, Tillich was profoundly influenced by Freud, and he in turn helped inspire an existential depth psychology in figures such as Erich Fromm, Rollo May, and R. D. Laing. This reading will step back, to trace Schelling's influence on Tillich, and then move forward to examine Žižek's cutting-edge reading of Schelling, which interprets the potencies as psychoanalytic drives, and finally Tillich and Schelling will be confronted with Lacan. One of the goals will be to show the relevance of Tillich's thought to contemporary theoretical debate, as indicated above, but another purpose is to demonstrate the significance of psychoanalytic theory for philosophical and theological thinking, which is the theme of this book in a general sense.

Most scholars and theologians who have studied Tillich know that he wrote two dissertations on Schelling, and that they deal with Schelling's late period, or positive philosophy. The second theological dissertation, *Mysticism and Guilt-Consciousness in Schelling's Philosophical Development*, is generally considered more significant in Tillich's own theological development, and it was the only one of the two published in German in the first volume of Tillich's collected works.[13] I argue, however, that the first dissertation, *The Construction of the History of Religion in Schelling's Positive Philosophy*, represents a more significant encounter with Schelling's middle period, which runs from about 1809 to 1820. The second dissertation, *Mysticism and Guilt-Consciousness*, does rely on the standpoint of Schelling's late philosophy (ca. 1827–54) to develop a contrast, important to Tillich's own theological thought, between mysticism and guilt-consciousness.

In the second dissertation, mysticism designates "the identity of God and man." Mysticism, for Tillich, is a religious term for a primarily philosophical achievement that refers to Leibniz and Spinoza but culminates in Schelling's early identity philosophy.[14] Guilt-consciousness, on the other hand, is a particularly Christian "religious expression for the absolute contradiction between God and man," associated with Kierkegaard as well as late Schelling.[15] Tillich sums up the alternatives: "Whereas the anthropocentric way (negative philosophy, as Schelling called it) by itself leads to mysticism, the theocentric way (positive philosophy) creates the possibility of a relation to God that is determined by guilt-consciousness."[16] Tillich relies on Schelling's late positive philosophy to make this distinction, and while he endorses the significance of guilt-consciousness as an advance over mysticism, he ultimately wants to reconcile the two in terms of history and spirit.

The Construction of the History of Religion in Schelling's Positive Philosophy, on the other hand, evinces Tillich's struggle to articulate his theoretical presuppositions amid a powerful encounter with Schelling's middle period. Tillich focuses most explicitly on the *Philosophical Investigations into the Essence of Human Freedom*, despite the dissertation title's apparent concern with positive philosophy. My periodization of Schelling is provisional and heuristic, but it is also useful for a thinker who underwent so many substantial shifts in his thinking. For the purposes of this essay, then, Schelling's early period constitutes the time from his arrival upon the post-Kantian philosophical scene in the mid-1790s, through the identity philosophy of 1804 and including both the *System of Transcendental Idealism* (1800) and the *Ideas for a Philosophy of Nature* (1797, revised 1803). The middle period stems from the 1809 *Philosophical Investigations into the Essence of Human Freedom*, through the *Ages of the World* drafts of 1811–15, and includes the *Stuttgart Private Seminars* of 1810. The middle period is primarily defined by Schelling's wrestling with the potencies or powers and his attempt to derive a finite world from the infinite or absolute. Žižek focuses on this period as the most fertile for psychoanalytic and philosophical thinking, and these are the themes that I am tracing in Tillich's thought. Finally Schelling's late philosophy begins in the late 1820s and continues to the end of his life, and includes the 1933–34 Munich lectures translated as *On the History of Modern Philosophy*, as well as the untranslated *Philosophy of Revelation* (1841–42).[17]

Tillich's first dissertation grapples with the potencies that are central to Schelling's middle period, although Tillich assimilates what I am calling Schelling's middle and late periods. Tillich interprets what he calls Schelling's positive philosophy, to advance a methodological framework for the history of religions. Even though Tillich refers explicitly to Schelling's positive philosophy, he explicates the potencies from the standpoint of a reading of the *Philosophical Investigations into the Essence of Human Freedom*. That is, Tillich works out a theoretical understanding of the potencies from Schelling's middle period, and then he follows the direction of Schelling's later philosophy by situating his own conception of the history of religion on top of that. This methodological concern leads Tillich to separate what was originally united in Schelling's middle period: the history of God and the history of the world. Tillich works out his own conception of the history of religions in the guise he calls the history of world-consciousness and distinguishes that from his earlier explication of the history of God-consciousness—Schelling's densely theological interpretation of the potencies. Tillich calls for a rational philosophy to understand the history of religions "after the potencies are deduced from the intellectual intuition of the concept of being."[18] In this vein he concludes that "whereas the mythological process is the history of God-consciousness, the rational process is the history of world-consciousness."[19]

Calling the history of God-consciousness mythological is to simplify Schelling's thought in both the *Philosophical Investigations into the Essence of Human Freedom* and the *Ages of the World* drafts. Yet Tillich works out a sophisticated understanding of the potencies, which ultimately influences the *Systematic Theology*. In the first dissertation, Tillich notes the original duality of the Schellingian will. Schelling's philosophy of identity presupposes an ultimate identity of that duality, and then attempts to derive the duality of human consciousness and seemingly objective nature from this presumed identity. Tillich sees that the ground of Schelling's philosophy of nature implies "that it is not enough to prove that the ego is everything; rather on the contrary, it must be understood that everything is like the ego." Instead of assimilating all of nature and reality to the self-conscious ego, as Fichte threatens to do, nature itself must be understood as parallel to self-consciousness. Tillich writes that "Nature is not an incomprehensible limit of action; it is itself action, creating will, becoming freedom, striving for consciousness."[20] Nature is not derived from human consciousness, nor is human consciousness derived from objectified nature; rather both are derived from an ideal absolute identity. Nature, however, is figured as unconscious in contrast to conscious humanity. And what is more, unconscious activity precedes and grounds conscious activity.

This scenario explains the derivation of two of the three potencies: nature becomes understood as a principle of unconscious ground, while human consciousness becomes a principle of essential self-awareness. Schelling wrestles with the exact relation of these two forces (as well as the third, which reconciles or resolves them) throughout his middle period, and in some ways the turn toward positive philosophy is generated out of Schelling's failure to adequately resolve this interrelationship. This attempted resolution takes its most complex form in the *Weltalter* drafts, and it is there that Žižek swoops in to offer his interpretation.

Tillich understands the basic point, however, which is that the grounding principle of unconscious activity is "real, expansive"; whereas "conscious action is ideal, repulsive."[21] Schelling posits an absolutely still and unmoving eternal will, which functions as the identity that underlies the duality of opposing forces or potencies. As soon as that absolute will that wills nothing (and in fact it cannot be properly called a will) differentiates itself and creates reality, it expresses itself as two opposing forces: expansion and contraction. One principle or potency functions as an unconscious ground, and it is this principle that strives to express itself in relation to the absolute will or absolute identity. The unconscious principle expresses itself negatively in relation to the absolute will but positively in relation to the generation of existence or matter.

The second principle — conscious form or essence — can be viewed as counter to the unconscious ground because it contracts being into a determinate appearance or form. The tension between these two opposing principles or potencies forms what Tillich later calls a polarity.[22] What Tillich recognizes in the first dissertation is that the priority of unconscious ground in the polar opposition introduces "an irrational principle" into philosophical thinking. Schelling therefore foreshadows what Nietzsche and Freud later emphasize, that "there is in the will itself an irrational moment, a 'potency' for self-contradiction. The real, dark principle of the philosophy of nature is nothing other than the actualization of this contradiction."[23]

The opposition of the potencies of unconscious ground and the conscious essence is not the final word. Schelling and Tillich affirm the resolution of this strife in a third potency that reconciles the first two. The third potency is called spirit, and it is also understood as freedom. This highest potency reinstates the calm of the original absolute identity, but the absolute is enriched by the process of the detour through self-differentiation. This process sounds Hegelian, and here Schelling is very close to Hegel, and is thereby constrained to articulate his distinction from, and hostility to, Hegel in forceful terms.[24] The major difference is that Hegel does not posit the fullness of absolute identity at the beginning of the process, as Schelling does, but rather understands absolute spirit as the accomplishment or construction of the process of world history and spiritual self-consciousness.[25]

Tillich explains his understanding of Schelling's three potencies. The first potency is the unconscious ground, which is also expressed as the reality of relative nonbeing, or Greek *me on*. Relative nonbeing is contrasted with absolute nonbeing, or *ouk on*, and it is relative nonbeing that is affirmed by both Schelling and Tillich. Relative nonbeing also expresses a pure potentiality for being. The second potency is necessary being, or the pure actuality of that which is. Necessary being is the contraction into determinate being of being that is for itself. Finally, "being must be posited a third time as subject-object that is free from the onesidedness of the two former principles," which is called spirit.[26]

Schelling in Itself

To more fully express the subtlety of Schelling's thought as well as its continuity with Tillich's, I will trace the development of this doctrine of the potencies in the second *Ages of the World* draft. In the 1813 draft, which Žižek claims is the culmination (and the failure) of Schelling's struggles to derive existence from the absolute, Schelling begins with the irreducible duality of experience and thinking. Although he writes from the standpoint of the Absolute, Schelling always focuses on the way humans must think about the Absolute to make sense of human experience and intuition. The only way Schelling can account for the duality of human experience, encapsulated by the first two potencies, is to relate them to a prior unity or identity. Yet the further he attempts to envisage this identity, the further Schelling is forced to introject the duality back into the heart of the Absolute.

The treatise begins with the demand for philosophical or scientific knowledge as well as the necessity to transcend empirical experience in order for that knowledge to be authentic. Schelling thus divides time into past, present, and future, to account for the differentiation of knowledge. All three of the *Weltalter* drafts only explicitly address the past because Schelling is engaged in a tremendous struggle to work out an articulation of the past that will issue in the present. As such, this task of articulating the past is an inductive and speculative activity, but it suggests important implications about the limits of theoretical thinking.

Schelling is forced by experience and the demands of thought to begin with "the unconscious presence of the Eternal," and to proceed to work out both the consciousness of the Absolute as well as conscious humanity in relation to physical nature.[27] This beginning is not the actual beginning of experience and thinking but rather the logical beginning that philosophical thinking is driven to adopt.

Schelling begins with struggle, conflict, and duality, and from this actuality he posits stillness or nothingness. The struggle refers to Schelling's contention that "whatever takes time only as it presents itself feels a conflict of two opposing principles in it; one strives forward, driving toward development, and one holds back, inhibiting and striving against development."[28] This conflict characterizes or constitutes everything that is, which Schelling calls being itself (*Seyn*). According to Schelling, "everything that is wants to be in itself and out of itself at the same time." As an entity strives to exist in itself in a contracting relationship, it "posits or collects itself together as what is [*als Seyendes*], as a subject."[29] To be a being, something must contract on itself to exclude everything else. At the same time, the expansive force that makes up its being drives it beyond itself as development and expansion.

There is a very subtle argument here, which repeats itself later in the treatise. In itself, expansion comes first as a logical principle, and this becomes clear in Schelling's initial discussion of the Absolute. The oppositional force to such expansion is the contraction into a determinate being, or what Schelling calls what-is or at other times "essence." Once existence occurs in time, however, the contraction into a being appears first because we encounter determinate beings, and in relation to this contracted essence we encounter an expansive force that pushes beyond the being. For Schelling, this expansive force repeats the initial expansion of being and makes up the third potency, spirit. This understanding is complicated because Schelling distinguishes between the development of the potencies as well as the Absolute both in relation to time both after time has taken place and in itself, prior to the existence of time. It is because Schelling has an interest in the way God appears in time at the end of the treatise that he is forced to dissemble and confuse the relations of the potencies as he deduces them in themselves. Another source of confusion is the fact that at the beginning of the *Ages of the World* draft the potencies are implicit and called wills, whereas it is only after he has already deduced the existence of the Absolute that Schelling explicitly introduces the three potencies.[30]

For Schelling, the understanding of the Absolute or the Highest is characterized by the fact that "it has all conditions of existence in itself"—that is to say, it is free to exist or not exist.[31] The only way he knows to define such a term is with the name "will," "for only pure will is free to become active or to remain inactive."[32] Schelling explains that the best way to conceive the Eternal is as a will that wills nothing: "only an immobile, divine . . . indifference is absolutely First," and any and all movement is only for the sake of this rest.[33] Pure freedom, or the highest possible will, is to have will "as if it did not have it," which raises the question whether the highest will is also the highest duplicity, as Nietzsche later suggests.[34] At the same time, this highest will is described in Heideggerian terms because it is "the pure freedom itself that does not grasp itself, it is the composure [*Gelassenheit*] that thinks about nothing and rejoices in nonbeing."[35] Finally, Schelling completes the circuit by foreshadowing Tillich's conception of God beyond God when he claims that "just as the will that wills nothing is Highest in man, so too in God himself—this very will is above God," (135).

In this state of absolute Eternity or pure freedom of a will that wills nothing, the Absolute cannot be said to be conscious of itself. Rather, "the more this composure is profoundly deep and full of bliss, the sooner must a quiet longing produce itself in eternity," (136). This first movement is described as "an unconscious, tranquil, self-seeking will," (137). Schelling posits a pure will that wills nothing, and then to get things moving he asserts that a second will disturbs this immobility with a silent longing that remains unconscious. This first will actualizes itself in relation to the will that wills nothing, but Schelling claims that it posits itself as negated and self-negating; that is, as lack. Even though it is tranquil and unconscious and essentially affirmative, "it can only posit itself as not being the essence, or what affirms, or what—(genuinely and by nature)—is," (138).

The first movement is the positing of eternal will as lack of essence, but it is affirmative in relation to the absolutely ideal will to nothing. This self-negating will then "generates essence in the authentic sense of the term . . . outside itself, as an essence distinct from it, free from it, indeed foreign and opposed to its nature" (139). Genuine essence is then presented in contrast to the self-negating will as a determinate, positive will. With this division into two opposing wills—negative and positive—Schelling reaches the point that Žižek calls the rotary motion of the drives. At this stage, the two potencies are in irreconcilable conflict, and only an external resolution accomplished by the third potency can dissipate this struggle.

If we regard nature in its initial stages, we find an attracting, inward-returning force in all corporeal things; this force never appears for itself alone, but only ever as the bearer of another essence, fastening it down and holding it together. This other essence is expansive by nature, and it is thus volitizing and spiritualizing. (139)

Žižek dramatizes this conflict with his description of the antagonism between the contractive and expansive wills, in which "God Himself . . . as it were, repeatedly dashes against his own wall: unable to stay within, He follows his urge to break out, yet the more He tries to escape, the more He is caught in His own trap."[36]

Schelling equates the unconscious will with the contracting first potency, while the generation of excessive essence is the second potency, but there occurs an extreme tension between what Schelling's words suggests and what he actually intends to say. It is the unconscious, self-negating will that is expansive and generates essence, as Tillich correctly understands in his first dissertation. The second will of actual essence is the contraction of identity into determinate being. Schelling carefully works this out from the supposition of an Absolute will to nothing. At the same time, Schelling wants to paint the unconscious potency as negative and negating, and thus ultimately contractive, in contrast to an expansive potency that is excessive and finally spiritual. For this reason he conducts a sleight of hand in the middle of the *Weltalter* draft by confusing the expansive and contractive forces to present expansive essence as illuminating and grounding being as dark and constricting. This reversal serves a theological agenda that desires to cast God as dark and threatening, while at the same time this dark unconscious ground is overcome by the expansive power of God's love. In fact things are much more complex because the will that wills nothing is purely ideal and cannot enter into conflict with the unconscious will that disturbs it. Both wills are essentially characterized as unconscious, such that unconsciousness is doubled and divided into a restful and moving unconscious will, which prompts the reader to wonder if they are not the same will.

Therefore the first potency is expansive and unconscious, and only indirectly posits a pure stillness. The second potency inserts essence into determinate being or what-is, which implies consciousness in the sense of an awareness of the conflict of the potencies but not self-consciousness. The third potency, however, is a return to the expansive power of the first potency, and Schelling wants spirit to occur as self-consciousness. The will seeks its initial indifference so it posits a unity between what-is and what-is-not, which Schelling now calls being. Schelling's phrase, "unity is spirit," recognizes the two opposed wills "as belonging to a single essence."[37] I will return to a consideration of the third potency later in the course of a discussion of Žižek, which will be related to a reading of the end of Schelling's treatise.

Here in the *Ages of the World*, Schelling introjects the potencies into the Absolute itself and its generation. This wrecks the system of identity philosophy proper because in his initial discussion of the potencies in the second edition of the *Ideas for a Philosophy of Nature* (1803), Schelling restricted the potencies to the world of nature and human consciousness, whereas the Absolute was purely and simply identity.[38] Here in the *Weltalter* drafts, the potencies invade the Absolute itself in a profound thinking of difference and differentiation, and it is this thinking that is profound and suggestive for both psychoanalysis and theology. However, Schelling cannot satisfactorily work out the development of the potencies within the Absolute, partly because of the reversals and complications I am pointing out.

Schelling for Tillich

In the next chapter, this reading of the potencies will be related to Žižek's interpretation of the second draft of the *Ages of the World*, to perceive the psychoanalytic stakes of such a reading and also to demonstrate how, despite his brilliance, Žižek follows Schelling's explicit interpretation too closely. But first I want to consider the impact of Schelling's thinking on Tillich's mature theology. In the first volume of the *Systematic Theology*, important traces can be found of the influence of Schelling's irrational principle on Tillich's conceptions of the depth of being and creation *ex nihilo*.

For Tillich the metaphor of depth drives his theology. In his *Theology of Culture*, he claims that "religion is not a special function of man's spiritual life, but it is the dimension of depth in all of its functions."[39] Tillich acknowledges the metaphorical aspect of the term "depth," but he indicates by this word a certain primordial manifestation that is not completely rational or conscious. As unconditional or ultimate concern, "religion is the substance, the ground, and the depth of man's spiritual life."[40] The use of the terms "ground" and "depth" echoes Schelling's language of the irrational ground of the

Absolute, even though Tillich affirms that such a ground is not completely irrational because it is never cut off from the rational aspect of reason or being.

Tillich describes the depth of reason as "the expression of something that is not reason but which precedes reason and is manifest through it."[41] Although the depth of reason is "essentially manifest in reason," it occurs as "hidden in reason under the conditions of existence."[42] The depth of reason is structurally similar to the unconscious here, and Tillich privileges this depth over the more superficial "structure" of reason. It is the depth of reason that in the *Systematic Theology* points toward revelation and a thinking of God as being-itself. The depth of reason raises the question of revelation because of its affinity with Tillich's second formal criterion of theology: "Our ultimate concern is that which determines our being and non-being."[43]

Robert P. Scharlemann explains that Tillich correlates "philosophical expressions of structure with religious expressions of depth," and that the difference between expressions of structure and those of depth is that "direct expressions of structure present the elements for what they are, whereas expressions of depth present the same structural elements as being there in spite of the fact that they need not be."[44] Because expressions of depth concern the possibility of expressions of structure, the depth of reason provides ground and meaning for the structure of reason and allows the structure to exist. Since the depth of reason concerns absolutes—our being and not-being, or human ultimate concern—for Tillich the depth of reason is more profound than the structure of reason because the possibility of the being and nonbeing of an object or person most fully resides in the depth of reason.

The depth of reason refers to the depth of being, which shows even more of an affinity with Schelling's thought. In what Tillich calls revelatory ecstasy, this ecstasy "unites the experience of the abyss to which reason in all its functions is driven with the experience of the ground in which reason is grasped by the mystery of its own depth and of the depth of being generally."[45] Finally, the mystery of the depth of being is expressed in language by means of what Tillich calls the Word of God. Tillich claims that something "shines through ordinary language which is the self-manifestation of the depth of being and meaning," (124).

In all of these passages the depth of reason and of being refers to the ground of existence, or Schelling's first expansive potency, which

Tillich in his first dissertation calls an irrational principle. The structure of both reason and being refers to Schelling's second potency, which expresses the essence or actuality of existence in a contracting form. Finally the two conflicting principles are united in spirit, which both Tillich and Schelling understand in terms of the *logos* or Word of God. What is important about Tillich's thought is the existence of Schelling's categories in slightly altered form, which testifies to the continuing influence of Schelling on Tillich as well as the significance of an unconscious principle that each thinker shares.

Schelling's doctrine of the potencies shapes Tillich's theology and leaves traces upon the architecture and central categories of the *Systematic Theology*. In a more specific sense, Schelling's thought influences Tillich's discussion of creation. In two important sections of the *Systematic Theology*, Tillich grapples with Schelling's distinction between being as *me on* (relative nonbeing) and *ouk on* (absolute nonbeing), and he struggles with the necessity of "positing a dialectical negativity in God himself." One of the examples of "the problem of dialectical nonbeing exerting influence on the Christian doctrine of God" is Schelling's first potency, although Tillich also refers to Jacob Böhme, Hegel, and Berdyaev (189).

The ontological question Tillich repeatedly insists upon is the question "Why there is something rather than nothing?" At the same time, the ontological question also raises the question of "the mystery of nonbeing," (186). Tillich rejects the simple exclusion of nonbeing from being, which he associates with Parmenides. A nondialectical exclusion of nonbeing from being is called *ouk on* in Greek: "*ouk on* is the 'nothing' which has no relation at all to being," (188). Arguing that the existence of anything finite is impossible without a dialectical relationship of nonbeing with being, Tillich claims that "there can be no world unless there is a dialectical participation of nonbeing in being," (187). This second alternative is Platonic and uses the Greek concept of *me on*, or "that which does not yet have being but which can become being if it is united with essences or ideas," (188).

After affirming the status of *me ontic* nonbeing, Tillich reveals that Christianity rejects "the concept of *me ontic* matter on the basis of the doctrine of *creatio ex nihilo*," (188). Creation *ex nihilo* represents creation out of nothing, or *ouk on*. This creation out of nondialectical nonbeing represents a rejection of the Greek concept of unformed matter existing with God, forming the primary material or stuff that God then uses to construct the universe. Tillich explains why Christianity makes this choice, but he implicitly criticizes it by noting that the dialectical problem of nonbeing continued to haunt Christian theology. He ends up considering existentialism, which heightens the threat of nonbeing to such a state that there is no way of conquering it. "The only way of dealing with it lies in the courage of taking it upon one's self: courage!" (189). Tillich concludes this brief section by drawing out the problem of nonbeing and setting it up in relation to the doctrine of creation *ex nihilo*, but he does not solve the problem. He affirms the situation of dialectical nonbeing because human finitude is inexplicable without a notion of *me on*, and yet this dialectical or *me ontic* nonbeing exists in tension with the orthodox doctrine of creation *ex nihilo*.

When he returns to the problem of creation *ex nihilo* in a later section, Tillich reaffirms this strange situation because he refuses to relate creation to either *me on* or *ouk on*, despite his evident desire for a dialectical or *me ontic* relationship with being in finitude. Tillich refers to the relative nonbeing as "finite creatureliness," while claiming that the formula *creatio ex nihilo* "expresses the relation between God and the world," (254). On the one hand, creation out of nothing expresses a negative meaning, which is the elimination of dualism. God "finds nothing 'given' to him which influences him in his creativity or which resists his creative *telos*," (253). If nothing refers to *me ontic* nonbeing in the classical Greek sense, then God would be set in opposition with the matter that God uses to create. On the other hand, "if *ex nihilo* meant the absolute negation of being, it could not be the origin of the creature," (253). Again, creation cannot exist in relation to absolute nonbeing if a finite world and finite human beings are to come into existence.

Tillich's affirmation of creation *ex nihilo* seems ambivalent and elliptic, but a consideration of Schelling's thought helps to clarify what Tillich is doing. *Me on* does not refer to matter or material outside of or in addition to God. God creates out of God's own nothingness, which is *me ontic*, as Schelling affirms in *Ages of the World*. Yet creation out of nothing is creation of finite creatureliness, which *is* or includes dialectical nonbeing. Tillich's insistence is on creation *ex nihilo* as finite creation, or creation of finitude. Although his account appears subjective and existential, Tillich affirms the ontological nature of this finitude.

Furthermore, the unconscious, negative principle is expansive, as Tillich notes in his first dissertation. God's decision to create is not a conscious, willed decision. God creates out of or via nothingness, which is unconscious, even to God.[46] The *me on* within divinity issues infinite creatureliness. Creation is an infinite process, while what is created is finite. Later in the *Weltalter* draft, Schelling reverses the terms of the potencies to claim that the essence is expansive rather than the mysterious ground. Yet Tillich understands Schelling's implications better than Schelling wishes to, even though Tillich is not completely clear in his explanation of creation *ex nihilo*. The first force or potency of creation is expansive and unconscious, while the second potency refers to the essence of what is created. Finite creation exerts a resistance toward the expansive creating force and sees it as destructive, which is why the first potency, affirmative in itself, appears as negative or negating.

In this chapter, I have read Tillich's *Systematic Theology* through the lens of Tillich's engagement with Schelling's *Ages of the World*, and shown how Schilling influences Tillich's doctrine of creation *ex nihilo*. This reading of Schelling and Tillich serves as a prolegomenon to reading Žižek's interpretation of Schelling in the next chapter, and finally I will offer a constructive understanding of creation *ex nihilo* in Lacan, which brings together Schelling, Tillich, Žižek, and Lacan around this central theological concept.

7

Ages of the World and Creation *ex Nihilo*, Part II

Žižek and Lacan

Schelling for Žižek

An account of Tillich's significance for contemporary theology, as well as the discussion of Tillich's appropriation of Schelling in the *Systematic Theology* in chapter 6, serves as background for the consideration of Žižek's interpretation of Schelling in this chapter. At the conclusion of this chapter I will reconsider Tillich's understanding of creation in relation to Lacan's discussion of creation in *The Ethics of Psychoanalysis*, in which creation *ex nihilo* refers explicitly to the creation of a signifier. In the meantime, Žižek's psychoanalytic reading of Schelling will be explicated and critiqued. On the one hand, Žižek provides an exciting interpretation that brings Schelling's philosophy into consideration for contemporary theoretical debate. On the other hand, Žižek partially misreads Schelling at the heart of the second *Weltalter* draft. This is a misreading that is also Schelling's misreading, but it is one that Tillich's thought enables us to correct. Although this remains a densely complicated topic, the whole discussion revolves around an understanding of the potencies.

When Schelling introduces the potencies in his revision of the *Ideas for a Philosophy of Nature*, it is in the context of his identity theory. The identity of the Absolute or God and its subsequent self-differentiation accounts for the derivation of the finite world and human consciousness. At first the doctrine of the potencies is kept separate from the initial identity of the Absolute. Later in his theoretical development, however, Schelling is forced to embed the thinking of the potencies deeper and deeper into the heart of the Absolute itself. According to Žižek, this climaxes in the second *Ages of the World* draft in 1813.

Žižek reads the potencies as psychoanalytic drives, and he shows how Schelling's failure to resolve the conflictual nature of the potencies testifies to Schelling's enduring significance for psychoanalytic theory and contemporary thought. In *The Indivisible Remainder*, Žižek characterizes Schelling's problem (as well as that of German Idealism in general) as one of beginning, which is also one of freedom. Beginning is the passage from a chaotic-psychotic universe of blind drives or forces that precedes an actual beginning, to language or a Word that represses or rejects the self-enclosed circuit of drives and opens up signification or desire. Žižek secularizes Schelling's theological language, but he retains the tension of the theological resonances that refer to both a human and divine language of beginnings when he writes "the true Beginning is the passage from the 'closed' rotary motion to 'open' progress, from drive to desire—or, in Lacanian terms, from the Real to the Symbolic."[1]

Freedom is a passage from unconscious drives to conscious or symbolic desire. The very resolution or beginning is what constitutes temporality because the unconscious drives do not exist in a literal past—they refer to a past that never actually existed but persists as a durable foundation of the present. Žižek makes a strong distinction between the middle Schelling, who struggles with unconscious drives or potencies, and the late Schelling, who regresses to a more traditional and reactionary ontology and theology to reach a solution to the problem of the drives, which is not a solution but rather an avoidance of the problems he creates in the *Ages of the World* drafts.

According to Žižek, God "contracts" being, which means to exist as God separated from the neutral indifference of a pure will that wills nothing, God must come to exist as a ground of existence. That is, God brings about God's own identity by means of a contracting or constricting force that excludes what is not divinity. Žižek refers to the image of a "'psychotic' mad God who is absolutely alone, a One who is 'all' since he tolerates nothing outside Himself—a 'wild madness, tearing itself apart,'" (24). God's madness occurs in the presupposition of the darkness of a ground of identity, which is required for divinity to exist. The significance of Schelling's middle period for Žižek is the insistence upon a terrifying intermediate stage between the blissful indifference of the primordial will and the free-dom of God as spirit and free creator that occurs in the pronounce-ment of the divine Word.

Žižek extracts the theological implications of Schelling's treatise with great subtlety and profundity and then relates those implica-tions to thinking about human freedom and subjectivity. "What comes in between the primordial freedom and God *qua* free Subject is a stage at which God is already a Subject," Žižek writes, "but not yet a *free* one." He explains that for Schelling, "At this stage, after contracting being, God is submitted to the blind necessity of a con-stricted rotary motion, like an animal caught in a trap of its own mak-ing and destined endlessly to repeat the same meaningless motions," (37). Schelling is forced by his logic and the intensity of his thinking to posit a "moment of blindness, even of 'madness', in the divine life" that he is unable to resolve in a satisfactory way, so he ultimately abandons his *Ages of the World* project and turns toward a positive philosophy in which God already possesses free being in advance, in which "the process of Creation therefore concerns another being, not the being of God Himself" (37).

The process of creation involves the creation of God or divinity itself, rather than the creation of something else by God already cast as a determinate being. This is what Tillich undertakes in a more ex-plicitly theological sense in the *Systematic Theology*, the introjection of *me ontic* being into the heart of divinity, which necessarily results in the production of creaturely finitude. Žižek shows that "the blind ro-tary motion of God [is] prior to the pronouncement of the Word," and that the actual Beginning is the very issuance of the Word that constitutes time and represses the rotary motion into an eternal past (31). The rotary motion of the drives is unconscious because once temporality occurs they are relegated to a timeless past. At the same time, the conflict of the rotary motion is still felt after the pronounce-ment of the Word, because it leaves a trace upon the very Beginning or creation that represses it, as a return of the repressed experienced as present conflict and tension.

The rotary motion of the drives casts the conflicting potencies as forces of affirmation and negation that so strongly oppose themselves and each other that no beginning or creation is possible. Although Schelling posits an evenly matched duality of drives, one could envi-sion this duality as metonymically representing a potentially infinite multiplicity of forces that mutually oppose each other. This opposi-tion founds time for Schelling because the rotary motion of the drives is always experienced as past, not simply as a day proceeds from present to past, but "past from the beginning of time," (32). The present is the awareness of the split between an unconscious past of rotary motion and the immediate existence of conscious temporality and language. Finally, for Schelling the future represents the projected eventual reconciliation of past and present, unconscious conflict and conscious decision.

Žižek shifts from a more theological discussion of God to a more anthropological discussion, but both he and Schelling want to hold onto the tension and ambiguity of the ability of this process to refer to both humanity and divinity. Žižek explains the generation of the Word:

> Since there is nothing outside God, this — "crazy God" — the antagonistic rotary motion of contracted matter — has to beget out of Himself a Son, that is, the Word which will resolve the unbearable tension. The undifferentiated pulsation of drives is thus supplanted by the stable network of differences which sustains the self-identity of the differentiated entities: in its most elemental dimension, the Word is the medium of self-differentiation. (32)

Creation is thus the free act of primordial decision that is generated through language. God ejects the rotary motion of the drives into an eternal past and creates time. This free act of God, however, cannot be logically deduced or explained; it is completely irrational and occurs out of love. God opts for creation over the contracting power that strives to maintain God in God's being against anything external to God. This free act is at the same time "a primordial act of repression," and what is more, lies "in strict analogy with the primordial act of decision by means of which man chooses his eternal character," (33). That is, God becomes a free subject by choosing to create something external to Godself, which is a repetition of the original creation of God. This act of creation or expansion beyond the confines of being places God "in exactly the same position as man on the verge of his timeless act of choosing his eternal character," (33). For Christianity the primordial act of decision by God for expansive creation of the world is considered "good," while humans inevitably "choose" evil, or contracting self-identity. This is the significance of the Fall. Žižek emphasizes, however, that beyond the moral valuation of the choices involved is the structural identity of an unconscious act of decision or creation that is both free and forced. "What is truly 'unconscious' in man," Žižek explains, is "the very founding gesture of consciousness, the act of decision by means of which I 'choose myself'—that is, combine this multitude of drives into the unity of my self," (33).

What is central here is the process of creation, which applies to both divinity and humanity. Psychoanalytic theory reinforces the significance of this unconscious act in Schelling, and its relation to the rotary motion of conflictual drives. The act of creation, which can be called freedom only in a counterintuitive sense, involves the repression of the rotary motion of the drives, which occurs in the pronouncement of a signifying Word or word—that is, in language. This understanding of language in terms of its intimate relation with, and constitution of, human subjectivity, is Žižek's inheritance from Lacan's work. Žižek stresses that "in this precise sense, freedom is atemporal: a flash of eternity in time." The flash of eternity "explains" the atemporal abyss of identity and refers to the passage from an abstract freedom to a free subject, "from the impersonal *Es* of 'there is freedom' to 'Him', a God [or person] who is free," (35). What is at stake is an understanding of a process of creation that is at the same time psychological and theological. Žižek enables one to see how Schelling's logic pressures modern human self-understanding and leads to dense epistemological aporias at the heart of thinking about both God and humanity.

In *The Abyss of Freedom*, Žižek reiterates his interpretation of Schelling's *Ages of the World*. Žižek values the generation of the Word that puts an end to the rotary motion of the drives and their deadlocked opposition. He claims that the "logic of presymbolic antagonism, of the rotary motion of the drives," deals with a "failed logic, with an endlessly repeated effort to begin."[2] For Žižek this presymbolic antagonism is nihilistic and meaningless precisely because it is presymbolic, and it can only take on significance in light of the resolution of this conflict in a free act of primordial decision. Although this act is not undertaken with any conscious freedom, Žižek follows Schelling's language in affirming the language of freedom because even if it is not voluntary, it is absolutely necessary and must be affirmed to have any existence or consciousness at all. For this reason, Žižek distinguishes sharply between the destructive rotary motion of the drives that cannot begin, cannot create, and are thus unproductive, from the creation of desire, which occurs with the pronouncement of the meaningful word. At the same time, Žižek recognizes the persistence of traces of that rotary opposition despite their relegation to a time eternally past the unconscious. The trace of this unconscious conflict persists and reoccurs as a return of the repressed that horrifies humans struggling with the split between conscious desires and their awareness of unconscious forces, albeit as always already eternally past. The rotary motion of the drives persists not in its ideal form, which prevents beginning or time, but in a muted repetition. This repetition of the rotary drives within time opens what Žižek calls the Real, following Lacan. The "gap that separates reality from the Real" is the gap that separates the past from the present, or unconscious drives from conscious desires (22). The persistence of the rotary (death) drives provides the minimal resistance that allows reality to function, and from the gap between reality and the Real emerges brute stuff, matter as such. But the existence of this "stuff" generated by the repetition of rotary drives is experienced as excessive and horrific, and thus "the kernel of reality is horror, horror of the Real," (23).

Žižek attempts to fashion his own future, his own spiritual reconciliation, at the end of *The Abyss of Freedom*, by shifting from a language of desire that attempts to restore or reconcile the original will that wills nothing in a Schellingian way, to a language of drives that do not function in terms of rotary motion. According to Žižek, Schelling's idealized restoration of a negative will that wills nothing and a positive will that wills God leads to a world in which everything is impossible and gives way to an unquenchable longing. On the other hand, Žižek himself invokes a postlinguistic understanding in which "drive is closed, absolutely immanent," but not thereby unproductive and rotary (84). Drive functions in consciousness in a way that ignores the existence of the Other, that is, the object of desire that animates me and prompts striving for symbolic recognition. Žižek opens the possibility of a pure drive beyond this desire for symbolic recognition, which would be a creative drive in itself, purified of the unproductive rotary opposition and occurring after language and the pronouncement of the word has taken place. Although he challenges the solution adopted by Schelling's positive philosophy, Žižek asks whether his understanding of the subject as a "being of drive" does "not point towards the Schellingian Reconciliation?" (87).

Schelling for Itself

Žižek basically accepts Schelling's characterization of God as contracting ground versus expansive essence, which Tillich allows us to question. To understand what is at stake in Schelling's subtle reversal, I want to consider more closely the end of the second edition of the *Ages of World*. This reading will flesh out Žižek's interpretation, and also allow me to question Schelling's valuation of divinity in the resolution of the conflict of drives or potencies in a free act of creation.

According to Schelling, spirit as the third potency affirms both the opposition of the first two potencies and at the same time resolves their opposition. The potencies develop through a law of progressive increase by means of opposition. It is the progressive increase that Žižek casts doubt upon, and the notion of progressive increase by opposition is where Schelling comes closest to Hegel. At the same time, the opposition of forces does not simply exhibit the brutal strife that Žižek describes while characterizing the rotary motion of the drives. Schelling argues that "the forces interact with each other" in such a way that "the forces become perceptible to each other, but without fighting each other. This is the first pure joy of mutual finding and being."[3] From the standpoint of spirit, this opposition is not destructive but exhibits rather a discordant accord and "serves as an eternal pleasure [*Lust*]," (145).

So in a manner both superficially Hegelian and at its core profoundly un-Hegelian, the opposition of forces serves as an eternal pleasure principle for the unity of spirit, which appropriates the tension of unconscious conflict for the sake of a self-conscious unity and reconciliation. At the same time, however, the opposition remains eternal, even if it is eternally past from the standpoint of spirit. Žižek provides a way of understanding this conflict in a less edifying way, but what is central for both Žižek and Schelling is how unity proceeds from duality. Schelling insists that it is "in the nature of spirit to insist constantly on division," but in this very insistence, "a view [*Blick*] of unity rises out of the division," (153). For Žižek, the unity of spirit issues in a Word that resolves the conflict of the rotary motion of unconscious drives. Yet Schelling's language also holds onto a more philosophical notion of spirit as a vision, glance, or view that flashes out and rends the opposition inoperable. Schelling actually fuses Athens (light or vision) and Jerusalem (speech or hearing) here, assimilating the Platonic idea to the "language that introduces Wisdom in speech," (161, 164).

In the climax of the *Ages of the World* draft, after which Schelling abandons the piece because it falls into "utter falsehoods," the resolution of the conflict of two opposing wills by and into spirit is explained more specifically in terms of God. As Žižek asserts, the struggle between the will that desires to will out of itself and the will that desires to contract in on itself in aseity is evenly matched. God is caught between the desire (or drive) to remain God and the desire to create a world. The stasis produced by the two opposed yet active wills — one negating, the other affirming — produces "the highest contradiction" and "an absolute decision is demanded," (169).

Spirit is called for as a free unity, but such unity is impossible. Schelling identifies God's will as a will that wants to remain within itself with "that barbaric term aseity," which is "an eternal wrath that tolerates nothing, fatally contracting but for the resistance of love," (171). God's love, on the other hand, is the expansive force that strives to create something outside of divinity. Again, these forces of self-concealing wrath and expansive love or generative fecundity are absolutely equal. This creates, as Žižek has emphasized, "a strain of forces, when life hangs in the balance," which "only the deed can decide," (172).

The deed is the free act, which cannot be explained or deduced in any way. The opposition of forces reaches such a level that a "moment of sudden need" arises. This crisis demands a resolution, a free act of decision, based upon an "uncomprehensible mutual knowledge" that "can only happen in a flash." Again, as Žižek relates, this moment of divine determination is analogous to the assumption of character in a person. Schelling claims "that nobody can be given character, and that nobody has chosen for himself the particular character he bears. . . . everyone recognizes and judges character as an eternal deed and attributes to a man both it as well as the action that follows it," (175). This decision of character is unconscious and terrifying, and at the same time it is the essence of freedom. "But most men shy away from this freedom that opens like an abyss before them," Schelling explains, and Žižek echoes this passage with the title of his book, *The Abyss of Freedom*.

All Schelling can say is that the conflicting wills are united in a flash or moment (*Augenblick*), through an instantaneous, all-illuminating action.[4] In some inexplicable way, a sort of miracle, "love swayed the first of the wills standing open," (176). That is, love persuades the negative will to give way and go first, to become the past so love can exist as present and allow spirit to unify the two in a futural eschatology. For time to exist, the opposition must give way to temporal differentiation. For creation to occur, the negative, contracting will must agree to go first so expansion can follow it. The first potency, negating and contracting, is divine wrath or aseity. This is the inscrutable ground of divinity, which tolerates nothing to exist outside of itself. The second potency is the affirmative will, expansive love, which is the drive to create. The only way Schelling can resolve a contradictory struggle he has set up is via a flash of spirit that somehow tips the balance and allows love to overcome wrath, so creation can occur. "If there were no decision," Schelling argues, "then there would only be mute eternity and God without revelation," (180). This is Schelling's answer to Tillich's question why there is something and not nothing.

This act is the only way a beginning, or creation, is possible, a creation out of nothing except the tension of the absolute opposition of two equal forces or wills. This "primordial deed" of freedom occurs once and immediately after "sinks into the night of unconscious," (181). It flashes up and its shadow leaves traces that become time. Schelling explains both the generation of God's identity and human subjectivity in this way. Human character merely repeats the original, primordial deed. Žižek has drawn out the compelling psychoanalytic implications.

And yet there remains a difficulty that is related to Schelling's early explication of the two wills. To follow the reading of the end of the *Ages of the World* is to lead directly to Žižek's profound interpretation. At the same time, Schelling (and Tillich after him) originally characterizes the negative, unconscious force as the expansive, generating one. Schelling also argues that contraction into an essence establishes subjectivity. Here is a strange reversal of the potencies; Schelling conducts a subtle reversal within the *Ages of the World* treatise. If unconscious ground is expansive, and essence is contracting, what does that imply for creation?

Schelling and Tillich both inject nonbeing into the heart of creation. If spirit or *logos* is somehow the resolution of creation, then language resolves the opposition of forces. The resolution, however, is not simply the persuasion of a negating will to go first and give way to an affirming will of expansive creation. The unconscious, seemingly negative will is already creative! Or, this expansive, negative, unconscious will provides the motivating force for creation, and it generates creation out of the tension it encounters when it meets itself as it resists itself in essence. There are not two wills; there is one will that doubles itself when it folds up into a determinate contractive essence. The contractive essence provides the friction or resistance necessary for creation but not by means of an extrinsic persuasion. This is not simply a monism of will, as Schopenhauer's philosophy would suggest, but the force of Schelling's thought and its affinity with Freud's refuses to permit duality to imply dualism. Freud constantly creates distinctions and differentiations of principles (life and death, pleasure and reality) but he always insists that these opposing principles never dissolve into a simple dualism.[5] If Schelling's thought admits a complex engagement with multivalent forces or potencies, it is because although he is forced to give up his extreme system of identity, the alternative is never dualism. If the unconscious expansive force is "the same," or identical with itself, then it cannot be fecund, it cannot create. A Deleuzian logic of a repetition of difference applies here, which understands the potencies as different aspects of the same will while recognizing the dependence of the awareness of this will as conscious on something beyond itself.

Alfred North Whitehead echoes Schelling by invoking Plato when he writes, "the creation of the world . . . is the victory of persuasion over force."[6] The mistake is to posit an irreducible opposition between persuasion and force, to imagine that persuasion is not a force, and to believe that force cannot persuade. Persuasion is a folding or doubling of force that makes it effective in a different way and at a different level. Another name for persuasion is sublimation, to return to the reading set forth in chapter 1. Force in itself is unconscious; persuasion in itself is conscious, but the fundamental act of persuasion is inaccessible to conscious will or voluntary freedom. It is assumed to occur secondarily. To posit the victory of persuasion over force in the way that Schelling does is to insert an extrinsic mechanism to regulate the outcome rather than to admit the seemingly irrational possibility that such a victory was either pure chance or worse, that the victory of persuasion over force is actually a victory of force itself that has multiplied in an uncanny way to emerge victorious whatever the outcome. Creation is once again either blind luck or blind necessity. On the other hand, conscious creation does not occur except as meaningful signification. How can one penetrate the sublime ignorance that forever veils the process of creation and separates us from the Thing that is created?

Lacan and Creation *ex Nihilo*

Tillich's thought concerning polarities and creation allows a more sophisticated understanding of Schelling, and Tillich's thought is itself enriched in an encounter with the language and concepts of psychoanalysis. One of the important implications of this chapter is that creation refers directly to a process of language and only secondarily to an actor or referent, whether God or a human being. In terms of Lacan, the contention that "the unconscious is structured like a language" forces us to grapple with the question of creation *ex nihilo* in a new way. For Lacan the question of creation primarily involves the creation of a signifier.

Lacan develops his notion of creation at the center of *The Ethics of Psychoanalysis*. Although he affirms that Freud's *Moses and Monotheism* implies that "the myth of the murder of the father is the myth of a time for which God is dead," Lacan also claims that "the idea of creation is cosubstantial with your thought. You cannot think, no one can think, except in creationist terms."[7] For Lacan the question of creation revolves not around God but around the Thing, as we saw in chapter 3. The Thing (*Das Ding*) refers to an object in the Real that can only be approached negatively by means of symbolic signification. Language is the realm of the symbolic, and within language "the Thing is that which in the real, the primordial real, I will say, suffers from the signifier" (118).

I am invoking Lacan's famous typology of Real, imaginary, and symbolic. As discussed at the beginning of chapter 3, in his early seminars and writings Lacan stresses the distinction between the imaginary and the symbolic, where the Real refers to the brute reality left behind with the functioning of language. The central ethical issue is the passage from the imaginary, narcissistic workings of language, to the symbolic proper that recognizes the mediations brought about by the fact that language always functions in relation to an Other. In *The Ethics of Psychoanalysis*, however, Lacan returns to a consideration of how the Real returns amid symbolic language by grappling with the Thing, which marks the limit of the symbolic. The Thing poses a challenge to traditional ethical language because it lies beyond good and evil considered in a utilitarian or symbolic sense. I discussed the difficulty of traditional ethics in light of Lacan's thought in chapter 3, and I will return to Lacan's critique of utilitarianism and the good in chapter 8 by way of a critique of Jean-Luc Marion.

Lacan claims that creation of a signifier occurs because "an object, insofar as it is a created object, may fill the function that enables it not to avoid the Thing as signifier, but to represent it," (119). As I mentioned in chapter 3, Lacan refers to Heidegger's famous essay on "*Das Ding*," where Heidegger discusses the nothingness that makes a vase a vase and allows it to function. Yet Lacan figures Heidegger's discussion differently by explicitly using Biblical language, that of a potter and a clay pot. Lacan follows Heidegger in affirming that "if the vase may be filled, it is because in the first place in its essence it is empty." Lacan continues, however, by making an analogy with speech: "And it is exactly in the same sense that speech or discourse may be full or empty," (120). Here Lacan shifts to the example of the mustard pot, and he develops the analogy in reference to ancient philosophy. The traditional problem of ethics, which is the central issue of theodicy in theology, is the viewpoint of the pot in relation to the potter: "if a reasonable power created the world, if God created the world, how is it that whatever we do or don't do, the world is in such bad shape?" (121).

Lacan continues by illustrating how the traditional argument proceeds:

> The potter makes a pot starting with a clay that is more or less fine or refined; and it is at this point that our religious preachers stop us, so as to make us hear the moaning of the vase in the potter's hand. The preacher makes it talk in the most moving of ways, even to the point of moaning, and makes it ask its creator why he treats it so roughly or, on the contrary, so gently. But what is masked in this example of creationist mythology . . . is the fact that the vase is made from matter. Nothing is made from nothing. (121)

So long as matter is conceived as eternal—as external to God—then the insoluble problem arises. The ancient Greek understanding, that nothing is made from nothing, prevents the possibility of a creation *ex nihilo*. At the same time a traditional Christian theological understanding remains indebted to this view because it assumes that matter is created out of pure nothingness, or *ouk on*, which is both logically absurd and inconceivable. The potter/pot scenario remains tied to a persistent but unrecognized image of the eternality of matter.

Schelling and Tillich both fight to escape the vicious alternatives implied in Greek logic and Christian theology. Here God's creation out of nothing is self-creation out of God's own nothingness, which is somehow intrinsically tied to human self-creation. Lacan takes this view further by tying it to the creation of language. "The fashioning of the signifier and the introduction of a gap or hole in the real is identical," according to Lacan, because a signifier is created out of nothing, and this nothingness in exemplary form refers to a Thing. The Thing is an object that metonymically represents the Real, or that which escapes symbolic representation. So the production of the signifier that signifies a Thing opens up a hole in reality because it brings to light the difference between the Thing and what it is supposed to represent. And this is the essence of creation: "The introduction of this fabricated signifier that is the vase already contains the notion of creation *ex nihilo*. And the notion of the creation *ex nihilo* is coextensive with the exact situation of the Thing as such," (122).

Lacan goes on to consider the nature of the work—the function of the vase—and he asserts that it is good and holds together, but our "optimism can in no way be justified by the way things function in the human world, nor by what is born of its works," (122). The reason we cannot be satisfied with works, or rather the meanings generated by creation, is that once created or signified, "the perpetuity of matter" becomes "the site of evil," (124). Lacan refers to the medieval Cathars to suggest not only that evil can be associated with matter—the eternal material created by the process of creation—but also that "evil may be in the Thing," (124). That evil may be in the Thing refers to the existence of the wrath of God or the negative principle in Schelling's thought. All of these references to created or natural evil concern the anxiety that issues from the body of God that I described in chapter 5. Lacan here calls this evil the presence of the human factor, however, and claims that the Thing is defined by the fact that it defines the human factor, even though we can never fully determine or define what this human factor is. What is "evil" or the essential human factor is not only the substantialization of particular creations into "matter," but the inevitability of this process and the difficulty of becoming aware of it. It is the matter sloughed off in the process of creation that causes enormous anxiety because it is what is rejected in identifying with the ego or agent of creation: God or self as *cogito*.

"The language forged by philosophical discourse," Lacan writes, "is such that, as you see, I cannot but constantly slip back into this world, into this presupposition of a substance that is permeated with the function of being."[8] He grapples with what extent our conceptions of matter and being are suffused by language, and the misplaced concreteness that results when we imagine that matter and being are the most concrete notions and yet are the most abstract. We are constantly being duped or are duping ourselves with the duplicity of language that is also incredibly uncanny and even horrifying.

Again, as we saw in chapter 3, the Thing defined in this way testifies to a beyond of the pleasure principle, where the pleasure principle is understood in terms of human happiness in an Aristotelian sense, and which is related essentially to being, or Aristotelian substance. The Thing disrupts this economy, and allows the questioning of the process of language and the Real, as a way of thinking about what is at stake in creation—that is, the creation of a Thing. Lacan uses the term sublimation to refer to the process of signification where the human being fashions a signifier in the image of the Thing, "whereas the Thing is characterized by the fact that it is impossible for us to imagine it."[9] Therefore the Thing is (the) sublime. At the end of the seminar, in his reading of *Antigone*, Lacan associates sublimation with the creation of a beauty that is fatal to traditional moral considerations of good and evil. I will take up some of the ethical implications of Lacan's reading of *Antigone* in relation to Anselm's proof of the existence of God and Jean-Luc Marion's reinterpretation of Anselm to suit Lacan's project of a thinking of God without being in the next chapter. Nevertheless, the central section "On Creation *ex nihilo*" opens up a site of convergence with Tillich and Schelling, even as it shifts their discourse into different semantic registers.

What does this foray into Lacan imply for thinking about creation? For Schelling there are the two opposing forces or potencies, which apply to creation and/or freedom for both divinity and humanity. Tillich wrestles with Schelling's thought, and in his *Systematic Theology* goes far to associate the process of creation *ex nihilo* with the creation of finite being when he writes, "finitude unites being with dialectical nonbeing."[10] Lacan introduces the notion of the signifier, and, despite his restriction to the human being, shows how creation *ex nihilo* fundamentally involves the creation of meaning rather than simply matter. Finite being is the substance of human interaction and signification. At the same time dialectical nonbeing pushes us to the limits of signification because it forces us to ask about the process of creating a signifier (the Real) rather than the use of prefashioned signifiers (the symbolic). Schelling's determinate potencies ($a = b$, etc.) are modes of (human) signification that function symbolically to regulate the play of meanings along ethical lines. However, the potencies themselves invade the process of signification. In addition, the identity Schelling posits as the will that wills nothing is the Lacanian Real that is always already disrupted by the "holes" introduced or opened by the attempt to signify the Thing.

To create such meanings is often seen as a divine task, too lofty for puny humans. At the same time, to create a signifier involves the relativization of established moral norms. For these reasons, theology is usually seen as essentially and rightly conservative, engaged in preserving, protecting, and promoting established doctrines and dogmas rather than creating new ones *ex nihilo*. Or if imaginative theological thinking is valued, it is generally the skill of devising new ways to justify the same old solutions or results. To really think theologically is dangerous because it implies playing god with the realm of the symbolic. Yet the return of the Real in the guise of the Thing reminds us that every creation of a signifier opens, rather than covers, a hole in the Real. Schelling and Tillich are both courageous in their attempts to fashion new meanings and new creations, despite the risks and the difficulties involved. Tillich is unique because despite his efforts to correlate Biblical answers with existential cultural questions, he was willing (however implicitly) to distort these traditional answers from the inside to transform what theology means and does.

Creation *ex nihilo* involves the creation of theological ideas—out of nothing. This is similar to what Deleuze and Guattari suggest is the task of philosophy—the creation of concepts.[11] Even if creation *ex nihilo* is (strictly speaking) impossible because nobody can create an idea without reference to previous ideas, texts, and traditions, it may still function as a task and a demand. In fact the creation out of nothing is not temporal in a linear sense. Creation involves a dynamic becoming of the ideas, concepts, or Things themselves out of nothingness, out of the nothing (in an eternally substantial sense) that is the event of thinking. Works, products, and practices are good—they work, they get things done, and they move us from one place to another. They even provide us with the ability to survive and breathe. But such works do not justify. Creation *ex nihilo* does not justify either, if one means the justification of a creator, philosopher, or theologian. What is justified, if anything, is the creation itself. And this creation lies beyond good and evil.

In his *Seminar XX, Encore*, Lacan claims that whether they realize it or not, "only theologians can be truly atheistic, namely, those who speak of God."[12] The atheism involved is not simply a denial of the Real, but a distancing from symbolic representations of God and a willingness to create conceptions of divinity. Lacan claims that "God is the locus where, if you will allow me this wordplay, the *dieu*—the *dieur*—the *dire*, is produced. With a trifling change, the *dire* constitutes *Dieu*." The translator explains the complexity of the French:

The French, *Pour un rien, le dire ça fait Dieu*, is far more polysemic than my translation here; by translating it as "For a nothing, the saying amounts to God," one can see speech's godlike power to create *ex nihilo*. . . . *Dieur*, in the last sentence, is a neologism, but since it is constructed like many other French terms, it can literally be understood to mean "sayer" or "speaker" (thus, the speaking god or the speaker as god).[13]

Out of nothing, the saying (signifier) creates God. Besides Tillich, are there theologians who possess the courage to think this untimely but most theological of thoughts? Unfortunately one of the most influential contemporary theologians, Jean-Luc Marion, shies away from this insight because he not only wants to read *God Without Being*, but he wants to free God from any entanglement in being. Marion follows Heidegger in separating a thinking of God from a thinking of being, but he does not want to detach God from the Good. In chapter 8 I will use Lacan's thought to critique Marion's theology, specifically his reading of Anselm's proof of the existence of God.

8

God Without Being (God)

A Lacanian Critique of Jean-Luc Marion

Introduction

How can we think about God, especially in light of psychoanalytic theory from Freud to Lacan? Postmodern theology is currently assessing notions of God liberated from the constraints of being, stimulated by the work of Jean-Luc Marion. Does Lacan's thought provide resources to think differently about some of these important discussions inspired by Marion concerning God without being?

With the publication and translation of *God Without Being*, Jean-Luc Marion has emerged as one of the significant voices in postmodern theology. In response to Heidegger, Marion provides a thinking of God that exceeds ontological difference or the distinction between being and beings. For Marion, God is not limited by ontological difference, but the restriction of thinking about divinity within the constraints of ontology makes God into an idol, and then God becomes questionable. However, by shifting that idolatry and questionability to Being, Being is suspended, and God is freed from primarily having to be. Instead God can be thought of primarily as giving and as loving: "God does not fall within the domain of Being, he comes to us in and as gift."[1]

According to Marion, God "does not have to be." The gift, the giving or loving that God fundamentally expresses, "does not have first to be, but to pour out in an abandon that, alone, causes it to be;

God saves the gift in giving it before being."[2] Being is not nullified, it is suspended and deferred. Being is an effect of God's loving/giving. God "crosses" being, and this crossing "traces a cross over ontological difference, a cross that abolishes it without deconstructing it, exceeds it without overcoming it, annuls it without annihilating it, distorts it without contesting its right."[3] God grants existence as a donation or a gift that "delivers Being/being."[4] The gift is associated with the incarnation and crucifixion of Jesus Christ and is experienced paradigmatically in the Eucharist.

The attempt to rescue God from Being is a contemporary postmodern theological response to Heidegger's work, particularly his analysis of ontotheology. "Onto-theo-logy," a Heideggerian term, refers to the logic of thinking about God in relation to being and vice versa, and this term is seen to encapsulate and incorporate Heidegger's critique of metaphysics.[5] Many postmodern theologians attempt to meet the challenge of ontotheology by articulating conceptions of God that are not constrained by determinate interpretations of Being. Marion's work is paradigmatic in this venture, and has gone far in the direction of overcoming ontotheology.

In challenging the priority of being as a name or property of God, Marion replaces Being with the Good. The implication is that the gift is good because it is a granting and a loving, the result of a superabundant charity on the part of God. Against St. Thomas, who defines God fundamentally as *ens* (existing being), Marion cites Dionysius, who "following Christ, says that the Good is God's primary name."[6] This emphasis upon God as gift, the overcoming of ontotheology, and the turn toward Christian mysticism or negative theology in the form of pseudo-Dionysius (as well as Meister Eckhart and others) in the discussions of postmodern theology in the 1990s, reflects the importance of Marion's work, which is indebted to both Heidegger and Derrida.[7] In fact *God Without Being* prompted Derrida's address in Jerusalem, "Denegations: How to Avoid Speaking," which represents a sea change in the interpretation of Derrida's thought and kicks off his more explicitly religious turn that has been commented upon and discussed at length at conferences and in books.[8]

Marion provides a reading of Anselm's famous proof of the existence of God in an essay published in his book *Cartesian Questions*. I will critique Marion's reading of Anselm's proof in the context of Marion's philosophical-theological project. Furthermore, I will suggest a reading of Anselm's formulation, God as "that than which greater cannot be conceived," that troubles Marion's interpretation by using insights from Lacan. I will also borrow insights from Edith Wyschogrod's Lacanian reading of Anselm's proof in her essay "Recontextualizing the Ontological Argument: A Lacanian Analysis." Finally I will return to the conclusion of Lacan's *Seminar VII* to consider what happens to the notion of God as good in Lacan's reading of *Antigone*.

Marion on Anselm

Marion is also an important historian of philosophy, and the translation of *God Without Being* in 1991 was eventually followed by *Reduction and Givenness: Investigations of Husserl, Heidegger and Phenomenology* in 1998. Marion is also an influential scholar on Descartes. In 1999 two of his books dealing with Descartes were published in English: *On Descartes' Metaphysical Prism* (French 1986), and *Cartesian Questions* (French 1991). Although the latter work primarily deals with philosophical issues and problems in Descartes, the last chapter, "Is the Argument Ontological?" introduces a careful reading of Anselm's proof of the existence of God. Marion argues that Anselm's argument is not necessarily or primarily ontological, but, set within a context of faith and prayer, it provides an indication for how to think about God.[9] It is rather the modern reception of this arguement from Leibniz to Kant that understands Anselm's argument as essentially ontological. Furthermore, Marion suggests that Descartes's proof of God's existence in *Meditation III* is faithful to the original spirit of Anselm's argument, whereas the later proof in *Meditation V* is more traditionally and problematically ontological.

According to Marion, Anselm's argument does not rely on a concept of divine essence. It relies on a "nonconcept. . . . since it rests precisely on the acknowledged impossibility of any concept of God."[10] In the *Proslogion*, God represents the upper limit of what is thinkable, the maximum, that than which greater cannot be thought. God must always be thought as the nonconcept lying beyond the limit of the concept, which brings to mind Žižek's deployment of the Lacanian distinction between the exception and the "not-all" discussed in chapter 5. This reading threatens to allow God to be figured as conceptual—as an exceptional extension of the limit of the concept—even though this reading is what Marion supposedly wants to prevent.

The rule is: whatever two possibilities present themselves, God must be thought as the greater of the two. So surely whatever is that than which greater cannot be thought must not rest solely in the understanding but must exist in reality. Again, this is not a proof of an object's existence, but a method or rule for thinking of God as greater. Whatever lies beyond understanding must exist in reality or, in a Lacanian sense, in the Real. Marion emphasizes the Latin term *majus* (maximum) and claims that "God is actually experienced only when thought acknowledges, without conquering it, the transcendent that surpasses this limit," (149). Anselm thinks of God as maximum by asserting and then respecting a limit, even though he also claims to be able to think of God paradoxically as beyond this limit. In any case, "the Anselmian project never claimed to achieve a knowledge of the divine essence by means of concepts," (150). God cannot be perceived by the senses or by the intellect, but can be known with certainty as the "something" greater than can be thought," (151).

At this point in the essay, Marion notes a shift in the *Proslogion* from greater (*majus*) to better (*melius*). In a second formula, God is "that than which nothing better can be thought." Marion argues that the term *melius* extends and completes *majus*. God is not simply whatever is greater in terms of maximum, but whatever is better in the sense of moral goodness. Therefore God is beyond essence in a very specific way, a way that culminates and completes or ratifies essence from a standpoint beyond essence, a superabundant essence that is (the) Good.

> God excepts Himself from essence, just as He was already transcending the concept. God surpasses essence through the same gesture that frees Him from the concept—because He can only be thought as He offers Himself, as sovereign good, as sovereign insofar as He is the good, rather than as Being. (152)

This turn away from Being and toward the good repeats the argument of *God Without Being*, since the good is a more primary name for God than Being. Essence, Being, or substance can be thought of only in light of goodness, which is partly an application of Levinas's thesis that ethics precedes ontology. God only is under the aegis of the good, and all Being must be solely seen in light of God's goodness as a function of *melius*.

Marion claims that "through the eminence of the good God transcends everything that exists," (155). One the one hand, we can ask questions about the adequacy of Marion's formulation of Anselm's maximum as an exceptional limit. On the other hand, Marion claims to free Anselm's argument—and thereby Anselm's thinking about God—from the accusation of ontotheology. Marion contrasts *majus* and *melius* (maximum and goodness). But since goodness functions to anchor and support greatness, determining and dispensing from/ the beyond of any limitation, cannot Marion be accused of "de-onto-theo-logy," playing on the ethical term deontology? A simple reversal of being and goodness does not avoid the problems of metaphysics that Heidegger has questioned throughout his philosophy. Further-more, from a psychoanalytic perspective, we desire (the) good, and we desire that God be good probably above all, probably even more than we desire that God exist and be powerful. And yet what reas-surance do we have that our thinking of God corresponds to God in any appropriate or adequate way? Or, to put it another way, how do we anxiously reassure ourselves about the proper relations of *melius* and *majus*?

Power, magnitude, maximum greatness of force or being, as ap-plied to God, nature, or humanity, can be encapsulated in the term *majus* here in Anselm's thought. This power must always be held under the sway and used only for and by *melius*, whatever is better, or good. Does not the distinction between *majus* and *melius* resemble the Kantian sublime? In the *Critique of Judgment*, Kant claims that "we call sublime what is absolutely large. . . . that is sublime in com-parison with which everything else is small."[11] In the mathematical sublime, the faculty of imagination reaches a limit (a maximum) and gives rise to an emotion of displeasure at the limit of human imagina-tion in the face of an absolute magnitude, while at the same time a counter-emotion of pleasure at the ability of human reason to break in and restore harmony with its ideas. The negativity represents an abyss confronted by the impotence of imagination in the face of the power of an absolute magnitude. Yet the moral elevation characteris-tic of the sublime refers to reason's ability to transcend the negative aspect of this conflict and restore a sense of harmony and conformity to our feelings. The result is an engendering of respect that "is ac-corded an object of nature that, as it were, makes intuitable for us the superiority of the rational vocation of our cognitive powers over the greatest power of sensibility."[12] It is not simply the force or power, but the moral elevation that characterizes the feeling of the sublime for Kant. Reason's ability to act in the name of moral ideas links it to *melius* for Kant, while the limits of imagination in the face of an absolute limit confers an experience of *majus*. *Melius* controls and contains *majus* here in a way similar to Marion's analysis of Anselm's argument.

Furthermore, this relationship between force and goodness cuts across both versions of the Kantian sublime. In the dynamical sublime, the object of human experience is more obviously nature's might, but it produces the same subjective effect. Here it is more explicitly the dignity of the human person and her superiority over nature. This dignity is manifest in the ability to judge nature aesthetically but ultimately morally. "Hence nature is called sublime," Kant writes, "merely because it elevates our imagination, making it exhibit those cases where the mind can come to feel its own sublimity, which lies in its vocation and elevates it even above nature."[13] In another essay Marion argues that the Kantian sublime is a prime example of what he calls a saturated phenomenon; that is, a phenomenon that exceeds all formal requirements laid down as conditions for the possibility of knowing or intuiting a phenomenon. The saturated phenomenon corresponds to "the possibility of a phenomenon in which intuition would give *more, indeed immeasurably more*, than intention ever would have intended or foreseen."[14] Kant's aesthetic idea is here "overexposed" by an "excess of light." The saturation given by the overabundant givenness of the phenomenon is lighted by *melius*, which guides and determines being as both essence and power.

The sublime can be read in this way, particularly if one over-saturates it with theological goodness. But tracing the sublime from Kant to Freud as I have done through this book allows a more suspicious reading not only of the Kantian sublime but of the goodness of the good, and furthermore all theological ethics, even and especially the ethics of a thinking of God "beyond being." Marion engages in a hermeneutics of retrieval, rescuing Anselm's argument and claiming "a thought of God that is absolutely free," a thought of God that furthermore becomes enchained to metaphysics in and through modernity.[15]

I have read Marion's reading of Anselm's proof to complicate his notion of God without Being.[16] My critique of Marion is that he disavows any negativity in theology; to preserve an understanding of God as good, Marion is unable to think of God as "beyond good and evil." Futhermore Marion is constrained to subordinate *majus* to *melius* in the same way that Kant harnesses the disturbing power of the sublime to the moral ends of reason. To assess the theological implications of a psychoanalytic reading of Anselm, I will turn to an essay by Edith Wyschogrod in which she conducts a Lacanian analysis of Anselm's ontological argument. Finally, to more explicitly engage the notion of the good operative in Marion's theology, and to further specify the contribution of Lacanian psychoanalysis for contemporary theological and ethical thinking, I will return to Lacan's seminar on *The Ethics of Psychoanalysis* and his critique of utilitarianism.

Wyschogrod on Anselm

In "Recontextualizing the Ontological Argument," Edith Wyschogrod enacts a therapeutic reading of Anselm's text that produces disturbing and fascinating results. She claims at the start of her essay that this reading "is good for nothing," and yet "Lacan opens up the possibility for linking the unconscious to theological discourse."[17] By treating the text like an analysand and interpreting the distinct voices in the text symptomatically, Wyschogrod argues that Anselm's proof "unfolds as a coming to consciousness of desire," (98). By distinguishing between the narrative voice of Anselm and his imaginary interlocutor, the Fool, and by incorporating Gaunilo's critique into the realm of the text, Wyschogrod attends to the different strands of textual development in the argument as it develops, and suggests that this "therapeutic structure" is "internal to the theological text itself," (99). This reading is a deconstructive one because instead of treating Anselm's voice as the conscious ego, Wyschogrod locates Anselm at the level of the unconscious, whereas the Fool and Gaunilo represent "ego ideals and mirages of the subject." By associating Anselm's voice with the voice of the unconscious she is able to read Anselm's prayer as a plea "for the ability to express discursively the love of God that is Anselm's deepest desire," (100). At the same time Wyschogrod sympathetically reads the development of the argument as a therapeutic process by identifying (perhaps even over-identifying) Anselm's voice, which is the voice of the unconscious, with or as the therapeutic strand of the argument. The danger of Wyschogrod's reading, then, is that the over-identification of Anselm's voice as the therapeutic strand of the text threatens to intensify the conscious aspects of the dialogue, in which case the retrieval subtly reinstates Anselm's narrative voice as ego. On the other hand, the value of Wyschogrod's reading is that its Lacanian analysis opens up Anselm's "proof" and shows it status as the expression of a profound desire. Wyschogrod combines an element of suspicion or deconstruction of the tradition with an element of retrieval in contrast to Marion, who is solely engaged in an effort of hermeneutic retrieval.

Wyschogrod suggests that the Fool is "a specular image thrown forth by the unconscious to negate the language of desire that declares God to be a being such that no greater can be conceived."[18] This figure represents "the text's expression of the mirror stage," because desire is here caught in its own reflection, a negation of itself that denies any external referent. In response, Anselm introduces a weak substitute (for himself), the Painter, "which now will be able to speak the language of Anselm's desire," (101). The analogy of a painter painting the name or definition of God does not refute the Fool, but it does push the dialogue ahead from a therapeutic standpoint. Ultimately "the statements of the unconscious are never directly accessible," which is why the Fool's formulation, "God is not," is untenable—it attempts to "transcribe unconscious content, God's plenary presence, directly," (106). So long as the assertion that God exists takes place at the level of conscious understanding, it is no more coherent than the denial of God's existence, even though Anselm undertakes an incredible effort to link faith and knowledge in his argument. What Wyschogrod understands, following Lacan, is that the discourse about God in the *Proslogion* is ultimately about the unconscious desire for God and the ability or inability to completely comprehend and express that insight in conscious discourse.

Although Wyschogrod's reading is therapeutic, it is not reassuring in a simple-minded way. The result of the impossibility of the nonexistence of God is anguish because being a conscious subject cuts off access to the direct experience of God, or *jouissance*. The Fool represents the conscious subject par excellence because he mistakenly persists in denying the reality of *jouissance*, even though he is technically correct in terms of conscious experience. It is only "when the I retreats—in theological language, 'dies to itself'" that "the Non-Being of the Other, discursively formulable only in negative terms, may actually become something boundless, inexpressible, *jouissance* without limit," (107). When Gaunilo takes on the part of the Fool to suggest a fantasy island that can be imagined but does not exist, Wyschogrod's Lacanian therapeutic perspective reveals that such an island can only be an *objet petit a* with no more than an *ontic* status. Furthermore, since *jouissance* is encoded in the divine name as "that than which greater cannot be conceived," God cannot be adequately thought of as the greatest or the Supreme Being, on which Marion and Wyschogrod all agree. Against Marion, however, Wyschogrod argues that "conceptualization of the divine name rests on difference: the difference between a highest being and a-being-such-that-a-greater-cannot-be-conceived, and difference is itself grounded in negation and lack," (110).

The thinking of the name or definition of God involves instantiating a radical negativity into conscious language because, as Lacan avers, God is unconscious. The word "God" becomes a master signifier if it refers to what cannot be directly accessible in and through conscious experience. The therapy is complete when Anselm, Gaunilo, and the Fool internalize the Law of the Father and recognize that "the fulfillment of primordial desire is barred," even as the master signifier is still able to invoke *jouissance* (110). Anselm distinguishes between understanding and conceiving, as both Marion and Wyschogrod point out. "For Anselm," Wyschogrod writes, "understanding is the faculty that grasps factual existence while the faculty of conceiving comprehends whatever is intelligible," (108). Understanding remains tied to symbolic conscious discourse, while in Lacan's terminology conception can range beyond understanding and is free to take up notions that may be imaginary or Real, in Lacan's terminology. I am tempted to apply Kant's distinction between apprehension and comprehension here. For Kant, comprehension is functions in terms of categories and concepts of the understanding. Apprehension, however, is associated more with the work of imagination, and, in the judgment of the sublime, imagination is said to be able to apprehend "to infinity."[19]

God as "that than which greater cannot be conceived" necessarily exists, or must necessarily be thought of as existing, according to Anselm's formulation. As a name of God, it "exists" in the Real (as *jouissance*), rather than in terms of the symbolic order of understanding, language, and being. This is what is meant by the determination of discourse about God as being the expression of an unconscious desire. The limit set by Anselm's formulation functions according to the Lacanian logic of exceptionality in Marion's analysis. The limit gives a beyond-the-limit, which draws the line and determines the limit as exception but also as extension. This limit is not simply greatness or magnitude, but goodness, ethics, or charity. The question, however, is where and how to draw the line. *Jouissance* is beyond the pleasure principle. What is the relationship between the Good and human goods? Is there a continuous, direct relationship, or is there a break between conscious and unconscious, good and goods, *jouissance* and pleasure? Even if we do not have to think of God as constrained by being, subject to ontotheology, is God still subtly and insidiously constrained by our notions of goodness, the conceptions of *melius* produced by our desires?

Lacan vs. Theological Utilitarianism

According to Lacan, traditional ethics from Aristotle through Mill (but not including Kant) are all varieties of utilitarianism. In *The Ethics of Psychoanalysis* Lacan claims that Freud's work constitutes a radical challenge to ethics because with Freud, for the first time, "the question of ethics is to be articulated from the point of view of the location of man in relation to the real."[20] In the *Nicomachean Ethics* Aristotle identifies happiness as the highest good, but for Lacan the significance is that happiness is intrinsically tied to pleasure, even if it is broader than a narrow hedonism. "In Aristotle the problem is that of a good, of a sovereign Good," Lacan writes. "We will have to consider why he emphasized the problem of pleasure, its function in the mental economy of ethics from the beginning," (11).

Ultimately the expansion of pleasure into the good, and its connection with a Sovereign Good, involves the establishing of an order. Human *Nous* or "mind" has to be made to conform

> to an order that from the point of view of Aristotle's logic has to be brought together in a Sovereign Good, a point of insertion, attachment or convergence, in which a particular order is unified with a more universal knowledge, in which ethics becomes politics, and beyond that with an imitation of the cosmic order. (22)

Pleasure is the guiding function of ethics, but it must be elaborated into the good to regulate our psychic life. Lacan assimilates the tradition of ethics from Aristotle onward to what Freud calls the Pleasure Principle. Kant is a precursor to Freud here because an understanding of Kantian thought in connection with Sade provides resources to envision a morality beyond the pleasure principle. For Lacan, "insofar as pleasure controls subjective activity, it is the good, the idea of the good, that sustains it," which is why he identifies Aristotle's ethics as a version of utilitarianism (34). Utilitarianism deals with goods, and Aristotle also specifies a plurality of goods appropriate to humans, but these goods are subservient to and regulated by the idea of the Sovereign Good, just as pleasure is subordinated to the Good.

The break with utilitarianism and the continuous relationship of pleasure and good comes not with the idea of the Sovereign Good, and certainly not with the idea of God as Supreme(ly) Good, but with the notion of the Thing (*das Ding*). As we saw in chapter 3, the Thing is beyond good and evil, at the limit of symbolic discourse, and constitutes a crisis of conventional morality because it calls the good into question. The question of the Thing touches on the Real and brings about *jouissance* under the name of the moral Law. Here is "the great revolutionary crisis of morality," the "culminating point for both Kant and Sade with relation to the Thing," (70). Lacan explains that for Freud, the desire for the mother represents the primary situation of the Thing. The maternal thing—the mother—occupies the original place of the Thing, and access to the mother in a sexual relationship is barred by the incest prohibition that founds culture. Lacan argues that it is telling that the ten commandments leave out the command not to engage in incest because that law is presupposed as the basis for all human speech:

> The ten commandments may be interpreted as intended to prevent the subject from engaging in any form of incest on one condition, and on one condition only, namely, that we recognize that the prohibition of incest is nothing other than the condition sine qua non of speech. (69)

If the moral law rests on a hidden basis—the desire for the Thing—this is a law that fundamentally opposes the pleasure principle and exposes the impossibility of the Sovereign Good. Freud, following Kant (along with Sade), turns the moral law on its head because he shows "that the Sovereign Good, which is *das Ding*, which is the mother, is also the object of incest, is a forbidden good, and that there is no other good," (70).

The reason Kant and Sade prefigure Freud here is because Kant purifies the moral law of pleasure in relation to the Thing-in-itself. Sade develops a consistent anti-morality that takes utilitarianism and pleasure to their limits and shows their resolution in pain. Pain is the result of the relation with the Thing, and Kant emphasizes the painfulness of duty to the moral law. The condition of reaching the supreme object of desire—the Thing—is not pleasure but pain. Lacan explains that "to the degree that it involves forcing an access to the Thing, the outer extremity of pleasure is unbearable to us," (80). The Law negatively reveals the Thing, which is why the Thing is usually figured as sin, fundamentally in the letters of St. Paul.

There is no access to *jouissance*, which is what the Thing mediates, without sin or transgression, at least in theory. That is "precisely the function of the Law," according to St. Paul. "Transgression in the direction of *jouissance* only takes place if it is supported by the oppositional principle, by the forms of the Law."[21]

Lacan attests here to the necessity and universality of sublimation, which occurs at the limit of utilitarian ethics and also incorporates an aesthetics of beauty, pushed to its limit, toward the sublime. The Thing opens up a gap in the Real and founds symbolic discourse—the discourse of conceptual conscious understanding. The moral Law, which ostensibly regulates control of pleasure and goods within the symbolic realm, ultimately refers to the Real, to the Thing as part-object of the Real, or the limit of Real as conceived/contained in the Thing. The Sovereign Good does not possess a continuous or affirmative relationship with human goods and pleasures, which is the nature of the break introduced by Freud between conscious and unconscious functions. Psychoanalytic theory allows or forces us to grapple with the dislocation of Good from good, Thing from things, Real from reality, in a negative sense. This is a kind of negative theology, but its discourse does not reside entirely or easily within a context of pious prayer, as the discourses of Pseudo-Dionysius and Anselm do. Faith and prayer cannot and should not be disallowed or disavowed, but they do not exhaust or saturate the field of desire in an over-determining way. To attend to the fidelity of the event of unconscious desire, even if it cannot be completely comprehended, is uncanny and disturbing in relation to discourses that attempt to contain their radicality and recover an ethical symbolic to restore belief, as Marion's theology essentially does.

Lacan says that sublimation is not simply an idealization of the subject's identification with its object, but rather "is precisely that which reveals the true nature of the *Trieb* [drive] insofar as it is not simply instinct, but has a relationship to *das Ding* as such, to the Thing insofar as it is distinct from the object."[22] Sublimation involves what Freud calls the death drive, although as I argued in chapter 4 the death drive is extremely complex and is not simply or consistently a death wish, but constitutes a beyond of the pleasure principle that Lacan claims involves the creation of a signifier *ex nihilo*, as we saw in chapter 7. Sublimation, as another name for the death drive, "points to the site that I designate alternately as impassable or as the site of the Thing," (213). Sublimation leads beyond the field of ethical utilitarianism toward aesthetic beauty.

Yet the beautiful, like the good, is also ultimately an obstacle or a barrier that "holds the subject back in front of the unspeakable field of radical desire," (217). Beauty leads the subject beyond ethics but then traps her and suspends her desire. "The appearance of beauty intimidates and stops desire," (238). The reading of *Antigone* that makes up penultimate section of *The Ethics of Psychoanalysis* reveals what happens when desire is pushed beyond beauty toward the sublime, even as the beauty or splendor of Antigone's sacrificial death, and her loyalty to an ethical desire beyond the moral law, threatens to capture desire and disarm it. At the same time, Sophocles diagnoses something inherent in human beings that Lacan translates as "he advances toward nothing." In that advance humans are always "artful" but also always "screwed," (275). Our inability to come to terms with death propels that advance, and at the same time we invent escapes, "an escape into *impossible* sickness." The problem is that we have not "managed to come to terms with death but he [man] invents marvelous gimmicks in the form of sicknesses he himself fabricates," (275). The advancing and the evasion are two sides of the same drive, and it is instructive to read theology in both traditional and postmodern forms as at once evasions and advances: "advances toward nothing," and "marvelous gimmicks," escapes into "impossible sickness."

I will not pursue the details of Lacan's reading further, except to note that he affirms that "the latent, fundamental image of Antigone forms part of your morality, whether you like it or not," (284). Antigone's tragedy is that she is caught between two deaths, until her own tragic death, of course. Her tragedy functions as an obstacle to work through to arrive at a proper understanding of psychoanalytic experience. Lacan draws conclusions about the tragic dimensions of psychoanalytic experience to conclude the seminar. The analysand asks the analyst for happiness:

> The question of the Sovereign Good is one that man has asked himself since time immemorial, but the analyst knows that it is a question that is closed. Not only doesn't he have that Sovereign Good that is asked of him, but he also knows there isn't any. (300)

To be faithful to the analyst's desire she must not reduce "the gap between the way in which the subject expresses his instinctual 'drives' and that way in which he would be able to express them if the processing of arranging and organizing them weren't available,"

(301). To hold onto this distance constitutes the core of the ethics of psychoanalysis, and I am suggesting that theological thinking should also attend honestly and faithfully to this irreducible gap between reality and the Real.

God is not good, at least in terms of human symbolic discourse. Our ideal of the Sovereign Good is not God, however much we desire that it should be. We resist these insights, these questions that "tend not to edification" (the Buddha) and are "good for nothing" (Wyschogrod). We eat to live, and as Whitehead puts it, "life is robbery." Because we can think and speak, because we can ask questions and design moral codes and laws, we sublimate. But in order for sublimation to work, "I definitely have to pay a price." "Sublimate as much as you like; you have to pay for it with something. And this something is called *jouissance*," (322). The price that one pays for the satisfaction of desire is the loss of the Good, understood as the object of desire par excellence.

Lacan sketches out a psychic economy where we do not get something for nothing. The essence of religion is the attempt to recuperate "the good which is sacrificed for desire," according to Lacan. I would not single out religion but extend his critique to all idealism, and therefore most philosophy and theology. Perhaps this is the essence of "metaphysics," or Platonism: the belief that somehow the scales are counterbalanced in the future, or in a future life. This restoration covers over a resounding and deeply felt conservatism, even as it sustains a vital liberalizing moral and political vision. Is religion essentially about recovering the good that has been sacrificed to desire? Is psychoanalysis the discourse that problematizes that effort? Not exclusively, or institutionally, but there is an element of Freud and Lacan's work that refuses consolation and challenges idealism. Is psychoanalytic theory from Freud to Lacan essentially suspicious to the extent that we could identify psychoanalytic discourse completely with the hermeneutics of suspicion, as Ricoeur does in *Freud and Philosophy*? Not necessarily, although I would suggest that much of the relevance and vitality of psychoanalytic theory derives from its suspicious edge, and even or especially when this suspicion becomes self-reflective.

Lacan's work challenges most traditional and much postmodern theological thinking beyond all efforts to contain it, label it, and dismiss it from the heart of theology itself. Lacan's thought provides insight into the paradoxical and, from an Anselmian viewpoint, quintessentially theological thinking of the limits of language and the understanding of God, or the Real. In chapter 9, I will turn to a consideration of the limits of language and its ability to express the Real, and to do so I will have to shift from *Seminar VII*, which has been privileged throughout this book, to *Seminar XX*, to work out Lacan's extremely complex understanding of language and the Real there. To reflect upon Lacan's topological theory about knots I will also read a novel by Herman Melville, *Benito Cereno*.

9

Expressing the Real

Lacan and the Limits of Language

> the proposition
> 'All forms point to the formless'
> is itself a formal proposition
>
> —R. D. Laing, *Knots*

Introduction

Taking the triad imaginary-symbolic-Real as representative of Lacan's consistent and core thought, one can detect a shift in emphasis from the symbolic to the Real over the course of his intellectual career, as described in chapter 3. From his conception of the mirror stage expressed in his addresses to the International Congress of Psychoanalysis to his early seminars in the 1950s, Lacan's early work focuses on the differentiation of the imaginary and the symbolic. The attention to symbolic discourse, and the identification of desire as the expression of the subject's speech, carries with it an ethical bent—to traverse the imaginary fantasy by breaking the mirror to break through to the symbolic order. This development reaches its fullest expression in *The Ethics of Psychoanalysis*, although this seminar also represents a turning in Lacan's thought, a turning away from the symbolic and toward a preoccupation with the Real. *The Ethics of Psychoanalysis* functions as a hinge for my interpretation of the theological resonances of Lacanian psychoanalysis throughout this book. At the same time, this shift culminates in the 1960s and 1970s in Lacan's obsession with mathemes and topographical knots as a suitable way to formalize the Real.

This chapter will turn from *Seminar VII* to *Seminar XX* in an attempt to follow Lacan's expression of the Real. Lacan's later work wrestles with the limits of language directly in an attempt to show what cannot be said, to put it in Wittgenstein's terms.[1] If Lacan's later work represents a strange return to the standpoint of the *Tractatus Logico-Philosophicus*, does this attest to a profound naiveté or a desire to escape the world? What is the significance of Lacan's turn to topology and mathematical theory? Is it symptomatic of the mental breakdown of a great thinker's intellectual powers? Does it represent a tragic but impossible attempt to directly express the Real?

Badiou and Žižek in the Shadow of Lacan

Perhaps philosophizing is a sickness, and of course theologizing is at least as unhealthy, especially without an assurance of God's existence and guarantee of theological discourse. Intense religious experience fails to conform to our models of scientific-psychological health and sanity, as William James points out in the first chapter of the *The Varieties of Religious Experience* on Religion and Neurology.[2] If someone finds herself in the grip of a theological fever, should she take medication to dull the intensity of the pain of asking provocative theological questions? We could say it is impossible to express the Real, but should that deter us from attempting the impossible?

The limit of language touches on the Real. We can choose to remain safely within the realm of symbolic discourse, or we can trace the boundary and risk madness—Real or imagined. The limits of language prescribe (and proscribe) the form of thought. The paradox is that the limit is not a thing that can be expressed with language; it is not an object and cannot be the content of a proposition. It can be shown but not said, and it takes the form of a shadow or a shadowy form.

> Any explanation of a symbol can do nothing but add to the symbol. Yet our notion of a symbol is that it points outside itself, to a shadowy being between symbol and fact, the shadow of its fulfillment, which is meant to mediate between symbol and fact. What kind of thing must this shadow be? "It is similar to the fulfillment." This explanation we saw would not do. To interpolate a shadow or the like between symbol or proposition and

fact will not do unless we have another shadow to mediate between that shadow and the fact; we have then an infinite regress, we are brought no nearer. As similarity does not explain the shadow, it does not explain the relation to fact either.[3]

We cannot posit or think of an infinite regress; we cannot allow the shadows to expand and engulf our facts and propositions, but can we simply exorcise this shadow?

In *Seminar XX* these shadows take the form of strings, and these strings form knots. Lacan's later musings on formalization, mathemes, and Borromean knots are easy to dismiss, especially for scholars working in the humanities. On the other hand, the growing significance of Alain Badiou's philosophy, which is indebted to Lacan's work, attests to a need to come to terms with what Lacan is doing. In his major work, *Being and Event*, Badiou attempts to formalize ontology in relation to set theory, and he does so explicitly along the lines of Lacan's mathematical formalization of knowledge.[4] In another essay Badiou explains that his project is an attempt to "rediscover a foundational style," which would reverse "the great linguistic turn of philosophy."[5] Badiou follows Lacan in *Seminar XX* in his investigation into the relationship between truth and the Real. He appeals to mathematics to provide a link between philosophical and psychoanalytic discourse: "mathematics is the science of being *qua* being."[6] Mathematical formalization in set theory, drawing on the work of Paul Cohen, allows Badiou to develop a nonlinguistic ontology that functions as the foundation or backdrop for a thinking of the event. Badiou claims that

> mathematics is precisely the thinking which has nothing to do with consciousness; it is the thinking which has no relation to *reality*, but which knots *letters* and the *real* together; a thinking faced with the void because it obeys the ideal of formalization.[7]

In pursuing a nonlinguistic ontology, Badiou misreads Lacan, who appeals to topology and string theory to offer a more general schema of the Real, but Lacan also affirms that "there's no such thing as a metalanguage," and mathematical formalization is still based on language, or writing.[8] Lacan would resist Badiou's attempt to dispense with language or at least to limit it in such a way. On the other hand, Badiou appeals to the formalizations of set theory to move beyond the modern, Cartesian subject. At the conclusion of *Being and Event*, Badiou claims that Lacan remains essentially Cartesian in his appeal

to a subject. Language fundamentally characterizes the human subject. Badiou writes: "What *still* attaches Lacan . . . to the Cartesian
epoch of science is the thought that the subject must be maintained in
the pure void of its subtraction if one wishes to save truth."[9] Badiou
abandons language in his impressive attempt to think being apart
from any subject who thinks being. The subject is rather the effect of
the event. Badiou opposes the linguistic turn in order to think ontology on the one hand, and on the other, the pure irruption of the
event, without any mediation. The question that remains, however,
is whether a logic or logics can be elaborated without getting caught
up in the problems of language. This question directly concerns *Logics of Worlds*, the "sequel" to *Being and Event*.[10]

Badiou's mathematical ontology represents a contemporary return
to Platonism to locate a secure place from which to think the event.
Badiou declares his fidelity to a certain form of Platonism without
the transcendence of the One, affirming Plato's "sharp, inaugural
awareness of what I call the 'conditions' of philosophy," which are
to be found "in obligatory dialogue with mathematics, with art and
poetry."[11] Badiou's engagement with Lacan's later formulations of
the Real creates a Platonic legacy for Lacan. I am critical of this Platonic interpretation of Lacan's significance despite a profound admi-
ration for Badiou's work. In the next chapter, as a counter-reading,
I will suggest a more Aristotelian context for thinking about Lacan,
with reference to Spinoza, Heidegger, Whitehead, and Deleuze.

Slavoj Žižek is an important influence upon the theoretical scene
with his brilliant analyses of films, politics, popular culture, and most
recently religion, and his philosophical insights are grounded in Lacanian thought. Furthermore, Žižek acknowledges the influence of
Badiou upon his work, particularly Badiou's book on St. Paul, although Žižek does not privilege the mathematical formalizations of
Lacan or the mathematical ontology of Badiou.[12] In *The Puppet and
the Dwarf* Žižek provides a compelling interpretation of universality
that contrasts with the seemingly more straightforward universalism
of Badiou. In *Saint Paul: The Foundation of Universalism*, Badiou affirms that grace is impossible without the law and that Paul creates
a new kind of discourse that configures the Real as pure event. This
event is always singular, and its conditions cannot be prescribed in
advance. On the other hand, universalism is an integral effect of the
proclamation of the event. Badiou writes, "for Paul, universality mediates identity. It is the 'for all' that allows me to be counted as one."[13]

Finally, "Paul demonstrates in detail how universal thought, proceeding on the basis of the worldly proliferation of alterities . . . *produces* a Sameness and an Equality."[14]

Although he cites Badiou positively, Žižek provides a more complex and nuanced account of Pauline universalism. According to a Hegelian reading of subtraction (Hegel read through Lacan), "universality is *aufgehoben* in singularity, not the other way around." Žižek argues that Judas functions as a precursor to Paul in the formation of Christianity, and he draws out the true significance of Paul's thought, which constitutes a "more Kierkegaardian betrayal . . . of the universality itself for the sake of the singular point of exception."[15] Žižek argues that the essence of politics repeats the founding gesture of Christianity and involves "a kind of short circuit between the Universal and the Particular," which consists of the identification of the "non-part" with the Whole.[16] Žižek's discussion of politics is similar to Badiou's, and both affirm the singularity of the event. Yet Žižek does not separate ontology and event to the same extent as Badiou, which allows a better articulation of movement, even though for both the event occurs as a subtraction from ontological being. Žižek claims, following Lacan in *Seminar XX*, that the Real is not separate from (or external to) the symbolic, but rather indicates a shift in perspective: "the Real is the Symbolic itself in the modality of non-All, lacking an external limit/exception."[17] Using language from *Seminar VII*, Žižek explains that

> The Real is thus simultaneously the Thing to which direct access is not possible and the obstacle that prevents this direct access; the Thing that eludes our grasp and the distorting screen that makes us miss the Thing. More precisely, the Real is ultimately the very shift in perspective from the first standpoint to the second.[18]

Badiou attempts to avoid the linguistic turn by formalizing the Real, by an appeal to set theory. Žižek more properly follows Lacan by showing that universal ontology "is" the shift from the Thing that represents the Real to the awareness that the Thing cannot represent the Real, not because the Real is beyond the Thing—as an exception beyond a limit—but because the Real is the movement itself, the turning from one perspective to another. Universality for Žižek is the abandonment of the universal for the particular, but it is not the particular in itself; rather it is the very movement from an abstract universality to a concrete particularity. Again, Badiou thematizes a similar relationship between being and event, but Žižek formulates this relationship in a less dichotomous manner.[19] To provide background for this contemporary relationship between Žižek and Badiou, I will take up a more direct consideration of *Encore*.

Encore

Lacan's *Seminar XX* deals with the limits of love and knowledge as well as feminine sexuality, even though "woman" does not exist inherently or as such. Lacan's famous discussion of God and woman's *jouissance* provides the impetus for contemporary discussions of feminist theology and mysticism spurred primarily by the work of Luce Irigaray, who elaborates upon "a jouissance of the body" that is "beyond the phallus."[20] Woman's *jouissance* envisions an alternative relationship to the Real beyond the conventional symbolic discourse ordered by the phallic signifier.

For Lacan there is never any question of direct access to the Real, but he becomes less optimistic about the nature of symbolic discourse. Here the signifier is duplicitous, even though it is "stupid"; we are always being duped by language and there is no simple cure. Lacan contrasts the "serious real" with the "stupid signifier."[21] *Jouissance*, which was more clearly located at the limit of symbolic discourse in *Seminar VII*, is in *Seminar XX* more explicitly caught up in the signifying relationship. *Jouissance* is always of the Other, and this is caused by the signifier, even if the signifier also limits, contains, and directs *jouissance*. Since "it is the Other who enjoys" every determinate relationship with a person or an object always involving other satisfactions, Lacan claims hyperbolically that the sexual relationship does not exist.[22] Again, *jouissance* has become more and more trapped in the machinery of the unconscious and symbolic desire, which is why Lacan is interested in positing another *jouissance*—woman's *jouissance*.

> It is insofar as her jouissance is radically Other that woman has more of a relationship with God than anything that could have been said in speculation in antiquity following the pathway of that which is manifestly articulated only as the good of man.[23]

The question is whether woman's God is different than the God constructed out of the Supreme Good of man, which is indubitably symbolic. This represents the promise and possibility of feminist theology beyond its necessary critique of traditional, patriarchal theology. Another question, however, is precisely how to situate the Real in relation to the imaginary and symbolic here. Lacan says the aim of his teaching is to dissociate the *objet petit a* and the *Autre* (Other) "by reducing the first to what is related to the imaginary and the Other to what is related to the symbolic." If the Real is not beyond either the imaginary or the symbolic, then it consists of the shift from one to the other, as Žižek suggests in *The Puppet and the Dwarf*. The ethical shift is from the imaginary *a* to the symbolic *A*. This is the basis for the universal, but Žižek follows Kierkegaard in arguing that the Real involves forsaking the universal and returning or reversing the movement back from A(*utre*) to a (*objet petit a*). The key is to write *A* into *a*, or to rework the symbolic back into the fantasy of imaginary part(icular), and it is this trajectory, properly speaking, that constitutes the Real.[24]

Lacan resorts to mathematical logic because "the real can only be inscribed on the basis of an impasse of formalization." At the same time, mathematical formalization is still based on language because it is "based only on writing," (93). He provides an image based on nature, for which he cites Spinoza's approval—the spider web, which is a writing that emerges out of the spider's belly. Specifically, writing is "what language leaves by way of a trace," (123). By following "the trace of these writings taking form" we can "grasp the limits, impasses, and dead ends that show the real acceding to the symbolic," (93). The matheme constitutes an ideal, not because it functions as a metalanguage, but because it provides a level of generality required to integrally transmit being. Yet Lacan claims that "no formalization of language is transmissible without the use of language itself," (119). We shape a particular kind of metalanguage, but we also use it as or in language, which is an inescapable horizon. Lacan attempts to sketch the limits of language in *Seminar XX*, which is similar in some ways to Wittgenstein's project in the *Tractatus*, except Lacan utilizes topology rather than logical propositions to trace this limit. Furthermore, the limit is more substantial and fixed in the *Tractatus*, while for Lacan the limit is much more dynamic, since it takes the form of a not-all and is thus not literally a limit.

Knots

Take a line of string and fold it to make a knot. There is no simple inside or outside of the string, and there are no holes or cuts in the string either. Lacan says that "the ideal string, the simplest string, would be a torus." You cannot form a knot from the surface of a torus, but "with the locus of a torus" you can. In this sense, "the torus is reason, since it allows for knots."[25] The torus is the locus for knots of string. Lacan multiplies the torus by three to form a Borromean knot, or a true ring of string. The key to the Borromean knot is that it allows the rings of string to be knotted to each other in such a way that if you cut one string, all three strings are set free. In addition, by bending the strings, an indefinite number of strings can be linked to form a chain, or a ring of strings.

This discussion is abstract, but a couple of points can be made. First, the ring of strings forms a chain, and this ring "is certainly the most eminent representation of the One, in the sense that it encloses but a hole." Here is the locus of Lacan's phrase, "There's such a thing as One" (*Y a ∂l'Un*), which also functions as a reading of Parmenides.[26] The ring or chain encloses a One, which represents the creation of a signifier in terms of language. Second, although the number of strings can be multiplied, the prime number is three, and the Borromean knot also represents the knot of desire as formed by the three strings of the Real, imaginary, and symbolic. The important issue here is not the representations, but the interrelationship among strands: imaginary, Real, and symbolic are entwined in such a way that to cut one is to release the others. The Real is partially the attempt to formalize these relationships using topology (knots and strings), but it is just as much the understanding that you cannot have any one (symbolic, imaginary, Real) in isolation from the others. Then the question is whether to cut the strings, or untie the knots and undo the chains of signification. The problem is that unbinding signification does not open to the Real but rather releases one into psychosis. Lacan references Schreber's language, in which "one of the links, when missing, sets all the others free, that is, withdraws them from the One," (128).

From the standpoint of signification, the extremes are psychosis (if the string is cut) and solitude because the One formed by the chain of signification has no substantiality and nothing to latch onto. The One is "there, we can assume, to represent solitude — the fact that the One doesn't truly knot itself with anything that resembles the sexual Other," because there is no other One, at least in terms of any particular chain of signification (128). The Other cannot be added to the One, it "can only be differentiated from it" — the Other is "the One-missing," (129). This is why Lacan concludes, pessimistically, that there can be no genuine sexual relationship, at least One-to-One.

Despite the language of mathematical formalization, and against certain aspects of Badiou's philosophy, I am arguing that language is still necessary and unavoidable for the expression of the Real. Language can be formalized into mathemes, propositions, and set theory up to a point, but not to the point that they become an autonomous metalanguage. In addition, literary language may be just as powerful and insightful, if not more so, in its expression of the Real. The Borromean knot is a special kind of knot, but most of Lacan's discussion is predicated on simple sailor's knots. Herman Melville's novel, *Benito Cereno*, also turns around sailors and knots.

Benito Cereno

Benito Cereno tells the story of a Massachusetts ship captain, Amasa Delano, who comes upon a mysterious Spanish vessel ostensibly commanded by Benito Cereno, carrying a cargo of African slaves to Peru. The novel focuses on the relationship between the two leaders, which is complicated by the fact that the Africans have revolted and taken over the ship, but have threatened Cereno and the few other Spanish sailors still alive with violent death if he gives away the secret of the ship. Captain Delano alternates in his confusion between trust and mistrust based on the conflicting signals given by Cereno, the other Spaniards, and the Africans on the ship, including Cereno's servant Babo and an imposing prisoner named Atufal. Finally Benito Cereno jumps aboard Delano's boat, reveals the secret of the mutiny, and the Americans overtake the Spanish ship and subdue the African rebels. The novel closes with a long deposition by Benito Cereno that reveals the circumstances of the revolt and discloses that Cereno himself has had a mental breakdown in the wake of the traumatic events.

Benito Cereno is an extremely psychological novel that can be read at many levels, and it also dramatizes certain aspects of Lacan's thought. Melville creates a strong sense of foreboding that pervades most of the novel: "shadows present, foreshadowing deeper shadows to come."[27] These shadows indicate the uncertainty and confusion that dominate the protagonist's consciousness throughout the text. Delano spots a stranger—a ship—through his glass, which "showed no colours" and only subsequently would reveal its true colors. The American wrestles with uneasiness, but he keeps reassuring himself that everything is as it appears because of his "singularly undistrustful good nature," (56). When the boat comes closer his impression of the colors of the men working it, with "throngs of dark cowls," leads him to picture it populated by monks. Delano expects to see white men on the ship, and when he sees the color black he imagines that they must be wearing black clothes. Finally "the true character of the vessel was made plain—a Spanish merchantman of the first class; carrying negro slaves, amongst other valuable freight, from one colonial port to another," (58). In addition the ship carried a figurehead that was hidden, wrapped in canvas, underneath which was written in chalk, "follow your leader." We later discover that the figurehead is the skeleton of the original captain of the ship, killed by the Africans in their revolt, and the phrase "follow your leader" functions as a warning to Benito Cereno and anyone else that they will share the same fate if they reveal the true situation to Captain Delano.

The novel builds very slowly and draws out the tense interaction between Delano and Cereno, showing through the American's eyes the conflicting signals and symbols that he does not know how to interpret. At one point Babo, the personal servant of Cereno, displays Atufal dressed up as a stubborn prisoner, and explains that he must ask Cereno's pardon before he can be freed, but Cereno refuses. "The slave there carries the padlock, but master here carries the key," Babo says. Delano naively remarks that padlock and key are "significant symbols, truly," but Cereno falters and remains mute. Delano continues to wrestle with his uncertainty and inability to discern the truth. At one point he concludes: "to the Spaniard's black-letter text, it was best, for a while, to leave open margin," (84). This oscillation between faith in the innocent nature of the situation (the cover story is that a plague killed most of the Spanish) and anxiety concerning the diabolical nature of Cereno increases but never touches the reality of the actual situation.

Finally the novel builds to a climactic event, in which "all this, with what preceded, and what followed, occurred with such involution of rapidity that past, present, and future seemed one," (134). Cereno jumps aboard Delano's ship in a desperate bid to escape and Babo follows with a dagger, but Captain Delano subdues him. All of a sudden, "a flash of revelation swept" over him, and Captain Delano saw, "now with the scales dropped from his eyes, saw the negroes, not in misrule, not in tumult . . . but with mask torn away, flourishing hatchets and knives, in ferocious piratical revolt," (135). Now action takes over, and Captain Delano leads a heroic capture of the Spanish ship, in which some of the Africans are killed but the majority are taken prisoner, and the boat is finally brought to Peru. The true story can now be told, with extracts from Spanish documents of the official investigation. We learn the original fate of the ship and the Africans' revolt, and eventually Benito Cereno's depression and mental breakdown because of his trauma and fear at being at the mercy of the blacks, especially Babo. Captain Delano reassures him, "you are saved; what has cast such a shadow upon you?" "The negro," says Cereno (162). We learn about the execution of the mastermind, Babo, whose body was burned to ashes and whose head was fixed on a pole. At the conclusion of the story we learn of the death of Benito Cereno, three months later, who "did, indeed, follow his leader," (164).

The temptation, and the danger, is to read *Benito Cereno* from the standpoint of Lacan's early distinction between the imaginary and the symbolic. In this reading the crossed signals and uncertainty in Delano's imagination during the first two-thirds of the novel give way to a breakthrough to the symbolic order when the true situation is finally revealed. This is a superficial reading, following a fairly generic and stereotypical plot resolution, although the tension at the beginning is drawn out almost interminably, and a contemporary (white) reader would probably both cringe at the racist language and excuse it as anachronistic, while perhaps resonating with it at a more primal level. Here the imaginary realm consists of a reversal of the proper order, and another reversal must be accomplished to set things right. The novel represents a reversal of the order of things, and this is encapsulated in the character of Benito Cereno, who is not really the captain. Captain Delano critically observes Cereno, judging that he is too strict in some way and too lenient in others. Delano, a true captain, is generous and trusting almost to the point of risking destruction, but he is rewarded with good fortune for his virtuousness.

The master is not really the master, and he is not in control of his ship or his cargo. The Africans' mutiny overturns the proper order of things and creates the perplexing situation that Captain Delano's actions finally resolve, even though his thinking could not. In terms of classical philosophy, and in accord with racial suppositions of the time, the Africans could be read as a collective id, which must be carefully controlled and contained by the (Caucasian) ego lest it revolt and take over. This reading, plausible as it may appear, fails to do justice to Melville's genius, and it ignores Lacan's criticisms of ego psychology. Reading the novel from the perspective of Lacan's later work reveals the pressuring of the symbolic by the Real and raises questions that indict the entire symbolic order in its racist operations. The reality of symbolic discourse is assumed and recovered, but the anxiety that Melville releases exceeds a complete recuperation. By forcing the reader to confront the racial language describing malevolence and the cleverness of the Africans, the good-hearted stupidity of the American Captain Delano, and the blurring of racial and national lines in the person of the Spaniard Benito Cereno, the novel forces a shift in perspective from the symbolic reality of the novel to the real nature of colors and leaders.

In *Seminar XX* Lacan focuses on women to articulate another *jouissance*—an alternative to the male symbolic order. At the same time, Lacan does not explicitly consider race or color in the configuration of symbolic discourse. In her book *Deconstruction, Feminist Theology, and the Problem of Difference*, Ellen Armour reads Derrida's essay "The Ends of Man," and considers how race and gender come together to shape a metaphysical humanism, which is the object of deconstructive critique. Derrida's essay is read in continuity with Derrida's essays on Heidegger entitled *"Geschlecht."* Armour suggests that the end of man "lies where race and sexual difference intersect." This end provides the opportunity to think about the closure of metaphysical humanism in terms of its racial and gendered categories, and to think of "race difference and sexual difference beyond the race/gender divide."[28] Racial categories always operate at the limits of humanity, making distinctions among humans that covertly function to delimit the humanity of other human beings. Certain ethnic groups or races are figured in terms of animals, and as lacking in authentic human "spirit," to distance them hierarchically from the goals of humanity. At the same time, Armour reads Derrida's essay on Heidegger and sexual difference as providing a way out of this impasse because *Geschlecht* is understood as an embodied dispersion proper to *Dasein*. The German word *Geschlecht* is technically untranslatable, but "gathers together several references including body, sex, race, genre, gender, lineage, family and generation."[29] One way to understand *Geschlecht* would be to use the term "mode," with its Spinozistic resonances. The dispersion of *Dasein* (which Derrida as points out in "The Ends of Man" cannot be simply translated as "man") in terms of *Geschlecht*, its modes of being, "funds current racial and sexual economies," but "it also prevents their closure."[30]

A racial economy dominates and determines symbolic discourse no less than gender does, although psychoanalytic theory has obsessively focused on the latter to the exclusion of the former. Furthermore, western discourse functions with binary categories that figure non-Western others as opaque—as colored—while the epistemological categories remain transparent, assuming white as a generic term and a colorless color. The conquest of the New World by Europeans, and the involuntary importation of African slaves, created a complex situation of cultural contact that was not the same for all of the participants involved. As the historian of religions Charles H. Long explains, "opacity of vision forces the vanquished to come to terms in a concrete manner with what has happened to them," but opacity has not been seen, and has been disavowed, by the conquerors.[31] This occurs not merely at the level of political history, but also at the level of language, the effects of which we are still feeling. Long points to the possibility of religious language to signify a new myth, one that avoids the vicious signification of others that preserves racial power structures. To possess the resources for a renewal of religious meaning we must come to terms with American colonial and imperialistic history—not simply what happened in a literal sense, but the reality wrought by signification and the possibilities for liberation on the part of the oppressed.

In Lacanian terms, the Real would constitute the critique of symbolic, signifying categories and the shift toward an opacity of vision, an opacity that would not be clear and transparent, but one that would acknowledge the necessity of W. E. B. Dubois's double-consciousness. We have become aware that language is not innocent, and we feel the effects in our words, in our actions, and in our bodies, however we are dispersed, even if we would prefer to deny this awareness. We are told to "follow our leaders," even to death, and the symbolic question then becomes, who is a true leader? During the battle when the Americans board the Spanish ship, one of Delano's mates cries out: "follow your leader!"[32] This cry resembles other battle crys, such as "Remember the Alamo!" or "Let's roll!" However, we should recall Lacan's caution about the aspiration to revolution, or even to revenge: "What you, as revolutionaries, aspire to is a Master. You will have one."[33] Lacan is not referring to himself, but to our desire for a master or a leader.

Christopher Columbus, sailing under the flag bearing the colors of Spain, discovered a New World. Although it was heavily populated with indigenous inhabitants, most of them quickly were decimated by overwhelming epidemics. For a majority of the peoples of the American hemispheres, Columbus is our leader, for better or for worse. Charles Long asserts that we still have not assimilated or understood the effects of that enormous encounter, which is paradigmatic for his notion of cultural contact. The European colonists and their descendents found themselves unable, for the most part, to acknowledge the full humanity of Native Americans and African-Americans, and this denial continues to function—mostly invisibily—in nearly every discussion of national identity. Long claims that "the basic problems that confront us [the United States] as a nation today result from the fact that we have not taken the integrity of nature seriously. The exploitation of our natural resources and of blacks and other racial minorities stems from this fact."[34] What is signified as nature, as natural resource, or as close to nature becomes subject to exploitation. Today this means "follow your leaders and deny the full humanity of Arab Muslims while you exploit global hydrocarbon reserves at an unsustainable rate."

In the novel, Benito Cereno recounts how Babo

> showed him a skeleton, which had been substituted for the ship's proper figure-head, the image of Christopher Colon, the discoverer of the New World; that the negro Babo asked him whose skeleton it was, and whether, from its whiteness, he should not think it a white's; that, upon covering his face, the negro Babo, coming close, said words to the effect: "Keep faith with the blacks from here to Senegal, or you shall in spirit, as now in body, follow your leader," pointing to the prow.[35]

The skeleton is that of the original captain, Aranda, who was killed in the revolt.

Why not revolt? Under the brutal circumstances of the slave trade, who in their right mind would not resist and attempt to return to their homeland? The Spanish skeleton substitutes for the figure of Columbus, whose lead so many white Europeans followed to the New World, and in whose name so many Indians and Africans were tortured and killed. The racial imaginary permeates the entire story and calls for a return to the symbolic order of whiteness as the proper order, and furthermore testifies to the heroism of the white Captain Delano whose color is not explicitly remarked upon; nonetheless Melville's novel touches on the Real, even as it points beyond the border of a self-contained novel. For if whiteness functions as the invisible anchoring of the proper ordering of colors, this very revelation provides tools to think about the exposure of this relationship, and above all the confusion represented by the Spanish non-captain, Benito Cereno, who is colored in relation to Delano, but still not racialized to the extent of the blacks. One way to read *Benito Cereno* is to see how the novel renders opaque the character of Benito Cereno, even as this process becomes unbearable and drives him mad. At the same time, in another, more famous novel, Melville reveals the insane pursuit of a great white whale. The whale, Moby Dick, can be understood in a more conventional theological manner as the representation of God, whose single-minded pursuit is doomed to fail, but at the same time, pressured by *Benito Cereno*, *Moby Dick* represents an indictment of the desire for whiteness, and again renders the process opaque.

The Final Cut

Finally, how does it stand with the Real? Is not this discussion, or any discussion, still too symbolic in terms of its attempt to describe reality? At the heart of *Benito Cereno* occurs a bizarre event involving a knot. Captain Delano is musing about how whites are shrewder and smarter than blacks when he comes across an aged sailor: "his hands were full of ropes, which he was working into a large knot."

> Captain Delano crossed over to him, and stood in silence surveying the knot; his mind, by a not uncongenial transition, passed from his own entanglements to those of the hemp. For intricacy such a knot he had never seen in an American ship, or indeed any other. The man looked like an Egyptian priest, making Gordian knots for the temple of Ammon. The knot seemed a combination of double-bow-line-knot, treble-crown-knot, back-handed-well-knot, knot-in-and-out-knot, and jamming-knot.
> At last, puzzled to comprehend the meaning of such a knot, Captain Delano addressed the knotter: —
> "What are you knotting there, my man?"
> "The knot," was the brief reply, without looking up.
> "So it seems; but what is it for?"
> "For someone else to undo," muttered the old man, plying his fingers harder than ever, the knot being now nearly completed.
> While Captain Delano stood watching him, suddenly the old man threw the knot toward him, and said in English, — the first heard on the ship, — something to this effect — "Undo it, cut it, quick."[36]

As Captain Delano stands dumbfounded, an elderly African explains that it is a harmless trick, and the knot is confiscated and tossed overboard. This elliptic exchange, at the center of the novel, symbolizes the entire situation, which takes the form of an incredibly complex knot. The Spanish sailor tries to symbolically communicate the situation to Captain Delano but pleads with him to cut the knot to grasp the reality of what is occurring. The deferred resolution breaks in a flash of revelation and action when Benito Cereno leaps aboard his ship, followed by the murderous Babo. At the same time, further strands suggest that the novel cannot be so neatly resolved or tied up again by symbolic discourse.

Do we remain tied up, confused in tracing the lines of rope or string as they coil among and across each other? Do we patiently attempt to untie or unravel the distinct strands that constitute imaginary, symbolic, ethical, scientific, logical, and theological discourses? Or do we cut the knot and risk losing our minds, being snatched away into the Real? Or is there another set of knots, a net or web to catch us in a deeper symbolic discourse? Melville's novel dramatizes a great deal of what is at stake in Lacanian knot theory as it attempts to grapple with the Real that is constituted negatively in the formation of a signifier—the Real that is revealed in and through the limits of language.

The attempt to directly express the Real ties us up in knots, but the attempt to untie the knot is inevitably unsuccessful, which leaves cutting it as perhaps the only option. Cutting the knot to undo it, however, risks madness, or even unleashes it. A psycho-theological thinking traces the strands of these efforts and lines without disavowing the Real that is inexpressible, and without renouncing the necessity for symbolic understanding and articulation. Even if we can still communicate, perhaps we are always already cut, snatched by the Real, or in a state of desperate insanity, as the political implications of *Benito Cereno* suggest. Tying and untying, binding and unbinding. Is the constant reworking of the knot a repetition compulsion—a manifestation of the death drive? Tying and binding of knots is a form of sublimation, a making of meaning, and of course a common etymology of religion means to re-bind or to bind back. At the same time, the sublime refers to the unraveling of ties, to being loosed into the Real. Radical theology attends not simply to the tying but also to the untying, the fraying and the cutting of psychosocial knots that opens a window to the Real.

We do not only attempt to reveal the Real by untying its knots. We also produce the sense of the Real through a substantial process of thinking that is tied to the creation of a signifier *ex nihilo*, as described in chapter 7. In chapter 10 I argue that this is more of an

Aristotelian process than a Platonic process, and I trace a line of theoretical thinking about substance from Aristotle through Spinoza to Whitehead, Lacan, and Deleuze. Furthermore, I claim that these attempts to express and process the Real are intrinsically theological because they deal with what is ultimate in a Tillichian sense: being and nonbeing.

Processing the Real

Sub-stance

Introduction

In the last chapter I discussed Lacan's *Seminar XX* as an attempt to express the Real that lies at the limit of language. I acknowledged the broadly Platonic aspect of Lacan's thought, which becomes more explicit in the work of Alain Badiou. At the same time, my reading of *Benito Cereno* is also a critique of Badiou's Platonism, or at least an effort to complicate the limit of language in a profound way. In chapter 8 I discussed Lacan's critique of Aristotelian utilitarianism; that is, an understanding of Aristotle's *Nicomachean Ethics* that privileges goods, or the Good, especially as it relates to God in Anselm and in Marion. In this chapter I want to provide a different Aristotelian context for understanding Lacan by thinking about Lacan's understanding of the Real in relation to Aristotle's substance. To think about substance in Aristotle and Lacan, I will have to provide a detour though Spinoza, Whitehead, and Deleuze to show how what Aristotle calls substance is really a process, and this process is a dynamic production of the Real. The production of the Real is a Deleuzian insight, and I am reading Spinoza and Whitehead through Deleuze to relate them to Lacan. Finally, I will return to *Seminar XX* to show the convergence of substance, language, and the Real in what Lacan calls *lalangue*, which is the source of *par-être* (para-being), or what appears. This chapter provides a Deleuzian interpretation of Lacan that is Aristotelian in a broad sense.

One of the key insights of Lacan's thought is that substance is far less substantial than we think, and the more we try to grasp it, the more it slips away in our language and in our being. Furthermore, substance is not matter qua matter, as opposed to signification, but rather it is created in the creation of a signifier *ex nihilo*, as discussed in chapter 7. In *Metaphysics* Aristotle conflates the substance of nature with the essence of thinking in a Lacanian way when he writes, "Therefore, as in syllogisms, substance is the starting-point of everything. It is from 'what a thing is' that syllogisms start; and from it also we now find processes of production to start" (1034a).[1] The starting point of everything — nature and language — is called *lalangue* by Lacan in *Seminar XX*. Lalangue is a kind of protolanguage, and in this chapter I am understanding *lalangue* "as" what Aristotle calls substance, although filtered through Spinoza, Whitehead, and Deleuze. At the end of his career Lacan is relatively pessimistic about the possibilities of grasping *lalangue*, although he continues to expend incredible effort to express it. We are constantly caught up in our determinate language, and essentially we are being duped by *lalangue*. At the same time, giving Lacan a Deleuzian twist allows us to positively view the production of *par-être* out of *lalangue*, the creation of being out of a substance that is so insubstantial that it is practically nothing.

Aristotle's Substance

One of the most difficult problems in the history of philosophy involves coming to terms with what Aristotle means by substance. According to Aristotle, philosophy begins because "all men by nature desire to know" (980a). He proceeds from sensation to understanding to wisdom, and declares that First Philosophy (which is later called metaphysics because Andronicus of Rhodes placed this work after the *Physics* in the first systematic editorial arrangement of Aristotle's corpus) is knowledge of first principles. The "nature of Wisdom," then, deals with "that which is in the highest sense object of knowledge, the science of *substance*" (996b). At the beginning of Book IV, Aristotle claims that this science "investigates being as being" (1003a). Substance as the object of study of being as being provides Heidegger with his notion of ontological difference — the difference between being and beings. Heidegger translates *ousia* as "being," and, following Franz Brentano, focuses on the variety of ways "being" is said or determined in Aristotle's work.

The problem is that it should be self-evident what substance is, but to read Aristotle on substance is to open up all sorts of aporias. First of all, as an unqualified term, "being" has several meanings, or manifests in at least four ways in chapter 2 of Book VI (1026a). One meaning is the accidental—that which happens—and the accidental cannot be object of scientific study. The second is as truth in opposition to what is false (non-being), and Heidegger argues in his commentary on Book IX that this determination of being as truth is the culmination of Aristotle's thought.[2] The third meaning of being as being refers to the figures of predication, or being according to the categories of quality, quantity, time, place, etc. Finally, "there is that which 'is' potentially or actually," being as *dynamis* and *energeia* (1026b).

Despite Aristotle's claim that there should be one science of first principles that deals with substance, when he analyzes being as being he uncovers an irreducible multiplicity. Metaphysics may be a unified inquiry, but being itself is not simply one, and Aristotle spends a great deal of time criticizing the naive Platonists and Parmenideans who declare that being is One. Furthermore, in his discussion of what substance or *ousia* "is," Aristotle runs up against a number of difficulties because of his prior commitment to the distinction between matter and form.

Substance is most immediate and concrete; it is that of which other things are predicated, but it is not predicated of something else. In *Categories*, species are said to be substances in a secondary sense, but not a primary sense (2a). Genera are even more abstract and qualify less as substances than species (2b). But species and genera are terms of classification or predication, and they can still be applied to more primary substances, the best example of which Aristotle gives as the "individual man." How is a particular individual a substance, and how does he express or manifest being as being?

In Book XII Aristotle states that "there are three kinds of substance—the matter . . . ; the nature . . . ; and again, thirdly, the particular substance which is composed of these two" (1070a). Here the nature refers to the form, but it also functions as the end or telos of the thing. On the one hand, a particular thing is a composite of form and matter, which would exclude it from consideration as primary substance. On the other hand, Aristotle argues that substance is what is most indivisible, individual, and particular. Many commentators have argued about what Aristotle meant by substance, whether his ideas about substance changed from the *Categories* to the *Metaphysics*, and whether he associated substance more closely with matter or with form.[3]

According to my reading, Aristotle's commitment to the notion of formal essence, and its significance for definition, forces him to over-identify form with substance. Because of substance's indeterminate nature, Aristotle is constrained to dissociate matter, prime matter, and matter as substratum from primary substance (1029a). At the same time, he conflates the formal cause with the final cause, even though they are clearly distinguished in the presentation of the four causes in the *Physics* (Book II, chapter 3). In Book XII of *Metaphysics*, Aristotle associates the combination of matter and form with priva-tion: Aristotle identifies three principles—"the form, the privation, and the matter"—that make up substance (1070b). According to the discussion in the *Categories*, substance should consist of the unity of formed matter, but here their combination and their alterability imply motion, so they are contrasted to that which does not move or change—the prime mover. The prime mover or uncaused cause is Aristotle's classic and famous definition of God. But it follows only from Aristotle's prior commitment to form as telos, and it violates the logic and integrity of Aristotle's inquiry into substance throughout most of *Metaphysics*. The famous definition of God as prime mover follows Aristotle's overemphasis on form because form is understood as eternal and changeless, whereas formed matter is temporal and temporary. If God is defined as uncaused cause or unformed form, then God can also be defined as absolute substance, and this inter-pretation is also closer to the traditional understanding of substance in Spinoza.

In Book VII Aristotle reveals a privileging of being determined as predication when he asserts that "there is an essence only of those things whose formula is a definition" (1030a). He concludes that "definition and essence in the primary and simple sense belong only to substances" (1030b). That's fine, but to claim that a formula or definition applies primarily to substances does not mean that a sub-stance is primarily a form(ula), or that primary substance is formal essence, as Aristotle seems to assume, if only by default. Aristotle says that matter can be stripped away from the thing, but a thing and its essence are one: "clearly, then, each primary and self-subsistent thing is one and the same as its essence" (1032a). He asserts that "what we seek is the cause, i.e. the form, by reason of which the mat-ter is some definite thing; and this is the substance of the thing" (1041b). The overemphasis on form also drives Aristotle to privilege *energeia* (actuality) over *dynamis* (potentiality) because matter is distinguished as potential and form as actual (1045a). Potentiality is distinguished by the privation or not-being that exists at the center or an individual thing as composite of matter and form.

I am reading Aristotle against Aristotle to associate substance more with particular being and its potentiality, composed of form and matter, than to the formal essence. An emphasis upon the latter—the formal essence—is more in line with Plato's philosophy, whereas thinking about substance as empirical being is more empirical. At the same time, this empiricism is complicated precisely because the empirical being includes its potentiality as well as its actuality. Furthermore, substance also implicates the nature of our logic and thinking—the syllogism, for Aristotle—as well as the nature of what we think and know, and this is where Aristotle is profoundly related to Lacan. To more directly relate Aristotle to Lacan, however, I have to briefly consider Spinoza's thinking on substance, at least as read through Deleuze.

Spinoza's Substance—Deleuze

When Descartes establishes modern philosophy on the basis of the subject he is forced to posit a dualism between thinking beings and extended beings. In the wake of Cartesian dualism, Spinoza constructs an impressive system of thinking that tries to restore the unity of substantial being as well as simplify the complexity of Aristotelian substance, rendering it more consistent. Spinoza consistently undermines and overcomes Cartesian duality to fashion a consistent and coherent substance. In a way, Spinoza remains faithful to the notion of Aristotelian substance, but he extends it infinitely and equates it with God. His masterpiece, the *Ethics*, quickly establishes the proposition that there is only one substance, which is God or "absolutely infinite being." Referring to Definitions, Spinoza claims that attributes are what we can perceive and understand as essential to substance, although we cannot experience substance in itself without qualification. Finally, modes are "the affections of substance; that is, that which is in something else and is conceived through something else."[4] The two modes pertaining to human understanding are extension and thinking, or body and mind. These are not two substances but two modifications of one substance: "by 'body' I understand a mode that expresses in a definite and determinate way God's essence in so far as he is considered as an extended thing; . . . by idea I understand a conception of the Mind which the Mind forms because it is a thinking thing."[5] The human being is formed by the coincidence of these two modes, but this is not a dualistic composition.

According to Deleuze, Spinoza's thought possesses enormous contemporary significance. First of all, Spinoza for the first time establishes a plane of immanence that locates all of existence on the same level. This is a move against transcendence and its split-level universe. What is involved is "the laying out of a plane of immanence on which all bodies, all minds, and all individuals are situated."[6] Spinoza claims in Proposition 18 that "God is the immanent, not the transitive, cause of all things."[7] The project of *Ethics* is fundamentally an ethical one of clarity and understanding that leads to right action. Spinoza's confidence is that the intellect can adequately understand God—at least the essential attributes of God—and therefore can attain adequate knowledge of the mind and correctly control and express our passions. At the same time, body remains opaque, as Proposition 24 explains that "the human mind does not involve an adequate knowledge of the component parts of the human body."[8] The mode of body is opaque to thinking, although the mode of thinking is open to the advancement of the intellect all the way to an adequate and eternal intellectual love of God (*amor intellectualis dei*), which would determine the "highest good of those who pursue virtue . . . common to all, and all can equally enjoy it."[9] The problem of the opacity of the body is supposed to be overcome by a redoubling of our efforts at intellectual understanding and by emphasizing the mode that does deliver adequate and clear knowledge. On the other hand, and despite Lacan's love of Spinoza, what psychoanalysis represents is the idea that there is something within human thinking that resists adequate knowledge and insists on a fundamental opacity of mind in a parallel manner to Spinoza's insistence on the essential unclarity of our conceptions of body. This opacity of mind and of body can be connected with Charles H. Long's discussion of "theologies opaque," as mentioned in chapter 9. Long claims that "the opacity of God forms a discontinuity with the bad faith of the other theological modes."[10] Body, mind, and God are all marked by opacity, and this is not simply an opacity that will soon give way to clarity, but is a constant constraint on our thinking. Clarity may be the goal, but the more psychoanalytic conceptions and unconscious processes are scrutinized, the more obscure they become. This is why Long argues that "it is at this point that theologies opaque must become deconstructive theologies—that is to say, theologies that undertake the deconstruction of theology as a powerful mode of discourse."[11] To cross traditional theology with psychoanalytic theory from Freud to Lacan is to deconstruct theology as a powerful mode of discourse, which does not mean to do away with it or simply to replace it with another kind of discourse.

Along with Spinoza's insistence on immanence, there also occurs, according to Deleuze, a prescription for thinking that precludes analogy. In *Expressionism in Philosophy*, Deleuze claims that Spinoza belongs to "the great tradition of univocity," which includes a "constant struggle against the three notions of equivocation, eminence and analogy."[12] The key issue here is the distinction between properties and attributes. According to Deleuze, traditional theological discourse on the properties of God focuses attention solely on the properties themselves and delimits God from these considerations. "Revelation concerns, in truth, only certain *propria*. It in no way sets out to make known to us the divine nature and its attributes," to the extent that a theology of revelation cannot make known anything about the nature or essence of God.[13] On the other hand, philosophy and theology as expression "expresses an essence, that is, a nature of the infinitive; it makes it known to us."[14] Attributes in turn express themselves in modes, which in Deleuze's later language consists of a direct unfolding of expression(s). Substance articulates itself in terms of its attributes and expresses itself in modes, and this process occurs directly rather than by means of analogy. An analogy retains the equivocity of being that delimits God as transcendent but it anchors the revelation of God in the world in an absurd and unknowable way.

If Spinoza's language of adequacy is read according to the logic of analogy, then it is constrained by an analogical notion of representation because we have to have a pre-understanding of an idea to measure its similarity against. On the other hand, if "an adequate idea is seen to be an expressive idea," then there is no prior model that is inaccessible to representation but nonetheless functions to guarantee the adequacy of representation according to an impossible notion of resemblance. Expression is direct and univocal as well as immanent and knowable, although not completely or finally.[15] The limits of expression should not be thought of in terms of analogy because that presumes both too much and too little. As Hume discusses in Part 2 of his *Dialogues Concerning Natural Religion*, every analogy is also a dis-analogy. Hume states that "from similar effects we infer similar causes," but my question is, what is the process and nature of this inference?[16] Spinoza's thought provides for Deleuze a philosophical alternative to the problematic detour of analogy. In a similar way, I am suggesting that a theological thinking that defines itself in terms of expression rather than analogy is actually more powerful and provides more understanding (if not more clarity) about God despite the fact that this notion is counter-intuitive for many people.

The problem with theological analogy is not what we do not know, it is what we think we know, and the leap that is made from one to the other. If we substitute expression for analogy and locate concepts and things (rocks, porcupines, God, etc.) along a plane of immanence, this does not simply set up an equivalence among such phenomena. For Deleuze's philosophy of difference, identity occurs in becoming—a repetition of difference that expresses substance. These processes are opaque, but it is not that body is opaque and can be simply illuminated with thinking, or vice versa. Later, in *Anti-Oedipus*, which is critical of Lacanian structuralism, Deleuze abandons the language of expression because it is too idealistic and adopts a more productive understanding whereby desire produces or creates the Real. On the other hand, I read Lacan through Deleuze in this chapter and to some extent in this book, and I argue that Lacan does provide resources to view the production of the Real as a process of creation *ex nihilo*, which is a substantial process, at least in terms of the reading of Aristotle I am unfolding here. What Aristotle calls substance is more akin to what Deleuze calls a singularity because it refers to the "difference" within a thing that makes it what it is. This difference is in becoming; it is a process, which is why substance should be understood as a process, and this is how Whitehead re-writes Aristotle in *Process and Reality*.

Whitehead's Process

Spinoza makes Aristotelian substance more complete and more direct, even though its expression is always multiple; it possesses many attributes and can be said in many ways. Analogy is more properly Platonic. Although Alfred North Whitehead states in *Process and Reality* that "the safest general characterization of the European philosophical tradition is that it consists of a series of footnotes to Plato," in some ways his thought is better appreciated as a quasi-Aristotelian expression of the univocity of substance in its becoming.[17] Whitehead distinguishes his philosophy of organism from Spinoza's thought by avoidance of "the 'substance-quality' concept." At the same time, "Spinoza's 'modes' now become the sheer actualities," such that "morphological description is replaced by description of dynamic process."[18] Whitehead in fact subjects Spinoza's system to a powerful dynamicity by opening up the notion of substance and demonstrating its intrinsic becoming.

Whitehead elaborates what he calls a "categoreal" scheme to flesh out his justification of speculative philosophy. There are eight categories of existence, but two "stand out with a certain extreme finality": actual entities and eternal objects.[19] Actual entities, also called actual occasions, are "drops of experience, complex and interdependent," while eternal objects are explained in terms of Platonic forms of pure possibility: "any entity whose conceptual recognition does not involve a necessary reference to any definite actual entities of the temporal world is called an 'eternal object.'"[20] Again, the Platonic language is misleading because the important things are not the final entities or objects but the processes of prehension and concrescence that make them up. Whitehead's scientific/metaphysical language describes a world in process, where process is reality and reality is process. The danger is to mistake Whitehead for an atomistic thinker by focusing too much on the particular actual entities and eternal objects. This danger represents another form of what Whitehead terms "the fallacy of misplaced concreteness." We substantialize reality, substance, or being probably more than anything else, and we struggle to articulate a causal efficacy that would be distinct from presentational immediacy.

The concrescence of actual entities in their becoming eternal objects can be read as a twentieth-century *entelechia*, which is Aristotle's term for the dynamic embeddedness of the Platonic forms in matter. Aristotle usually denigrates potentiality (*dynamis*) in favor of actuality (*energeia*), but one result of twentieth-century thought is the reversal of Aristotle's opposition and a profound grappling with the importance of potentiality. Deleuze calls it virtual rather than potential to work free of Aristotle's subjection of potentiality, and sets up a relation between the virtual and the actual. Deleuze claims that the virtual "does not have to be realized, but rather actualized; and the rules of actualization are . . . those of difference or divergence and of creation."[21] In *Parables for the Virtual* Brian Massumi explains that "it is the edge of the virtual, where it leaks into actual, that counts. For that seeping edge is where potential, actually, is found."[22] It is the seeping edge as such that matters, not necessarily the conditions or the results. At the same time, the edge is not simply between immanence and transcendence but must be thought along a single plane or level.

In his book *The Fold*, Deleuze reads Leibniz through Whitehead to assemble a thinking that is neo-Baroque. Whitehead's thinking focuses on the question, "What is an event?" which is why he "stands provisionally as the last great Anglo-American philosopher before Wittgenstein's disciples spread their misty confusion, sufficiency and terror."[23] Deleuze claims that "prehension is individual unity," it is what allows subjective form, and yet Whitehead broadens the notions of feeling and subjective form to include the entire universe. Furthermore, every prehension "is a prehension of prehension, and the event thus a 'nexus of prehensions.'"[24] Since prehensions are fundamental events or occasions, eternal objects are better understood as virtualities than as Platonic forms. According to Deleuze, "eternal objects are pure Possibilities that are realized in fluvia, but also pure Virtualities that are actualized in prehensions."[25] Eternal objects "ingress" into the events: the actual occasions that manifest themselves. The main difference between Leibniz and Whitehead is that in Whitehead's thought God does not remain aloof from the world, regulating and harmonizing its possibilities. Rather, God "desists from being a Being who compares worlds and chooses the richest compossible. He becomes Process, a process that at once affirms incompossibles and passes through them."[26] *Compossable* means what is actually possible in terms of the various entities and occasions that exist in the world and how they fit together. For Leibniz, we live in the best possible world, meaning the best one that can actually exist including everything that exists in it, which is compossible; this is not necessarily the best imaginable world. Deleuze reads Whitehead as radicalizing Leibniz, such that God is processed through compossibilities and even incompossibilities.

As Whitehead puts it, "God is an actual entity, and so is the most trivial fluff of existence in far-off, empty space."[27] In *Process and Reality*, God is disjoined into primordial and consequent nature. As primordial nature, God is unconscious, Real, or what Tillich calls being-itself: "He is the lure for feeling, the eternal urge of desire."[28] God is also consequence of concrescence, the sense-making of the world related to a special kind of eternal object. Whitehead also calls God "the presupposed actuality of conceptual operation, in unison of be-coming with every other creative act."[29] This dipolar nature of God can be folded back into the initial category of the Ultimate, whose notions are called creativity, many, and one. Here is Whitehead's fa-mous pronouncement, "The many become one, and are increased by one."[30] That is, become many, again and again.

Whitehead and Deleuze are both skeptical of language and threat-ened by its ambiguity, its duplicity, and the danger of losing the richness of variegated experience. Whitehead uses scientific and psy-chological language, and he retains the quasi-linguistic propositional form, but he does not participate in the linguistic turn. In *The Tran-scendental Imagination* Charles Winquist uses Whitehead's philosophy to complement Heidegger's thought to explore the ontological sig-nificance of the Kantian transcendental imagination. At the same time, Winquist claims that "Whitehead's analysis of language is on the ontic level, and for this reason he tried to penetrate beyond lan-guage to its presuppositions."[31] Whitehead is not explicitly con-cerned with the ontological significance of propositions that possess value in terms of higher phases of experience. At the same time, he has to import highly discriminative meanings to describe the percep-tions of the external world.

Deleuze prefers signs and semiotics as indicators of sense and meaning to language, an obsession of many of his French contempo-raries that he views as limiting and narcissistic. At the same time, a linguistic ontology understood in its broadest sense as signification is compatible with the philosophies of Whitehead and Deleuze. The charge that language becomes a prison house, keeping the subject trapped inside while the world goes about its business outside, is a red herring. There is never a question of something outside of, or other than, language—an extra-linguistic reality. The problem is that we can never signify it directly without some form of signification as making sense, which is what Derrida means by saying that there is no simple "*hors-texte*," at least one that can be purely and simply in-voked. Language is warp and woof of reality, and this is the basis of Whitehead's creativity and of Deleuze's emphasis upon fiction or the powers of the false. The problem becomes the problem of representa-tion if language is thought to mediate reality. For Deleuze, and for Whitehead (at least implicitly), and by extension a certain Spinoza and a certain Aristotle, language does not mediate anything, but di-rectly expresses, actualizes, and becomes or concresces. Language is a mode of being of a substantial mode of reality; it is symbolic, and this is a more productive way to read Lacan. If there are other modes, they are not isomorphic on a split-level plane of correspondence, but true alternatives that manifest otherwise.

Lacan and the Being of Language

The question Badiou poses, "language or being?" is a false opposition, and we should refuse a forced choice. What Lacan drives us to think in *Seminar XX* is the inextricability of language and being under the terms *lalangue* and *par-être*. The difficulty is the stubborn persistence of what Whitehead calls the fallacy of misplaced concreteness, which substantializes our language into being or disembodies language by supposing that being is somewhere "out there." According to Lacan, "the language forged by philosophical discourse" is composed in such a way that "I cannot but constantly slip back into this world, into this presupposition of a substance that is permeated with the function of being."[32] At the basis of our determinate, structured languages lies *lalangue*, a sort of proto-linguistic stammering or stuttering that precedes symbolic discourse. *Lalangue* (which is translated into English with the cumbersome word *llanguage*,) is a primal language that lies at the base of all actual language. *Lalangue* "serves purposes that are altogether different from that of communication," (138). Language itself is made up of *lalangue*, which makes it stupid. According to Lacan, *lalangue* is "knowledge's hare-brained lucubration about language," (139). *Lalangue* is similar to what Deleuze calls delirium in *Anti-Oedipus* and elsewhere.

Language both reveals and conceals being, as Heidegger would say; or better, language gives being with and as itself, but this gift is always ambiguous and ambivalent. We can write language into a formalized, quasi-mathematical system, and we can presume a simple, immediate access to being, but either strategy exposes us to the risk of profound duplicity because we are always trying to write *lalangue* or write about being. "Isn't it thus true that language imposes being upon us and obliges us, as such, to admit that we never have anything by way of being?" (44). Or at least we never have the being we want to have, only a misplaced concreteness, since concreteness is misplaced and we can never set ideas down and have them remain where they are put.

Being does not stay put. It wanders around, as Aristotle supposed the woman's hysterical uterus did. Being leaks or takes flight, even if it alights. It appears as *par-être* or "para-being." According to Lacan, "what we must get used to is substituting the 'para-being'—the being 'para,' being beside—for the being that would take flight," (44). Substance is *lalangue*, which expresses itself as para-being. With substance we articulate a place, "the Other as the locus of truth," which is the place where God is created as an effect of symbolic discourse because God is presupposed to sustain any symbolic discourse. We are all theologians because "it is impossible to say anything without immediately making [God] subsist in the form of the Other," even if "only theologians can be truly atheistic, namely, those who speak of God," (45).

Following Freud and Lacan, any genuinely radical theological thinking must be atheistic; that is, it must accept the death of God or the break between all symbolic discourse about God and the Real. Theology expresses substance: the articulation of creative and substantial language that makes being appear beside itself as para-being. As I suggested in chapter 7, this is a contemporary version of the traditional theological doctrine of creation *ex nihilo*. Radical theology, which I called a psychotheology in the introduction, is informed by psychoanalytic insights from Freud to Lacan and Žižek, even as it adopts a Deleuzian or quasi-Aristotelian vision of an *entelechia* of substantial becoming—an expression of the sublime and not merely a sublimation. There is no outside of language in a simple spatial sense; or rather, the outside is already inside language as llanguage. The desire to resist and delimit the linguistic turn may evidence a conservative nostalgia for an immediate and simple being, while embracing a simplistic linguistic constructivism as the absolute freedom to create and bestow meanings is a dangerous fantasy. The genuine alternative is to open language, turn it inside out, and plumb its intersection with the Real, whether it is called substance, *lalangue*, being, or some other name.

Conclusion

Differences and distinctions are not necessarily oppositions. Three strands of French thought that are currently influential in terms of philosophy and cultural theory are often assigned the proper names Derrida, Deleuze, and Lacan.[33] Many English-speaking commentators and disciples play off one against the other(s): Derrida against Deleuze, Deleuze against Lacan, Lacan against Derrida, etc. These polemics are useful to understand the fine-grained distinctions at stake in their respective works, but they often become reduced to repetitive slogans and willful misreadings. If I have privileged Lacan and, to a lesser extent, Deleuze, in this book, this in part reflects a pragmatic intervention into contemporary religious thought and theology, where discussions of Derrida often predominate, but it should in no way be read as a rejection or dismissal of the significance of Derrida's thought. In fact we can envision a triangulation of Derrida, Deleuze, and Lacan beyond disciples and polemics in service to the production of creative theological thinking, or the creation of what Deleuze calls an image of thought. Here Deleuze, Derrida, and Lacan could occupy respectively the place of the imaginary, symbolic, and Real. The problem with constructing a narrative placing each of these thinkers, however, is that each one will not stay put, and they shift, switch, or rotate in relation to differential aspects of discourse. Now Derrida occupies the place of the Real, Deleuze affects a new symbolic, and Lacan's insights are completely imaginary. The important thing is to sustain the model of triangulation without collapsing it into two, which is the temptation and the danger, even in this book where just as Derrida is underrepresented, the role and site of the imaginary is downplayed to emphasize the confrontation between the symbolic and the Real and its importance for theological thinking. Writing substantial expression is psychotheological in nature and essence, and its attributes are multiple even if substance itself possesses an imaginary unity.

We live when and where we live, and if we are alive to living and to thinking, then the challenge is to create a theology responsive to the demands of the world, its sense and non-sense, while at the same time preserving an untimely tension in relation to that which is unnamable, unthinkable, unforeseeable, that which Derrida claims is always "to come."

When we think, when we act, when we write, we always have to do with works of love, and, as Freud and Lacan have taught us, love is uncanny and always involves transference and counter-transference. Reading and writing are broadly therapeutic, although not technically equivalent to clinical analysis. The practical questions of therapeutic and analytic technique are not divorced from the theoretical issues and implications of psychoanalytic theory, however pragmatically they can be distinguished for the purposes of postmodern religious theory and theological thinking. Love is at stake and at risk in all of our work, and the identifications we make are important, difficult, complex, and potentially dangerous.

The stable division of analyst and analysand cannot be sustained as theological thinking interrogates itself. We are called to respond and to be responsible, but not by a solitary voice; rather by and in a multitude or cacophony of voices, and we split off schizzes as we take up, one after another, problems, persons, concepts, questions, obligations, and assimilations. This means that we never achieve a unitary being, rendered as it were by effects of love and hate because there is always the potential for reversion of any passion into its opposite. If these simple oppositions (love and hate, analyst and analysand, inner and outer, nature and culture, language and reality, etc.) are deconstructed and continue to deconstruct themselves even as they maintain themselves in force precisely as they submit to deconstruction, then we lack purchase on any stable position from which to assess and apply such distinctions, implicated by and within them as we are. A psychotheology sustains itself in and as a theological pragmatics without thereby neutralizing the importance of language and its effects, including that of truth. Finally critique, affirmation, and neutrality also form a triangle—not quite a circle—more like a knot along which we crawl and slip in and out among symbolic, imaginary, and Real discourses in a passage of transferential love.

Conclusion

The problem of thinking is a problem of sublimation. To have language, meaning, and thereby religion, science, culture, and art, there must be sublimation in a broad sense. This book has traced some of the intricacies of sublimation through psychoanalytic theory as it impresses upon theology. Sublimation means that meaning is not direct and unmediated but consists of a detour. At the same time, my readings of theology, continental philosophy, and psychoanalytic theory suggest that sublimation is not an elevation above a material reality. In chapter 1, I appealed to Deleuze to question the two-level model of reality that sublimation often presumes. Sublimation is a detour through force or body, a displacement of force that produces an excess of force that constitutes meaning. This repetition does not occur on a higher plane of existence, and it does not deny material reality, at least according to my understanding of sublimation.

In chapter 2 I raised the topic of psychosis or schizophrenia to illustrate the incredible complication between words and things. Schizophrenia is the result of the attempt to refuse language and cling to the object itself—the Real—and this is not simply the result of an individual choice but also the result of a social and political situation. The metaphor of the black sun encapsulates the situation of schizophrenia because language is disoriented by the pull of a dark sun that distorts meaning. Furthermore, such distortion is theologically revealing. In some ways schizophrenia is the opposite of sublimation because it occurs when sublimation does not work, but it also functions as a possibility at the heart of language and sublimation. Chapter 3 proceeds into the ethics of psychoanalysis because desire is not simply the desire for objects within the compass of symbolic reality, but directly relates to what Lacan calls the Thing. The Thing represents the edge of language, where it touches the Real, and the Thing is sublime because it also disorients symbolic thinking, even as it orients it. The Thing possesses a quasi-schizophrenic intensity, holding onto the tension between the Real and the symbolic, making the desire for the Thing is a theological desire.

I return to the problem of psychosis in chapter 4, where the notion of foreclosure short circuits meaningful sublimation in a way. But I also appeal to Kristeva to develop an understanding of foreclosure that represents an artistic production. The foreclosure of God is similar to the foreclosure of Being in a Heideggerian sense, and both situations represent the challenge of responding to the refusal of Being or God to reveal themselves to humans. Kristeva's solution—a kind of aesthetic foreclosure of foreclosure, and a particular form of sublimation—constitutes a desperate psychoanalytic response to a general ontological or theological situation. So chapter 4 picks up on themes from chapter 2 and draws them out a little further in relation to the question of psychoanalytic and theological desire. Then chapter 5 attends to the anxiety that necessarily results from such a response. That is, to take on the task of generating aesthetic and theological meaning through the production of an icon, in light of the withdrawal of Being or the refusal of God to appear, is an enormous challenge fraught with risk.

Anxiety is not simply a result of the repression of desires threatening to the subject, but in some ways anxiety produces the subject. Anxiety generates an aesthetic subject that appears as cogito at the same time that it splits off a bodily remainder that takes the form of slime. Theological thinking is caught between two choices: to repress its own material form, its origin, and disavow the slime that is internal to it but is rejected as the body of God; or to attend to its own materiality, embodiment, and sliminess, which takes the form of a writing of the body of God. This writing is a theological production as well as an aesthetic production, as Kristeva suggested in chapter 4. What is the nature, and what are the stakes involved in the generation of meaning, which is an artistic and a theological project? Chapters 6 and 7 plunge deep into the abyss of creation *ex nihilo* by reading Schelling through both Tillich and Žižek. Chapter 6 focuses on Tillich's appropriation of Schelling for his theology and begins the task of unraveling Schelling's *Ages of the World* draft. Chapter 7 critically engages Žižek's important interpretation of Schelling and brings Tillich, Schelling, and Žižek together with a reading of Lacan on creation *ex nihilo*.

In addition to the specific readings of philosophers and theologians, chapter 7 is the fullest investigation into the question of the theological generation of meaning, which is a process of sublimation. In some ways chapters 6 and 7 constitute the center of the book because they incorporate nearly all of the theoretical issues involved, even though further clarifications of the concepts of God, the Real, and substance are deferred to later chapters. Creation involves the creation of a signifier, following Lacan, and this process of creation is theological because it implicates God and being as well as desire and meaning, and produces incredible anxiety. These chapters attempt to wrest significance out of the sublime depth of unconscious will, which is neither simply material nor simply immaterial, but is at once both and neither. Creation is a struggle for meaning that takes place out of nothing, or out of its own nothingness. Nothingness is not absolute, or *ouk on*, but relative nothingness, *me on*. Nothingness is already potentially pregnant with meaning, and that meaning takes the form of thought as well as body. The edge or limit of the representation of the source of that meaning is the sublime, but it can also be figured as God, Real, or substance.

Chapter 8 elaborates a thinking of God without being but also without conventional morality, following Lacan's reading in *The Ethics of Psychoanalysis*. I use Kant and Lacan to critique Jean-Luc Marion's understanding of *God Without Being*, and I also appeal to Edith Wyschogrod to provide an alternative reading of Anselm's famous proof of God's existence that counters Marion's. God is a name for the sublime, as is the Real, which is the subject of chapter 9. Here I turn toward Lacan's later thought as it appears in *Seminar XX* to think about how the Real traces the limits of language. For this discussion I appeal to a novella by Herman Melville to think about what it means to configure the Real in the form of a knot. Knots are important in mathematics, physics, and also as metaphors, and they express the Real in its intricate implication—one with political and theological effects. Another term that attempts to capture reality is substance, and substance is a word that refers to both reality (in a symbolic sense) and the sublime. The sublime traces the edge of symbolic reality, and substance—when thought of under the pressure of

Aristotle, Spinoza, Whitehead, Deleuze, and Lacan—becomes less substantial and more linguistic. Here substance is deeply linguistic, with depth serving as a metaphor for the link to the unconscious and the Real. Substance is sublime because the word "sublime" is a postmodern word that names the link between signification and what it signifies. The sublime is that which resists signification as well as makes it possible, and the sublime possesses both psychoanalytic and theological implications.

This book attempts to answer the question What happens to psychoanalysis and theology if you bring them together around an understanding of sublimation that dispenses with the notion of two hierarchical planes? That is, if spirituality is not layered on top of materiality, then sublimation becomes much more complex, and this reading, following Deleuze, Lacan, Žižek, Kristeva, and Derrida, possesses important theological implications. Sublimation concerns the attempt to generate meaning while recognizing that being is already shot through with language. Every iteration is a sublimation. But sublimation should not dispense with, forget, or disavow force, forces, or the physical play of bodies that both founds and resists language. The embodied source of sublimation is the sublime.

Sublimation is a creation, a creative force, and the creation of meaning. Creation is necessarily *ex nihilo*, as we saw in chapter 7. Creation *ex nihilo* is not the magic trick of making a world appear out of nothing on the part of an omnipotent God, but rather the generation of meaning out of what seems like nothing because it is materially insubstantial or incorporeal. At the same time, meaning always appears out of corporeality in a way, but still in material and physical existence. The relationship between language and materiality exceeds any simple relationship between inside and outside or container and contained.

Creation out of nothing always leaves a trace: some kind of bodily remainder. As I suggested in chapter 5, this remainder can take the form of slime. Most theologians prefer clean, well-lighted rooms to slimy messes. Theological thinking is creative thinking, just as for Deleuze and Guattari philosophy concerns the creation of concepts, but that does not mean one is free to simply invent whatever one wants idealistically or fantastically. Creation takes place under certain conditions, pressured by enormous restraints. This book works to create a psycho-theological thinking by working through dense texts and concepts. Theological thinking "works" best when it can operate under conditions of its own choosing, but I claim that it then sacrifices honesty and credibility. A radical theological thinking pressured by the insights of continental philosophy and psychoanalytic theory grapples with the Real in a non-idealistic way. To remain in the realm of sublimation and lose the connection with the sublime is to take cover in an idealism that forgets the insistence of the Real.

Sublimation follows the sublime. In this book I have written the Kantian sublime into Freud to grapple with the Freudian sublime as it is expressed by Lacan, Kristeva, and Žižek, and to show how it affects theological thinking. The sublime is the trace of the material in signification, the kernel of (meta)physical being that cannot be completely absorbed or represented in language, but that continues to exert distorting effects.

The sublime is religious because religion is what resists the attempts of philosophical representation, and this is the paradigmatic theoretical understanding of religion in the modern world. In Kant's *Critique of Judgment*, the sublime cannot be subsumed under the conceptual categories of the understanding, which leads ultimately to a crisis of reason that is both taken up and covered up by Romantic Idealism. What Freud's investigations into the nature of the unconscious demonstrate is that the sublime is not simply inert and passive, but actively resists representation, and that process of resistance generates significant effects. Furthermore, what a structuralist-inspired psychoanalysis discovers is that the unconscious and the sublime are not objects or entities—they are processes. They are substantial processes, according to the logic of substance I develop in chapter 10, and they are also dynamic—that is, post-structural.

The sublime is the motor of sublimation; it is what drives the process of sublimation. The sublime is religious, and therefore the interpretation of the process of sublimation is a theological interpretation. Here theology is understood in an extremely broad sense. According to Tillich, theology is second-order reflection upon religious experience. Furthermore, theology is ultimate concern: it concerns our being and non-being. Freed from dogma and unharnessed from any positive revelation, theology becomes a powerful interrogative force for asking urgent and important questions. Most theologians are conservative, whether they desire to be or not. They contain and constrain the force of theological questioning and delimit the world to make it conform to a pre-established vision, truth, or faith-commitment. Most radical theorists dispense with and despise theology, and perhaps rightly so, because they cannot see the subliminal edge that inhabits the underside of theological expression. Here psychoanalytic theory becomes a powerful tool to intervene into traditional theological discourse as well as a creative resource for a truly open and visionary theological thinking. In and around the interstices of the sublime, I have assembled fragments for a psychotheology that avoids hypostatizing or idealizing the psyche.

Theology shares with psychoanalysis (and philosophy) a dual nature. On the one hand, analysis and thinking are critical, interrogative, and unsettling. They radically upset our established truths and confront us with difficult and disturbing realities. On the other hand, there is a therapeutic task for analysis as well as theory, and perhaps this therapeutic or pastoral aspect is overdetermined in theology. Theologies are supposed to help, to do good, to edify. The Buddha reportedly said that some questions tend not to edification. This is undoubtedly the case, but how do we know which questions edify and which do not prior to asking them? And if we ask them, and they are not edifying, do we have the option of simply un-asking them? Furthermore, how do we know what is edifying if more than conscious intentionality is at issue? Edifying for whom, or for what? Do we really know what we desire? As Žižek suggests, and as I mentioned in the introduction, do we really want to know the truth about our desires?

The Thing, the Other, the Real—these are theological concepts because in psychoanalytic theory they implicate what we understand by divinity, even though they are not simply equivalent to God. By exfoliating and unfolding these conceptions as they occur in psychoanalytic, philosophical, and theological texts, we can gain better purchase on the nature and stakes of postmodern sublimation. Our postmodern world is a profoundly religious world, and this is becoming clearer and more undeniable by the day, for better or for worse. Psychoanalysis and theology both attend to desire and its complexity. We yearn for truth, justice, simplicity, and the good in an unevenly globalized world marked by confusion, conflict, and brutality. Perhaps we really desire power and wealth, and perhaps our ethical desires simply mask this fact. Or perhaps we genuinely and sincerely desire both. Perhaps we will destroy ourselves, and create our own religio-secular Armageddon.

What good is thinking for? We do not know, even if we may hope. This book is a missive: a prayer to hope that one's thought makes a difference for the better, however that may be understood or measured. Our world is *en procès*, on trial, as Kristeva writes about the subject. Psychoanalytic truths are not evaluated and assimilated for their scientific validity, but for their ability to open up ideas, bodies, and texts like abysses for pragmatic operations.

God is dead, even if belief in God is back, which means that everything is questionable. Radical theology is free to ask questions, unanchored by a grounding in a substantial God. Even substance is not substantial. Questions swirl, spiral, and intertwine. Sublimation means making meaning. The sublime both gives meaning to language and resists meaning. The sublime is the source of sublimation.

Dark forces are at work. Illumination is partial, at best.

Notes

Introduction

1. Kathleen Biddick, *The Typological Imaginary: Circumcision, Technology, History* (Philadelphia: University of Pennsylvania Press, 2003), 95.

2. A re-reading of the Wolf Man case should also attend to its explicit religious significance, since the Wolf Man imagines himself as Christ to make sense of his imagined sufferings at the hands of his father, who is of course God the Father. Freud states that he found "an incomparable sublimation . . . in the story of the Passion of Christ." In Sigmund Freud, *Three Case Histories*, ed. Philip Rieff (New York: Macmillan, 1963), 309.

3. Tomoko Masuzawa, *In Search of Dreamtime: The Quest for the Origin of Religion* (Chicago: University of Chicago Press, 1993), 170.

4. Sigmund Freud, *Moses and Monotheism*, trans. Katherine Jones (New York: Vintage Books, 1967), 112.

5. Ibid., 116–17.

6. Ibid., 114.

7. Andrew Shanks, *God and Modernity: A New and Better Way to Do Theology* (New York: Routledge, 2000), 111. Despite some good insights and suggestions, the book does not necessarily live up to the promise of its subtitle.

8. Carl Raschke, *Deconstruction and Theology*, Thomas J. J. Altizer et al. (New York: Crossroad, 1982), 27.

9. See Mark C. Taylor, *Erring: A Postmodern A/theology* (Chicago: University of Chicago Press, 1984).

10. See Charles E. Winquist, *Epiphanies of Darkness: Deconstruction in Theology* (Aurora, Colo: Davies Group, 1999).

11. Charles E. Winquist, *Desiring Theology* (Chicago: University of Chicago Press, 1995), ix.

12. Phillip Blond, introduction, *Post-Secular Philosophy*, ed. Phillip Blond (London: Routledge, 1998), 45.

13. See John D. Caputo, *The Prayers and Tears of Jacques Derrida: Religion without Religion* (Bloomington: Indiana University Press, 1997). More recently, however, Caputo has come out of the closet as a theologian. See *The Weakness of God: A Theology of the Event* (Bloomington: Indiana University Press, 2006). I celebrate this event, and argue that by embracing his role as a theologian, Caputo possesses better resources to intervene in important religious and theological debates, even though his theology, while Derridean, is not explicitly informed by psychoanalysis.

14. See, for example, Merold Westphal, ed., *Postmodern Philosophy and Christian Thought* (Bloomington: Indiana University Press, 1999).

15. See Gianni Vattimo's formulation, *"credere di credere,"* or "belief in belief," an affirmation of belief in itself without subscribing to any particular beliefs. This phrase is compressed in the title of the English translation, *Belief*, trans. Luca D'Isanto (Stanford: Stanford University Press, 1999).

16. In *Prayers and Tears*, Caputo provides a careful reading of many of Derrida's later works, including *Archive Fever: A Freudian Impression*, but he focuses mainly on Yosef Hayim Yerushalmi's discussion of Freud's Jewish identity, and does not consider Freud's deep and continuing influence on Derrida's thought. See "Is Deconstruction Really a Jewish Science?" 263–80.

17. Diane Michelfelder and Richard E. Palmer, eds., *Dialogue and Deconstruction: The Gadamer-Derrida Encounter* (New York: SUNY Press, 1989), 53.

18. Ibid., 56.

19. See Paul Ricoeur, *Freud and Philosophy: An Essay on Interpretation*, trans. Denis Savage (New Haven: Yale University Press, 1970).

20. At the same time, this book does not adopt a position of orthodoxy in regard to Freudian or Lacanian psychoanalysis, in terms of their ideas or their conclusions. In her biography of Lacan, Elizabeth Roudinesco talks about the secularization of Lacan's thought in philosophical and academic discourse, as opposed to "the psychoanalytic movement itself," in which "Lacan's work is treated as if it were holy writ." Elizabeth Roudinesco, *Jacques Lacan*, trans. Barbara Bray (New York: Columbia University Press, 1997), 435. My perspective is explicitly aligned with the former orientation. and has no intention of simply reducing the phenomenon of religion to basic physical drives, or explaining it according to a literal, "scientific," psychoanalytic explanation.

21. See Clayton Crockett, *A Theology of the Sublime* (New York: Routledge, 2001).

22. See ibid., 459–493. At the same time, Ricoeur cautions that "the danger for the philosopher . . . is to arrive too quickly, to lose the tension, to become dissipated in the symbolic richness, in the abundance of meaning" (495).

23. Biddick, *The Typological Imaginary*, 82. Biddick cites Mladen Dolar's essay in *Gaze and Voice as Love Objects*, ed. Renata Selacl and Slavoj Žižek (Durham: Duke University Press, 1996). At the same time as she complicates the periodization of psychoanalysis and its association with modernity by reading Kant along with Moses Mendelssohn.

24. Immanuel Kant, *Critique of Judgment*, trans. Werner Pluhar (Indianapolis: Hackett, 1987), 103–23.

25. See Jacques Lacan, *The Seminar of Jacques Lacan Book III: The Psychoses*, ed. Jacques-Alain Miller, trans. Russell Grigg (New York: Norton, 1993), 268.

26. See Alain Badiou, *Being and Event*, trans. Oliver Feltham (London: Continuum, 2006).

27. See Thomas J. J. Altizer, *The Gospel of Christian Atheism* (Philadelphia: Westminster Press, 1966).

28. Winquist, *Epiphanies of Darkness*, xvi.

29. See Robyn Ferrell, *Passion in Theory: Conceptions of Freud and Lacan* (New York: Routledge, 1996).

30. Ibid., 98–99.

31. Eric Santner, *The Psychotheology of Everyday Life* (Chicago: University of Chicago Press, 2001), 8.

32. Ibid., 8.

33. Slavoj Žižek: *Organs without Bodies: On Deleuze and Consequences* (New York: Routledge, 2004), 128.

34. Ibid., 9.

1. On Sublimation: The Significance of Psychoanalysis for the Study of Religion

1. An example of principled hostility to psychoanalysis occurs in Edith Wyschogrod's book, *An Ethics of Remembering: History, Heterology and the Nameless Others* (Chicago: University of Chicago Press, 1997). Wyschogrod skillfully grapples with complex issues of historical understanding and interpretation and their irreducible ethical resonances, but she disqualifies psychoanalytic explanations from the purview of the heterological historian. "The psychoanalytic interpretation of text, image, artifact, or living witness is, in this view," she writes, "always already an act of violence that sublates the other's alterity" (208). Although psychoanalytic interrogation is fraught with risk, so is interpretation in general. Any attribution of meaning or significance risks sublating the alterity of the other that performs the historical action or event. In fact, Wyschogrod's two indispensable moments of historical interpretation could apply to psychoanalytic interpretation. A heterological psychoanalysis can be envisioned which would be both metonymical—an explanation of an event may be undecidable among certain alternatives ("it could have been w, x, or y")—and also deictic—certain interpretations may be excluded ("it could not have been z").

2. Sigmund Freud, *Civilization and Its Discontents*, trans. James Strachey (New York: Norton, 1961), 15.

3. Ibid., 20.

4. Ibid., 29–30.

5. Ibid., 30.

6. James J. DiCenso, *The Other Freud: Religion, Culture and Psychoanalysis* (London: Routledge, 1999), 41.

7. Ibid., 108.

8. See Jacques-Alain Miller, "An Introduction to Seminars I and II: Lacan's Orientation Prior to 1953 (II)," in *Reading Seminars I and II: Lacan's Return to Freud*, ed. Richard Feldstein, Bruce Fink, and Maire Janus (Albany: SUNY Press, 1996), 15–25, 19.

9. Paul Ricoeur, *Freud and Philosophy: An Essay on Interpretation*, trans. Denis Savage (New Haven: Yale University Press, 1970), 149.

10. Ibid., 19.

11. Ibid., 495. Ricoeur's opposition derives from Hegel's famous discussion of force and understanding in the *Phenomenology of Spirit*. See G. W. F. Hegel, *Phenomenology of Spirit*, trans. A. V. Miller (Oxford: Oxford University Press, 1977), A, III, 79–103.

12. Ibid., 497.

13. See Friedrich Nietzsche, *On the Genealogy of Morals*, trans. Walter Kaufmann (New York: Vintage Books, 1967), 160–63.

14. Sigmund Freud, "The Unconscious," in *General Psychological Theory*, ed. Philip Rieff (New York: Macmillan, 1963), 116.

15. Freud, "Instincts and Their Vicissitudes," in *General Psychological Theory*, 81.

16. Ibid., 87–88.

17. Ibid., 91.

18. Jacques Lacan, *Écrits*, trans. Bruce Fink (New York: Norton, 2006), 225.

19. Freud, "The Unconscious," 150.

20. Ibid., 149–50.

21. Freud, "Repression," *General Psychological Theory*, 126.

22. Ibid., 127.

23. Ricoeur, *Freud and Philosophy*, 135.

24. Freud, "Repression," 126.

25. Ricoeur, *Freud and Philosophy*, 144.

26. Ibid., 149.

27. Ibid., 492, 497–98.

28. DiCenso, *The Other Freud*, 95.

29. Gilles Deleuze, *Difference and Repetition*, trans. Paul Patton (New York: Columbia University Press, 1994), 105.

30. Ibid., 103–4.

31. Ibid., 104.

32. Brian Massumi, *Parables for the Virtual: Movement, Affect, Sensation* (Durham, N.C.: Duke University Press, 2002), 35.

33. See Charles H. Long, *Significations: Signs, Symbols and Images in the Interpretation of Religion* (Aurora, Colo.: Davies Group, 1999).

34. See Jean-Luc Marion, "Descartes and Onto-theology," in *Post-Secular Philosophy*, ed. Phillip Blond, trans. Bettina Bergo (London: Routledge, 1998), 82.

35. Blond, "Introduction," *Post-Secular Philosophy*, 15.

36. See my reading of the Kantian sublime in Clayton Crockett, *A Theology of the Sublime*. See also Jean-François Lyotard, *Lessons on the Analytic of the Sublime*, trans. Elizabeth Rottenberg (Stanford: Stanford University Press, 1994); and Gilles Deleuze, *Kant's Critical Philosophy*, trans. Hugh Tomlinson and Barbara Habberjam (Minneapolis: University of Minnesota Press, 1984).

37. Immanuel Kant, *Critique of Judgment*, 115.

38. Blond, introduction, in *Post-Secular Philosophy*, 15.

39. Kant, *Critique of Judgment*, 106.

40. Sigmund Freud, "The Uncanny," in *The Standard Edition of the Complete Psychological Works*, ed. James Strachey (London: Hogarth Press, 1955), 17:238.

41. Jacques Lacan, *The Four Fundamental Concepts of Psychoanalysis*, trans. Alan Sheridan (New York: Norton, 1977), 58.

42. Ibid., 275. See also my discussion of Spinoza in chapter 10.

2. **We Are All Mad: Theology in the Shadow of a Black Sun**

1. In the context of understanding schizophrenia as a medical and cultural condition, see the critique of the psychiatric establishment by Thomas Szasz, *Schizophrenia: The Sacred Symbol of Psychiatry* (Syracuse: Syracuse University Press, 1976).

2. See Freud, *Standard Edition* vol. 12; and Daniel Paul Schreber, *Memoirs of My Nervous Illness*, trans. Ida MacAlpine and Richard A. Hunter (Cambridge, Mass.: Harvard University Press, 1955).

3. Freud, *Standard Edition*, 12:20.

4. Ibid., 50–51.

5. According to Vincent Crapanzano, Schreber's account is not simply a psychological problem but more importantly a "hermeneutical problem" whose main elements are communicative and discursive. For Crapanzano, Schreber represents a dramatic case of "interlocutory collapse," which is ultimately based on a confounding of "representation and experience." See Vincent Crapanzano, "'Lacking Now Is Only The Leading Idea, That Is — We, the Rays, Have No Thoughts': Interlocutory Collapse in Daniel Paul Schreber's *Memoirs of My Nervous Illness*," *Critical Inquiry* 24 (Spring 1998): 737–67 (quotes 743, 749). Crapanzano criticizes Freud, but ends up with a

quasi-Lacanian interpretation because he argues that Schreber is unable to negotiate a proper relationship with the law. The difficulty is that Schreber's mental illness is seen primarily from the standpoint of individual responsibility.

6. Lacan, *Écrits*, 470. For a more extended discussion of the Freudian term *Verwerfung*, which is significant for both Lacan and Julia Kristeva, see chapter 4. The Lacanian term, "Name-of-the-Father," or *nom du pere*, designates the symbolic order, which is also the realm of the Law. Lacan follows Freud's myth of the primal horde in asserting that it is the authority of the dead father that authorizes and upholds the realm of symbolic and social (conscious) discourse.

7. Freud, *Standard Edition*, 12:22.

8. Ibid.

9. Ibid., 12:20.

10. Freud, "The Unconscious," *General Psychological Theory*, ed. Philip Rieff (New York: Macmillan, 1963), 143.

11. Ibid., 12:144.

12. See also Sander L. Gilman, *Freud, Race and Gender* (Princeton: Princeton University Press, 1993), for a critique of Freud's study of Schreber that under-emphasizes the anti-Semitic aspects of Schreber's writings in favor of a consideration of sexuality and Schreber's homosexuality in relation to his father. Gilman says that "Freud's reading of this most complicated text ignores all of Schreber's 'homosexuality,' his delusion of castration and of being transformed into a woman" (161).

13. Freud, *General Psychological Theory*, 145.

14. Ibid., 146.

15. Ibid., 147.

16. Ibid., 147, 149.

17. Ibid., 149–50. Another dimension must also be considered, which is vision, although that raises extremely important theoretical questions that I do not take up here. Apparently there is no such thing as a blind schizophrenic. Mark Pendergrast explains in *Mirror Mirror: A History of the Human Love Affair with Reflection* (New York: Basic Books, 2003) that "in the single known case where a long-term schizophrenic went blind, she went into remission within a few days" (360). The function of the gaze is also crucial, and it intersects the split between word and thing. For Freud, the act of looking at male and female genitalia is at the basis of the neurosis of the castration complex. The rays of Schreber can also be compared to the solar metaphors at the end of this chapter.

18. See Louis A. Sass, *The Paradoxes of Delusion: Wittgenstein, Schreber, and the Schizophrenic Mind* (Ithaca: Cornell University Press, 1994), for an intriguing comparison of schizophrenia with philosophical solipsism, or absolute idealism. Sass, like Crapanzano, claims that Schreber's fantasies are

ultimately epistemological rather than psychological, which is a critique of Freud. Following Ricoeur's *Freud and Philosophy*, I am trying to show that Freud's writings are profoundly epistemological, and that such issues are not exclusive of psychological or libidinal understandings. Sass isolates the problem of solipsistic schizophrenia and overlooks its entrenchment in all philosophy, not merely in Wittgenstein's thought.

19. Julia Kristeva, "The True-Real," in *The Kristeva Reader*, ed. Toril Moi (New York: Columbia University Press, 1986), 218.

20. Ibid., 227.

21. Ibid., 230.

22. See Julia Kristeva, *Revolution in Poetic Language*, trans. Margaret Waller (New York: Columbia University Press, 1984), 37, 43–45.

23. See R. D. Laing, *The Divided Self: An Existential Study in Sanity and Madness* (New York: Penguin Books, 1990 [1959]), passim.

24. Ibid., 194. He writes of her earlier situation, "Julie's shreds of sanity at this stage depended on the possibility of being able to lodge some bad in her actual mother. The impossibility of doing this, in a sane way, was one of the factors that contributed to a schizophrenic psychosis."

25. A similar crossing of neurotic and psychotic categories is Kristeva's use of the image of black sun as the title of her powerful book on depression, which is classically considered a neurotic illness. For Kristeva, the depressed narcissist mourns not simply an object, but rather a Heideggerian Thing, and she petitions Nerval's "dazzling metaphor . . . the Thing is an imagined sun, bright and black at the same time." Julia Kristeva, *Black Sun: Depression and Melancholia*, trans. Leon S. Roudiez (New York: Columbia University Press, 1989), 13. This loss of the real Thing, which gleams darkly, necessitates symbolic substitutions and sublimatory solutions that act as lucid counterdepressants.

26. Laing, *The Divided Self*, 196–97.

27. In my petition of an adequation of language to experience, I do not presuppose a standard of experience to which such a schizophrenic language would be adequate. In fact, the adequation is created along with the language, and even the meaning or value of experience is constructed by the creation of a language. Adequacy is merely a heuristic criterion applied after the fact; it is not "adequate" or enough, but it is all we have to evaluate. See Jacques Derrida's critique of Lacan's notion of truth as adequation, "Le Facteur de la Vérité," in *The Post Card: From Socrates to Freud and Beyond*, trans. Alan Bass (Chicago: University of Chicago Press, 1987), 413–96.

28. Friedrich Nietzsche, preface, in *The Genealogy of Morals*, trans. Francis Golfing (New York: Anchor Books, 1956), i.

29. Laing, *The Divided Self*, 203.

30. Ibid., 204.

31. Ibid.

32. Ibid.

33. Gilles Deleuze and Félix Guattari, *Anti-Oedipus: Capitalism and Schizophrenia*, trans. Robert Hurley, Mark Seem and Helen R. Lane (Minneapolis: University of Minnesota Press, 1983), 57.

34. Antonin Artaud, *Antonin Artaud, Selected Writings*, ed. Susan Sontag (New York: Farrar, Straus and Giroux, 1976), 555–71.

35. Ibid., 558–59.

36. One could argue, of course, that I am being reductive, by reducing the reality of external events and referents to language, but only if one possesses an extremely narrow and settled view of language, which I am trying to open up. The question of language is a question of intelligibility, and to simply impose our pre-established models of intelligibility upon other speakers raises tangled moral and political issues. How can we presume that we know the structure of intentionality of another culture, for example, when we bracket the question of the referent of that intention? If respect for others and openness to alterity are taken seriously rather than merely paraded like slogans, we must ask about alternative propositional and linguistic structures and anti-structures, rather than merely about different referents which are then viewed as literally absurd when judged by our experience. And I do not simply view the use of the term "we" in the last few sentences as in any way unproblematic.

37. Freud, *General Psychological Theory*, 147.

38. Jacques Derrida, *Margins of Philosophy*, trans. Alan Bass (Chicago: University of Chicago Press, 1982), 243.

39. Ibid., 243–44. Note also the affinity with Kantian language of the sublimity of "the starry heavens above me and the moral law within me," in Immanuel Kant, *Critique of Practical Reason*, trans. Lewis White Beck (New Jersey: Prentice Hall, 1993), 169. Kant, who as an astrophysicist helped to "discover" the Milky Way, also describes his theoretical work in the *Critique of Pure Reason* as a "Copernican revolution," in which objects conform to human understanding rather than vice versa. Once again, what is the epistemic status of such usage of language, here in a cosmological guise?

40. Derrida, *Margins of Philosophy*, 270.

41. Ibid., 271.

42. See Sigmund Freud, *The Interpretation of Dreams*, trans. James Strachey (New York: Avon Books, 1965), 311–12.

43. See Derrida, *The Post Card*, 480–83.

44. Derrida, *Margins of Philosophy*, 255.

45. Ibid., 235.

3. **Desiring the Thing: The Ethics of Psychoanalysis**

1. Jacques Lacan, *Écrits: A Selection*, trans. Alan Sheridan (New York: Norton, 1977), 129.

2. For resources on Lacan, in addition to the recent English translation of the entire *Écrits* by Bruce Fink (New York: Norton, 2006) and the seminars translated and cited in this book, major secondary sources available in English include John Muller and William Richardson, *Lacan and Language: A Reader's Guide to Écrits* (International Universities Press, 1994); Anika Lemaire, *Jacques Lacan*, trans. David Macey (London: Routledge, 1979); Elizabeth Roudinesco, *Jacques Lacan*, trans. Barbara Bray (New York: Columbia University Press, 1997); *Reading Seminars I and II*, ed. Bruce Fink, et. al. (New York: SUNY Press, 1995); *Reading Seminar XI*, ed. Richard Feldstein, et. al. (New York: SUNY Press, 1995); and *Reading Seminar XX*, ed. Suzanne Barnard and Bruce Fink (New York: SUNY Press, 2002); as well as the series *Lacanian Ink*, nos. 1–24/25.

3. Mark C. Taylor, *Hiding* (Chicago: University of Chicago Press, 1997), 54.

4. Jacques Lacan, *The Ethics of Psychoanalysis*, trans. Dennis Potter, *Book VII: The Seminar of Jacques Lacan*, ed. Jacques-Alain Miller (New York: Norton, 1992), 54.

5. Bruce Fink, "The Subject and the Other's Desire," in *Reading Lacan's Seminars I and II: Lacan's Return to Freud*, 76–77. See also Jacques Lacan, *The Four Fundamental Concepts of Psycho-Analysis*, trans. Alan Sheridan, ed. Jacques-Alain Miller (New York: Norton, 1977), 210–12.

6. Lacan, *Ethics*, 70.

7. See Ibid., 188–203, as well as Jacques Lacan, "Kant With Sade," *Écrits*, 645–668.

8. See John D. Caputo, *The Prayers and Tears of Jacques Derrida: Religion Without Religion* (Bloomington: Indiana University Press, 1997); Edith Wyschogrod, *An Ethics of Remembering: History, Heterology, and the Nameless Others* (Chicago: University of Chicago Press, 1998); and Wendy Farley, *Eros for the Other: Retaining Truth in a Pluralistic World* (University Park: Pennsylvania State University Press, 1996).

9. Caputo, *Prayers and Tears*, 52.

10. See Lacan, *Four Fundamental Concepts*, 235–36.

11. Jacques Lacan, "On Freud's '*Treib*' and the Psychoanalyst's Desire," in *Reading Seminars I and II*, 417–21: "desire comes from the Other, and jouissance is on the side of the Thing" (419).

12. Lacan, *Ethics*, 177.

13. Ibid., 177.

14. See Julia Kristeva, *Revolution in Poetic Language*, trans. Margaret Waller (New York: Columbia University Press, 1984) and *Powers of Horror: An Essay on Abjection*, trans. Leon S. Roudiez (New York: Columbia University Press, 1982).

15. See Gilles Deleuze, *Difference and Repetition*, trans. Paul Patton (New York: Columbia University Press), 239: "Difference is a matter of degree only within the extensity in which it is explicated; it is a matter of kind only with regard to the quality which covers it within that extensity—beneath

the two lies the entire nature of difference — in other words, the intensive. Differences of degree are only the lowest degree of difference, and differences in kind are the highest form of difference."

16. Ibid., 106.

17. Lacan, *Ethics*, 118.

18. Ibid., 126. Lacan's use of religious language in this section is striking, not because it reveals a religious allegiance, but because it affirms the necessity of understanding religion and religious ideas in interpreting creation, reality, signification, etc. Lacan affirms that "God is dead," but he also asserts that "you cannot think, noone can think, except in creationist terms."

19. Ibid., 282. Antigone's rejection becomes the basis of Kristeva's concept of rejection in *Revolution in Poetic Language*. See 147–64.

20. Ibid., 281.

21. Ibid., 314.

22. See Gilles Deleuze, *Bergsonism*, trans. High Tomlinson and Barbara Habberjam (New York: Zone Books, 1991), 109–11, where he discusses the small intercerebral interval between intelligence as individual egoism and quasi-instinctive social pressure which he calls, following Bergson, creative emotion.

23. See Alfred North Whitehead, *Process and Reality* (New York: Free Press, 1978), 29.

24. Daniel Keyes, *Flowers for Algernon*, (New York: Bantam Books, 1966), 197.

4. Foreclosing God: Heidegger, Lacan, and Kristeva

1. Too much has been made of Heidegger's elliptical statements that if he were to write a theology, he would not use the word "being," and his claim that "faith has no need for the thinking of Being," as if Heidegger were not already deeply theological in his thinking. In fact Heidegger has so severely problematized thinking Being itself that one cannot help understanding Being along the same lines as God, even if God does not possess Being and Being is not divine. The issue is the radical inaccessibility of each, which is perhaps most closely and explicitly related in the *Beiträge*. On Heidegger and Being in relation or nonrelation to God, see Jacques Derrida, "How to Avoid Speaking: Denials," trans. Ken Frieden, in *Derrida and Negative Theology*, ed. Harold Coward and Toby Foshay (Albany: SUNY Press, 1992), 73–142 (Heidegger quote 127).

2. See Martin Heidegger, *Contributions to Philosophy (From Enowning)*, trans. Parvis Emad and Kenneth Maly (Bloomington: Indiana University Press, 1999), 285–93. Emad and Maly translate the crucial term *Ereignis*, which means "event of appropriation" or "appropriating event" as "enowning."

3. Ibid., 57.

4. Ibid., 285.

5. See Martin Heidegger, *Discourse on Thinking*, trans. J. M. Anderson and E. H. Freund (New York: Harper and Row: 1966), 61. See also Reiner Schürmann's influential interpretation, *Heidegger on Being and Acting: From Principles to Anarchy*, trans. Christine-Marie Gros (Bloomington: Indiana University Press, 1987).

6. Martin Heidegger, *Contributions to Philosophy*, 285.

7. Ibid., 285.

8. Jacques Lacan, *Écrits*, trans. Bruce Fink (New York: Norton, 2006), 465.

9. See Sigmund Freud, "Repression," in Freud, *General Psychological Theory*, trans. James Strachey (New York: Macmillan, 1963), 106.

10. Sigmund Freud, "The Unconscious," in Freud, *General Psychological Theory*, 116.

11. Jacques Lacan, *Écrits*, 465–66.

12. Ibid., 466.

13. Jacques Lacan, *The Four Fundamental Concepts of Psychoanalysis*, trans. Alan Sheridan (New York: Norton, 1978), 130.

14. Ibid.

15. Ibid., 131.

16. Ibid.

17. See Martin Heidegger, "The End of Philosophy and the Task for Thinking," in *Basic Writings*, ed. David Farrell Krell, (San Francisco: HarperCollins, 1993), 431–49.

18. See Friedrich Nietzsche, *The Gay Science*, trans. Walter Kaufmann (New York: Vintage Books, 1974), 181–82.

19. Sigmund Freud, *Beyond the Pleasure Principle*, trans. James Strachey (New York: Norton, 1961), 43.

20. See Sigmund Freud, *Civilization and Its Discontents*, trans. James Strachey (New York: Norton, 1961), 23–24.

21. See Immanuel Kant, *Critique of Judgment*, trans. Werner Pluhar (Indianapolis: Hackett Publishing, 1987), 99.

22. Freud, *Beyond the Pleasure Principle*, 48.

23. Immanuel Kant, "What Is Enlightenment?" in *Kant: Political Writings*, 2nd ed., ed. Hans Reiss, trans. H. B. Nisbet (Cambridge: Cambridge University Press, 1991), 59.

24. See Ursula Goodenough, *The Sacred Depths of Nature* (New York: Oxford University Press, 1998), 149, for a contemporary discussion of the germ/soma distinction within the context of her religious naturalism: "So our brains, and hence our minds, are destined to die with the rest of the soma. And it is here that we arrive at one of the central ironies of human existence. Which is that our sentient brains are uniquely capable of experiencing deep regret and sorrow and fear at the prospect of our own death, yet it was the invention of death, the invention of the germ/soma dichotomy, that made possible the existence of our brains."

25. Julia Kristeva, *Revolution in Poetic Language*, trans. Margaret Waller (New York: Columbia University Press, 1984), 148.

26. See Sigmund Freud, "Negation," in *General Psychological Theory*, 213–17.

27. Kristeva, *Revolution in Poetic Language*, 148.

28. Ibid., 148. "Freud remarks that the symbolic function is instituted on the basis of expulsion (*Ausstossung*), referred to as *Verwerfung* [foreclosure] in 'Wolf Man.'"

29. Freud, *Beyond the Pleasure Principle*, 46–47.

30. Kristeva, *Revolution in Poetic Language*, 155.

31. Ibid., 156.

32. Ibid., 162.

33. Ibid., 164.

34. Julia Kristeva, "The True-Real," in *The Kristeva Reader*, ed. Toril Moi (New York: Columbia University Press, 1986), 217.

35. The French word for "disavowal" is *denegation*, which is also the term used by Derrida for the title of his famous essay on Negative Theology, which is usually translated as "Denials." Tracing the thread of nuanced meanings through French, German, and English is undoubtedly challenging and confusing, yet the complex of meanings and philosophical resonances associated with the notion of refusal/rejection lends rich resources for a theological thinking bent on honestly grappling with negativities of life and discourse.

36. Kristeva, "The True-Real," 227.

37. Ibid.

38. Ibid., 228.

39. See Jean-Luc Marion's valorization of the term "icon" in contrast with an idol in *God Without Being: Hors-Texte*, trans. Thomas A. Carlson (Chicago: University of Chicago Press, 1991), 7–24.

40. Kristeva, "The True-Real," 230.

41. See Gilles Deleuze, *The Logic of Sense*, trans. Mark Lester (New York: Columbia University Press, 1990). In an essay on Pierre Klossowski, Deleuze claims that language or "reasoning has a theological essence" because it is "the science of nonexisting entities" or surface effects (280–281).

5. Anxiety and the S(ub)lime Body of God

1. Jacques Lacan, *The Four Fundamental Concepts of Psycho-Analysis*, ed. Jacques-Alain Miller, trans. Alan Sheridan (New York: Norton, 1978), 235.

2. Immanuel Kant, *Critique of Pure Reason*, trans. Norman Kemp Smith (New York: St. Martin's Press, 1965), 43 (B2 in the German version).

3. Ibid., 538 (A652/B680).

4. Jacques Lacan, *The Ethics of Psychoanalysis 1959–1960: The Seminar of Jacques Lacan Book VII*, ed. Jacques-Alain Miller, trans. Dennis Porter (New York: Norton, 1992), 199.

5. Ibid., 208.

6. Sigmund Freud, "The Unconscious," *General Psychological Theory*, trans. James Strachey (New York: Macmillan, 1963), 126.

7. Danielle Bergeron, "Aliens and the Psychotic Experience," in *Lacan, Politics, Aesthetics*, ed. Willy Apollon and Richard Feldstein (Albany: State University of New York Press, 1996), 306.

8. Ibid., 307.

9. Ibid., 312.

10. Ibid., 312.

11. Julia Kristeva, "The True-Real," in *The Kristeva Reader*, ed. Toril Moi (New York: Columbia University Press, 1986), 218. See the discussion of this essay in chapter 2, above.

12. Slavoj Žižek, *Tarrying With the Negative: Kant, Hegel and the Critique of Ideology* (Durham: Duke University Press, 1993), 62.

13. Ibid., 62. See also Žižek's more extensive discussion of post-Cartesian subjectivity in *The Ticklish Subject* (London: Verso, 1999).

14. See Julia Kristeva, *Powers of Horror: An Essay on Abjection*, trans. Leon S. Roudiez (New York: Columbia University Press, 1982), chapter 1, 1–31.

15. Jacques Lacan, *The Seminar of Jacques Lacan: Book II The Ego in Freud's Theory and in the Technique of Psychoanalysis*, ed. Jacques-Alain Miller, trans. Sylvana Tomaselli (New York: Norton, 1988), 154–55.

16. Freud, *General Psychological Theory*, 129.

17. Ibid., 130.

18. Sigmund Freud, *Inhibitions, Symptoms, and Anxiety*, in *The Standard Edition of the Complete Psychological Works of Sigmund Freud*, Volume XX, ed. James Strachey (London: The Hogarth Press, 1959), 108–9.

19. Sigmund Freud, "Anatomical Sex-Distinction," in *The Standard Edition* (1961), 19:252.

20. Freud, *Inhibitions*, 109.

21. Jacques Lacan, *The Ego in Freud's Theory and in the Technique of Psychoanalysis*, 321.

22. See Luce Irigaray, *Speculum of the Other Woman*, trans. Gillian C. Gill (Ithaca: Cornell University Press, 1985). For a profound analysis of the ways in which categories of sex and gender are constructed and wielded, and particularly their intersections with those of race and class, see Judith Butler, *Bodies That Matter* (New York: Routledge, 1993). For a partial discussion of race in the context of psychoanalysis, see chapter 8.

23. Freud, *Inhibitions*, 109.

24. Elizabeth J. Bellamy characterizes psychoanalysis as a discourse of anxiety rather than desire, an "unlocatable excess of displacement," in her reading of *Othello* as a tale of epistemologically undecidable anxiety. Like the early Freud and most other psychoanalytic thinkers, however, she claims that "anxiety is the (unreadable) *failure* of repression." "Othello's Lost Handkerchief: Where Psychoanalysis Finds Itself," in *Lacan, Politics, Aesthetics*, 151–79.

25. Martin Luther, *The Freedom of a Christian*, trans. W. A. Lambert, in Three Treatises (Philadelphia: Fortress Press, 1970), 281.

26. See Erik H. Erikson, *Young Man Luther: A Study in Psychoanalysis and History* (New York: Norton, 1993).

27. *What Luther Says: An Anthology*, compiled by Ewald M. Plass (St Louis: Concordia Publishing House, 1959), vol. I, 336.

28. Žižek, *Tarrying With the Negative*, 53.

29. I am primarily dealing here with Žižek's discussion of Lacan's formulas of sexuation. For Lacan's presentation of this distinction, see Jacques Lacan, *On Feminine Sexuality The Limits of Love and Knowledge: The Seminar of Jacques Lacan Book XX Encore 1972–1973*, ed. Jacques-Alain Miller (New York: Norton, 1998), especially 64–81.

30. Ibid., 57.

31. This privileging of beyond over limit is the standard reading of speculative idealism, especially Fichte and Hegel, although Žižek conducts a very original, Kantian, and counter-intuitive reading of Hegel that claims that Hegel radicalizes the finitude Kant asserts rather than overcoming it. See *Tarrying With the Negative*, chapter 3: "Hegel's Logic of Essence," 125–61.

32. As Žižek acknowledges, this interpretation posits that "woman" is nothing in herself, but only what she is for "man's" enjoyment, or *jouissance*. Later in the book, however, Žižek conducts a Lacanian reversal of symptom and ground, which argues that contrary to the manifest reading, "Man himself exists only through woman qua his symptom," he "ex-sists" outside himself, through woman. Woman, being "not-all," does not exist in this manner; rather, "she insists, which is why she does not come to be only through man." *Tarrying With the Negative*, 188.

33. Lacan, *Seminar XX*, 77.

34. Žižek, *Tarrying With the Negative*, 47.

35. Jean-Pierre Changeux, *Neuronal Man*, trans. Laurence Garey (Princeton: Princeton University Press, 1997), 157.

36. Friedrich Nietzsche, *On the Genealogy of Morals*, trans. Walter Kaufmann (New York: Random House, 1967), 58.

37. See Henri Bergson, *An Introduction to Metaphysics*, trans. T. E. Hulme (New York: Macmillan, 1955), 27–28.

38. Gilles Deleuze characterizes the relationship among the Kantian faculties as a discordant or contingent accord in *Kant's Critical Philosophy*, trans. Hugh Tomlinson and Barbara Habberjam (Minneapolis: University of Minnesota Press, 1984), 54.

39. On the relationship of imagination and reason in the mathematical sublime, see Immanuel Kant, *Critique of Judgment*, trans. Werner Pluhar (Indianapolis: Hackett Publishing Co., 1987), 109–16.

40. The main distinction between Žižek and Lacan here is the notion of finitude because Lacan in *Seminar XX* relates the not-all to an infinite set in

order for it to not function as an exception (103). Lacan deals with classical Aristotelian logic, where any negation would have to constitute an exception, and it is on the other hand modern forms of "infinite" mathematics and logic that allow a thinking of negation or not-all, which would not fall into a logic of exceptionality. Here I am following Žižek by relating Lacan's distinction to a *philosophical* understanding of finitude, as opposed to a metaphysical infinite that could only function as an exception to worldly finitude understood as simply the realm of human experience.

41. Charles E. Winquist, *Epiphanies of Darkness* (Aurora, Colo.: Davies Group, 1999), 53.

6. Ages of the World and Creation *ex Nihilo*, Part I: Tillich and Schelling

1. See the discussion in Elizabeth Roudinesco, *Jacques Lacan*, trans. Barbara Bray (New York: Columbia University Press: 1997), 265.

2. For example, see Hent de Vries, *Philosophy and the Turn to Religion* (Baltimore: Johns Hopkins University Press, 1999).

3. Paul Tillich, "On the Idea of a Theology of Culture," in *What Is Religion?* trans. James Luther Adams (New York: Harper and Row, 1969), 177.

4. In an aside, many historians and sociologists of religion use an uncritical conception of culture that has been established by philosophers and theologians with acute metaphysical underpinnings. For a recent critique of Geertz, whose influential essay, "Religion as a Symbol System," still determines the field to a great extent, see Nancy K. Frankenberry and Hans H. Penner, "Clifford Geertz's Long-Lasting Moods, Motivations, and Metaphysical Conceptions," *The Journal of Religion* 79:4 (1999): 617–40. These criticisms are trenchant and needed, although the analytic language and logic tends to mask the complexity of the problem and promise a solution: even if Geertz fuses or confuses the symbolic and the conceptual—what language does not do—where is there a clear demarcation of conceptual and metaphorical language? On the possibility that this is not possible, see Jacques Derrida, "White Mythology: Metaphor in the Text of Philosophy," in *Margins of Philosophy*, trans. Alan Bass (Chicago: University of Chicago Press, 1978), 207–71.

5. Paul Tillich, *Biblical Religion and the Search for Ultimate Reality* (Chicago: University of Chicago Press, 1955), 7.

6. Paul Tillich, *Ultimate Concern: Tillich in Dialogue*, ed. D. Mackenzie Brown (New York: Harper and Row, 1965), 191.

7. Paul Tillich, *The Dynamics of Faith* (New York: Harper and Row, 1957), 1.

8. Paul Tillich, *The System of the Sciences According to its Objects and Methods*, trans. Paul Wiebe (Lewisburg: Bucknell University Press, 1981), 65.

9. On the influence of gestalt psychology upon structuralism, see Maurice Merleau-Ponty, *The Structure of Behavior*, trans. Alden L. Fischer (Boston: Beacon Press, 1963).

10. Ibid., 92.

11. In a way, a return to Tillich is also a return to Whitehead via a psychoanalytic understanding of Whitehead's distinction between the primordial and the consequent nature of God. The primordial nature of God is unconscious, and refers to what Lacan calls the real, or what Tillich calls being-itself, while the consequent nature of God is necessarily symbolic and refers to theology in itself. As the consequent nature of God, a radical and constructive theology consciously produces concepts of divinity through novelty and creativity. At the same time, theology should not lose sight of the tension between its formulation of discursive concepts and the intrinsic inaccessibility of the Real: God. Here is a different kind of correlation, that of primordial and consequent, real and symbolic. Are there theologians who possess the courage to venture beyond the Protestant principle to encounter the substance of the New Being, which according to a strictly Freudian logic is death, however we mark out and value the path that constitutes the detour of theological thinking? I consider Whitehead's philosophy in relation to Lacan and Deleuze in chapter 10.

12. See Martin Heidegger, *Schelling's Treatise on the Essence of Human Freedom*, trans. Joan Stambaugh (Athens: Ohio University Press, 1985), and Andrew Bowie, *Schelling and Modern European Philosophy: An Introduction* (London: Routledge, 1993).

13. Victor Nuovo, "Translator's Introduction," in Paul Tillich, *The Construction of the History of Religion in Schelling's Positive Philosophy*, (Lewisburg: Bucknell University Press, 1974), 11–12.

14. Paul Tillich, *Mysticism and Guilt-Consciousness in Schelling's Philosophical Development*, trans. Victor Nuovo (Lewisburg: Bucknell University Press, 1974), 30.

15. Ibid., 31.

16. Ibid., 101.

17. See Andrew Bowie, "Translator's Introduction," in F. W. J. von Schelling, *On the History of Modern Philosophy* (Cambridge: Cambridge University Press, 1994).

18. Paul Tillich, *The Construction of the History of Religions in Schelling's Positive Philosophy*, 98.

19. Ibid., 98.

20. Ibid., 45.

21. Ibid., 45.

22. On the polar character of the basic structure of being, which is the object of ontological analysis, see Paul Tillich, *Systematic Theology*, Volume One, (Chicago: University of Chicago Press, 1951), 164–65, 198–200. Tillich writes that "finitude is actual . . . in the ontological elements. Their polar character opens them to the threat of nonbeing. In every polarity each pole is limited as well as sustained by the other one," (198).

23. Paul Tillich, *The Construction of the History of Religions in Schelling's Positive Philosophy*, 48.

24. See F. W. J. Schelling, *On the History of Modern Philosophy*, 134–63.

25. On the difference between Schelling and Hegel, and for a defense of Schelling, see Andrew Bowie, *Schelling and Modern European Philosophy*, 127–77. For a more Hegelian reading of Schelling, see Alan White, *Schelling: An Introduction to the System of Freedom* (New Haven: Yale University Press, 1983).

26. Paul Tillich, *The Construction the History of Religion in Schelling's Positive Philosophy*, 53.

27. F. W. J. Schelling, "Ages of the World," trans. Judith Norman in Slavoj Žižek, *The Abyss of Freedom/Ages of the World* (Ann Arbor: University of Michigan Press, 1997), 119.

28. Ibid., 123.

29. Ibid., 123.

30. See Ibid., 144. The official statement of the potencies is as follows: the first potency is expressed in the formula, $a = b$, and refers the grounding state of the two opposing forces, positive and negative; the second potency is the essence or what-is expressed by the affirmation a^2. Finally, the implicit opposition between the first two potencies is resolved in the unity of the affirmation of both a and b, or a^3. The first potency expresses conflict, or what Žižek calls the closed rotary motion of the drives. The second potency affirms the essence of what is contested or struggled over. The third potency, which Schelling identifies with spirit, validates the affirmation of the whole process, carrying it forward in the generation of existence.

31. Ibid., 132.

32. Ibid., 132.

33. Ibid., 132.

34. Concerning Nietzsche and the Absolute will that wills nothing, see the conclusion of *On the Genealogy of Morals*, trans. Walter Kaufmann (New York: Vintage Books, 1967), 162–63. Writing from the standpoint of the human being, Nietzsche implicitly argues against a quiescent will that wills nothing as an actual possibility. Or rather, Nietzsche claims an ascetic will that wills nothing remains a positive will: "*a will to nothingness*, an aversion to life, a rebellion against the most fundamental presuppositions of life; but it is and remains a *will*! . . . And, to repeat in conclusion what I said at the beginning: man would rather will nothingness than *not* will."

35. Schelling, "Ages of the World," 134.

36. Slavoj Žižek, *The Indivisible Remainder: An Essay on Schelling and Related Matters* (London: Verso, 1996), 23. He suggests that "perhaps the best metaphor for this rotary motion is a trapped animal which desperately strives to disengage itself from a snare: although every spring only tightens the snare, a blind compulsion leads it to make a dash for it again and again, so that it is condemned to an endless repetition of the same gesture."

37. Schelling, "Ages of the World," 143.

38. See F. W. J. Schelling, *Ideas for a Philosophy of Nature*, trans. Errol E. Harris and Peter Heath (Cambridge: Cambridge University Press, 1988), 136–39.

39. Paul Tillich, *Theology of Culture* (London: Oxford University Press, 1959), 5–6.

40. Ibid., 8.

41. Tillich, *Systematic Theology*, 1:79.

42. Ibid., 80.

43. Ibid., 14.

44. Robert Scharlemann, *Reflection and Doubt in the Thought of Paul Tillich* (New Haven: Yale University Press, 1969), 113–114.

45. Tillich, *Systematic Theology*, 1:113.

46. In this thinking of creation *ex nihilo*, we could follow Derrida, and say that "divinity is *not* God. In a sense it is nothing." See Jacques Derrida, "Violence and Metaphysics," in *Writing and Difference*, trans. Alan Bass (Chicago: University of Chicago Press, 1978), 146. Although Derrida refers to Meister Eckhart here, this statement could be situated closely to Lacan's pronouncements on the death of God, and his claim that God is unconscious.

7. Ages of the World and Creation *ex Nihilo*, Part II: Žižek and Lacan

1. Slavoj Žižek, *The Indivisible Remainder*, 13.

2. Slavoj Žižek, *The Abyss of Freedom / Ages of the World*, 19.

3. Schelling, "Ages of the World," 145.

4. The German word *Augenblick* literally means "blink of the eye," although Schelling also uses it in different forms, including *blick* for view, and *Lichtblick* for flash, with varying emphases and resonances. *Augenblick* is a central term in Heidegger's philosophy, especially in his interpretation of *Augenblick* as Moment or Gateway in Nietzsche's doctrine of eternal recurrence. See Martin Heidegger, *Nietzsche*, vol. 2: *The Eternal Recurrence of the Same*, trans. David Farrell Krell (San Francisco: HarperCollins, 1984), 37–44, 176–83. For a consideration of the notion of the *Augenblick* in Heidegger in relation to ancient Greek philosophy, see William McNeill, *The Glance of the Eye: Heidegger, Aristotle, and the Ends of Theory* (Albany: SUNY Press, 1999). McNeill does not consider the existence of this term in Schelling, or the general question of the influence of Schelling's thought on Heidegger.

5. See Jacques Derrida, "'To Do Justice to Freud': The History of Madness in the Age of Psychoanalysis," *Critical Inquiry* 20:2 (Winter 1994): 227–66, which offers the theme/figure of the spiral to think of a "spiralled duality," which would avoid the alternatives of monism and dualism (266).

6. Alfred North Whitehead, *Adventures of Ideas* (New York: The Free Press, 1967), 83.

7. Jacques Lacan, *The Ethics of Psychoanalysis 1959–1960*, ed. Jacques-Alain Miller, trans. Dennis Porter (New York: Norton, 1992), 177, 126.

8. Jacques Lacan, *Encore: On Feminine Sexuality The Limits of Love and Knowledge 1972–73*, ed. Jacques-Alain Miller, trans. Bruce Fink (New York: Norton, 1998), 44.

9. Jacques Lacan, *The Ethics of Psychoanalysis*, 125.

10. Paul Tillich, *Systematic Theology*, 1:189.

11. See Gilles Deleuze and Félix Guattari, *What is Philosophy?* trans. Hugh Tomlinson and Graham Burchell (New York: Columbia University Press, 1994), 2: "Philosophy is the art of forming, inventing, and fabricating concepts."

12. Jacques Lacan, *Encore*, 45.

13. Ibid.

8. God Without Being (God): A Lacanian Critique of Jean-Luc Marion

1. Jean-Luc Marion, *God Without Being*, trans. Thomas A. Carlson (Chicago: University of Chicago Press, 1991), 3. It was originally published in French in 1982 as *Dieu sans l'être: Hors-texte*.

2. Ibid., 3.

3. Ibid., 95.

4. Ibid., 101.

5. Heidegger develops his notion of ontotheology in his 1936 lecture course on Schelling. He calls it a "continuous playing back and forth between the theological question of the ground of beings as a whole and the ontological question of beings as such, an onto-theo-logy revolving within itself." See Martin Heidegger, *Schelling's Treatise on the Essence of Human Freedom*, trans. Joan Stambaugh (Athens: Ohio University Press), 66. For two recent theological discussions of ontotheology, see Merold Westphal, *Overcoming Ontotheology: Toward a Postmodern Christian Faith* (New York: Fordham University Press, 2001), and Jeffrey W. Robbins, *Between Faith and Thought: An Essay on the Ontotheological Condition* (Charlottesville: University of Virginia Press, 2003). Westphal follows Heidegger's critique of ontotheology by advocating a Christian theology free from ontotheology, while Robbins argues that the ontotheological condition is in some ways inescapable, and he adopts a phrase from Levinas in proposing a theological strategy that is "otherwise than overcoming" in relation to ontotheology.

6. Marion, *God Without Being*, 75.

7. For an excellent study of negative theology in relation to Heidegger, see John D. Caputo, *The Mystical Element in Heidegger's Thought* (Athens: Ohio University Press, 1978). For a good discussion of mysticism and negative theology in the context of postmodern philosophy, see Thomas Carlson: *Indiscretions: Finitute and the Naming of God* (Chicago: University of Chicago Press, 1999).

8. See Jacques Derrida, "How to Avoid Speaking: Denials," trans. Ken Frieden, in *Derrida and Negative Theology*, ed. Harold Coward and Toby Foshay (Albany: SUNY Press, 1992). For discussions of Derrida's turn to religion, see John D. Caputo, *The Prayers and Tears of Jacques Derrida: Religion*

Without Religion (Bloomington: Indiana University Press, 1997) and Hent de Vries, *Philosophy and the Turn to Religion* (Baltimore: Johns Hopkins University Press, 1999).

9. It should be noted that Karl Barth's reading of Anselm's argument in *Anselm: Fides Quaerens Intellectum* (Richmond, VA: John Knox Press, 1958) rests in the background for both Scharlemann's and Marion's interpretations. Barth suggests that Anselm's argument is less of a logical proof for the existence of God than a rule for how to properly think about God. Wyschogrod's essay, discussed later, explicitly mentions Barth's book on Anselm.

10. Jean-Luc Marion, *Cartesian Questions: Method and Metaphysics*, trans. Jeffrey L. Kosky (Chicago: University of Chicago Press, 1999), 146.

11. Immanuel Kant, *Critique of Judgment*, trans. Werner Pluhar (Indianapolis: Hackett Publishing Co., 1987), 105.

12. Ibid., 114.

13. Ibid., 121.

14. Jean-Luc Marion, "The Saturated Phenomenon," trans. Jeffrey L. Kosky and Thomas A. Carlson, in *Phenomenology and the "Theological Turn": The French Debate*, (New York: Fordham University Press, 2000), 195.

15. Marion, *Cartesian Questions*, 160.

16. It is interesting to read Robert Scharlemann's essay, "The Being of God When God is Not Being God: Deconstructing the History of Theism," in *Deconstruction and Theology*, Thomas J. J. Altizer et al. (New York: Crossroad, 1982), 79–108, in conjunction with Marion's theology. Scharlemann conducts a Heideggerian reading of Anselm's ontological proof and levels a critique against traditional theism:

> The theistic picture does not depict the experience of the time of negation—namely that worldly being (the being of what is not God and what God is not) is the being of God when God is not being God; it does not depict the phenomenon of the world as a moment of time in the being of God (95).

Anselm's formulation expresses a tension between the demand to think of God as "that than which greater cannot be thought" and the traditional theistic understanding of God as being. The metaphysical understanding of being as being limits God, as Marion demonstrates in *God Without Being*. The reason is that "'being,' in the theistic picture, comprises both God and what is not God" (97). In this case being is greater, at least quantitatively, than God. But this violates Anselm's rule: always think of God as the greater of any two possibilities. So the alternative follows that "either being is God and God is not truly God or, in anxiety before this prospect, one must desist from thinking being at all, one must forget being to save the God of the theistic picture," (97).

In many ways, Scharlemann's thought parallels Marion's because both attempt to think about God beyond the limits of being. Scharlemann presses further, however, because although Marion wants to free God of the limits of Being, he does not truly conceive of God as not-being, and he disavows atheism as idolatry. In his radicality Scharlemann claims that the only way to escape the aporia and self-contradiction of theism is to think of God as being-itself: "only if God includes a theism as well as an atheism with respect to the theistic picture is God one than whom something greater cannot be thought," (98). In order to think of God in a different way, "that is to think of the relation between God and being by incorporating time and negation into deity," Scharlemann draws attention to the word God as the instantiation of a radical negativity (105). God has no objective referent as an entity, but God is an expression of language straining to express what it cannot express, because what it attempts to express is always greater than its finite ability of expression. The challenge is to truly think of God as not being, as not-a-being, and this occurs solely in language, or word. According to Scharlemann, "God *is* what language *means*, and language is what God means" (102). The word, God, refers to what God as being is not. Anselm's radical formulation propels itself and us beyond Anselm's theistic metaphysics. Language is "the being of God when God is not being God," and this insight incorporates time and negation into a thinking of deity in a way that distorts traditional theism more powerfully and provocatively then Marion's theology does. For Marion, God gives language and being, without reserve, but there is no negativity because God is always a surplus that re-founds and re-funds being. God never exhausts his ability to give, and his gifts are always good.

17. Edith Wyschogrod, "Recontextualizing the Ontological Argument: A Lacanian Analysis," in *Lacan and Theological Discourse*, ed. Edith Wyschogrod, David Crownfield, and Carl A. Raschke (SUNY Press, 1989), 97.

18. Ibid., 101.

19. See Kant, *Critique of Judgment*, 111.

20. Jacques Lacan, *The Seminar of Jacques Lacan Book VII: The Ethics of Psychoanalysis*, ed. Jacques-Alain Miller, trans. Dennis Porter (New York: Norton, 1992), 11.

21. Ibid., 177. See Alain Badiou, *St. Paul: The Foundation of Universalism*, trans. Ray Brassier (Stanford: Stanford University Press, 2003). Although Badiou acknowledges that "without the law, there is no liberated, autonomous, automatic desire" (82), the event breaks with the law that reigns over being. Badiou affirms Paul as the thinker with the greatest fidelity to the purest event, which is the Resurrection (73, although Badiou himself does not believe in the Resurrection). Badiou opposes the law to grace, with its concomitant faith, hope, and love in an almost-dualistic way: "Grace is the opposite of law insofar as it comes without being due" (77). In *The Puppet and the Dwarf* (Cambridge, Mass.: MIT Press, 2003), Slavoj Žižek attends to the "perverse core of Christianity" in St. Paul in a more Lacanian way because he does not distinguish between law and love in Paul: "Christian

love is a violent passion to introduce a Difference, a gap in the order of being," in which "violence is already the love choice as such, which tears its object out of its context, elevating it to the Thing (33)." The essence of the Law is this love, this violence, in a direct and nondualistic way. See chapter 9 for further discussion of Badiou and Žižek and their respective understandings of universalism.

22. Lacan, *The Ethics of Psychoanalysis*, 111.

9. Expressing the Real: Lacan and the Limits of Language

1. One could develop an interesting comparison between Wittgenstein and Lacan, although it goes beyond the scope of this book. If Lacan's trajectory shifts from the symbolic to the real, then Wittgenstein moves in the opposite direction. The *Tractatus Logico-Philosophicus* expresses an attempt to formalize the real in propositional form, while the development of Wittgenstein's later philosophy moves in the direction of the symbolic. From the standpoint of the *Philosophical Investigations*, the preoccupation with language games and "forms of life" shows a more practical and explicitly therapeutic interest in the nature of symbolic language. Here language is a tool, and logic simply refers to the prescription of a rule. As Wittgenstein puts it in *The Brown Book*, "we need have no reason to follow the rule as we do," and it is a misplaced desire to search for reasons in the same manner that we ascribe causes to effects. See Ludwig Wittgenstein, *The Blue and Brown Books* (New York: Harper and Row, 1958), 143.

2. See William James, *The Varieties of Religious Experience* (New York: Mentor Books, 1958), Lecture 1, 21–38.

3. Ludwig Wittgenstein, *Wittgenstein's Lectures: Cambridge, 1930–32*, ed. Desmond Lee (Totowa, N.J.: Rowman and Littlefield, 1980), 32.

4. See Alain Badiou, *Being and Event*, trans. Oliver Feltham (London: Continuum, 2006).

5. Alain Badiou, *Infinite Thought: Truth and the Return of Philosophy*, trans. Oliver Feltham and Justin Clemens (New York: Continuum, 2003), 50.

6. Ibid., 89.

7. Ibid., 88.

8. Jacques Lacan, *On Feminine Sexuality, The Limits of Love and Knowledge: The Seminar of Jacques Lacan, Book XX: Encore 1972–73*, ed. Jacques-Alain Miller, trans. Bruce Fink (New York: Norton, 1998), 118.

9. Badiou, *Being and Event*, 432.

10. See Alain Badiou, *L'Etre et l'événement : Tome 2, Logiques des mondes* (Paris: Seuil, 2006).

11. "Politics and Philosophy: An Interview with Alain Badiou," Appendix to Alain Badiou, *Ethics: An Essay on the Understanding of Evil*, trans. Peter Hallward (London: Verso, 2001), 119.

12. See Žižek's extended discussion of Badiou in *The Ticklish Subject: The Absent Centre of Political Ontology* (London: Verso, 1999), 127–70. Žižek

claims that ultimately Badiou is too Kantian because "he limits the scope of truth" by detaching it from being (166). "For this reason," Žižek concludes, "one should stick to Lacan's thesis that 'truth has the structure of a fiction': truth is condemned to remain a fiction precisely in so far as the *innomable* Real eludes its grasp" (167). Badiou goes a little too far in formalizing the Real.

13. Alain Badiou, *Saint Paul: The Foundation of Universalism*, trans. Ray Brassier (Stanford: Stanford University Press, 2003), 97.

14. Ibid., 109.

15. Slavoj Žižek, *The Puppet and the Dwarf: The Perverse Core of Christianity* (Cambridge, Mass.: MIT Press, 2003), 17.

16. Ibid., 65.

17. Ibid., 69.

18. Ibid., 77.

19. These intersecting yet diverse relationships among the work of Lacan, Žižek, and Badiou form an interesting knot, although this is not the explicit topic of this chapter. A serious reading would have to account for the interrelations among politics, psychoanalysis, and philosophy for all three, and could then suggest religion as the invisible Real that knots these together.

20. Lacan, *Seminar XX*, 74, 76. See Luce Irigaray, *Speculum of the Other Woman*, trans. Gillian C. Gill (Ithaca, N.Y.: Cornell University Press, 1985), especially the section "Volume-Fluidity," 227–240. For a more contemporary discussion of the issues involving feminist theology and mysticism, including a consideration of the significance of Irigaray's work, see Amy Hollywood, *Sensible Ecstasy: Mysticism, Sexual Difference, and the Demands of History* (Chicago: University of Chicago Press, 2002).

21. Lacan, *Seminar XX*, 23.

22. Ibid., 24.

23. Ibid., 83.

24. One way to read *Anti-Oedipus* is to see it as a reading of *a* over *A*; Deleuze and Guattari deploy the object *a*, or the part-object, against the signifier, albeit in a more violent, anti-psychoanalytic way. See their discussion with Serge Leclaire in Gilles Deleuze, *Desert Islands and Other Texts 1953–1974*, trans. Michael Taormina (Los Angeles: Semiotext(e), 2004), 221–22.

25. Ibid., 123. For a relatively nontechnical discussion of some of the mathematical and physical implications of knot theory, see Alexei Sossinsky, *Knots: Mathematics with a Twist*, trans. Giselle Weiss (Cambridge, Mass.: Harvard University Press, 2002).

26. Lacan, *Seminar XX*, 127. Lacan's reading of Parmenides occurs at almost the same time as Heidegger's consideration of Parmenides, and his valorization of Parmenides over Heraclitus in his 1973 *Zähringen Seminar*. See

Martin Heidegger, *Four Seminars*, trans. Andrew Mitchell and François Raffoul (Bloomington: Indiana University Press, 2003), 77–81. For Heidegger it is not a question of the One, but of a presenting of unconcealment.

27. Herman Melville, *Bartleby the Scrivener, Benito Cereno and Billy Budd, Foretopman* (New York: Quality Paperback Book Club, 1996), 55. A fascinating fact is that the infamous political and legal theorist Carl Schmitt referred to *Benito Cereno* a number of times in the late 1930s and 1940s, and Schmitt even went so far as to sign a letter written on his fiftieth birthday as "Benito Cereno." As Tracey Strong relates in his foreword to Schmitt's *Political Theology*, Schmitt explains that "Benito Cereno, the hero of Herman Melville's story, was elevated in Germany to the level of a symbol for the situation of persons of intelligence caught in a mass system" Schmitt apparently identified with Benito Cereno and, at least after his disillusionment with the Nazis, equated the Nazis with the blacks in the novel. See Carl Schmitt, *Political Theology: Four Chapters on the Concept of Sovereignty*, trans. By George Schwab (Chicago: University of Chicago Press, 2005), vii.

28. Ellen T. Armour, *Deconstruction, Feminist Theology, and the Problem of Difference: Subverting the Race/Gender Divide* (Chicago: University of Chicago Press, 1999), 156.

29. Ibid., 157.

30. Ibid., 162.

31. Charles H. Long, *Significations: Signs, Symbols and Images in the Interpretation of Religion* (Aurora, Colo.: Davies Group, 1999), 118.

32. Melville, *Benito Cereno*, 139.

33. Jacques Lacan: *Television: A Challenge to the Psychoanalytic Establishment*, ed. Joan Copjec (New York: Norton, 1990), 126.

34. Long, *Significations*, 160.

35. Melville, *Benito Cereno*, 149.

36. Ibid., 100.

10. Processing the Real: Sub-stance

1. *The Basic Works of Aristotle*, ed. Richard McKeon, *Metaphysics* trans. W. D. Ross (New York: Random House, 1941), 689–926. Parenthetical citations refer to the standard Berlin Academy pagination.

2. See Martin Heidegger, *Aristotle's Metaphysics Θ 1–3: On the Essence and Actuality of Force*, trans. Walter Brogan and Peter Warnek (Bloomington: Indiana University Press, 1995).

3. For a discussion of substance in Aristotle, see Russell Dancy, "On Some of Aristotle's First Thoughts About Substances," *The Philosophical Review* 84, no. 3 (July 1975): 338–73, and his follow-up, "On Some of Aristotle's Second Thoughts About Substance: Matter," *The Philosophical Review* 87, no. 3 (July 1978): 372–413.

4. Baruch Spinoza, *Ethics*, trans. Samuel Shirley (Indianapolis: Hackett Publishing Company, 1992), 31.

5. Ibid., 63.

6. Gilles Deleuze, *Spinoza: Practical Philosophy*, trans. Robert Hurley (San Francisco: City Light Books, 1988), 122.

7. Spinoza, *Ethics*, 46.

8. Ibid., 82.

9. Ibid., 218, 173.

10. Charles H. Long, *Significations: Signs, Symbols and Images in the Interpretations of Religion* (Aurora, Colo.: Davies Group, 1999), 209.

11. Ibid., 209–10.

12. Gilles Deleuze, *Expressionism in Philosophy: Spinoza*, trans. Martin Joughin (New York: Zone Books, 1990), 48–49.

13. Ibid., 56.

14. Ibid., 57.

15. Ibid., 133.

16. See David Hume, *Dialogues Concerning Natural Religion* (London: Penguin Classics, 1990), 53–58.

17. Alfred North Whitehead, *Process and Reality* (New York: The Free Press, 1978), 39.

18. Ibid., 7.

19. Ibid., 22.

20. Ibid., 18, 44.

21. Gilles Deleuze, *Bergsonism*, trans. Hugh Tomlinson and Barbara Habberjam (New York: Zone Books, 1988), 97. See also Alain Badiou, *Deleuze: The Clamor of Being*, trans. Louise Burchill (Minneapolis: University of Minnesota Press, 2001), 50: "It would be just as wrong to conceive of the virtual as a kind of indetermination, as a formless reservoir of possibilities that only actual beings identify. . . . The couple virtual/actual would start to resemble the Aristotelian couple of matter and form. . . . Virtualities, like problems, are perfectly differentiated and determined, and are just as real as actual beings, in the same way that problems are just as real as solutions."

22. Brian Massumi, *Parables of the Virtual: Movement, Affect, Sensation* (Durham NC: Duke University Press, 2002), 43. Giorgio Agamben conducts a more Heideggerian transformation of potentiality by taking potentiality to its limit in impotentiality. In his essay "On Potentiality," he claims that *adynamia* belongs to all *dynamia*. True potentiality, or impotentiality, occurs "only where the potentiality to not-be does not lag behind actuality but passes fully into it as such." Impotentiality "preserves itself as such in actuality." See Giorgio Agamben, *Potentialities: Collected Essays in Philosophy*, trans. Daniel Heller-Roazen (Stanford: Stanford University Press, 1999), 183.

23. Gilles Deleuze, *The Fold: Leibniz and the Baroque*, trans. Tom Conley (Minneapolis: University of Minnesota Press, 1993), 76.

24. Ibid., 78.

25. Ibid., 79.

26. Ibid., 81.

27. Whitehead, *Process and Reality*, 18.

28. Ibid., 344.

29. Ibid., 345.

30. Ibid., 21.

31. Charles E. Winquist, *The Transcendental Imagination, in The Surface of the Deep* (Aurora, Colo.: Davies Group, 2003), 70.

32. Jacques Lacan, *On Feminine Sexuality, The Limits of Love and Knowledge: The Seminar of Jacques Lacan, Book XX: Encore 1972–73*, ed. Jacques-Alain Miller, trans. Bruce Fink (New York: Norton, 1998), 44.

33. Another way to schematize the contemporary theoretical landscape would be to distinguish broadly among (1) post-Heideggerians, which would include Derrida, Agamben, Nancy, etc.; (2) post-Lacanians, including Žižek and Badiou, and (3) post-Deleuzians, which would include Antonio Negri. This distribution would fail to do justice to the important *political* similarities and differences along and across these quasi-epistemological lines, as well as take into account the resurgence of a certain Marxism in Žižek, Badiou, and Negri (and a certain "spirit" of Marxism in Derrida).

Index

Perspectives in
Continental Philosophy Series

John D. Caputo, series editor

14. Mark C. Taylor, *Journeys to Selfhood: Hegel and Kierkegaard*. Second edition.

15. Dominique Janicaud, Jean-François Courtine, Jean-Louis Chrétien, Michel Henry, Jean-Luc Marion, and Paul Ricoeur, *Phenomenology and the "Theological Turn": The French Debate*.

16. Karl Jaspers, *The Question of German Guilt*. Introduction by Joseph W. Koterski, S.J.

17. Jean-Luc Marion, *The Idol and Distance: Five Studies*. Translated with an introduction by Thomas A. Carlson.

18. Jeffrey Dudiak, *The Intrigue of Ethics: A Reading of the Idea of Discourse in the Thought of Emmanuel Levinas*.

19. Robyn Horner, *Rethinking God as Gift: Marion, Derrida, and the Limits of Phenomenology*.

20. Mark Dooley, *The Politics of Exodus: Søren Keirkegaard's Ethics of Responsibility*.

21. Merold Westphal, *Toward a Postmodern Christian Faith: Overcoming Onto-Theology*.

22. Edith Wyschogrod, Jean-Joseph Goux and Eric Boynton, eds., *The Enigma of Gift and Sacrifice*.

23. Stanislas Breton, *The Word and the Cross*. Translated with an introduction by Jacquelyn Porter.

24. Jean-Luc Marion, *Prolegomena to Charity*. Translated by Stephen E. Lewis.

25. Peter H. Spader, *Scheler's Ethical Personalism: Its Logic, Development, and Promise*.

26. Jean-Louis Chrétien, *The Unforgettable and the Unhoped For*. Translated by Jeffrey Bloechl.

27. Don Cupitt, *Is Nothing Sacred? The Non-Realist Philosophy of Religion: Selected Essays*.

28. Jean-Luc Marion, *In Excess: Studies of Saturated Phenomena*. Translated by Robyn Horner and Vincent Berraud.

29. Phillip Goodchild, *Rethinking Philosophy of Religion: Approaches from Continental Philosophy*.

30. William J. Richardson, S.J., *Heidegger: Through Phenomenology to Thought*.

31. Jeffrey Andrew Barash, *Martin Heidegger and the Problem of Historical Meaning*.

32. Jean-Louis Chrétien, *Hand to Hand: Listening to the Work of Art*. Translated by Stephen E. Lewis.

33. Jean-Louis Chrétien, *The Call and the Response*. Translated with an introduction by Anne Davenport.

34. D. C. Schindler, *Han Urs von Balthasar and the Dramatic Structure of Truth: A Philosophical Investigation*.

35. Julian Wolfreys, ed., *Thinking Difference: Critics in Conversation*.